Political Economy, Literature & the Formation of Knowledge, 1720–1850

This edited collection, *Political Economy, Literature & the Formation of Knowledge 1720–1850*, aims to address the genealogy and formation of political economy as a knowledge project from 1720 to 1850. Through individual essays on both literary and political-economic writers, this volume defines and analyses the formative moves, both epistemological and representational, which proved foundational to the emergence of political economy as a dominant discourse of modernity. The collection also explores political economy's relation to other discourses and knowledge practices in this period; representation in and of political economy; abstraction and political economy; fictional mediations and interrogations of political economy; and political economy and its "others," including political economy and affect, and political economy and the aesthetic.

Essays presented in this text are at once historical and conceptual in focus, and manifest literary critical disciplinary expertise whilst being of genuinely broad and interdisciplinary interest. Amongst the writers whose work is addressed are Charles Dickens, Elizabeth Gaskell, David Hume, Thomas Malthus, Jane Marcet, J. S. Mill, David Ricardo, and Adam Smith. The introduction, by the editors, sets up the conceptual, theoretical, and analytical framework explored by each of the essays. The final essay and response bring the concerns of the volume up to date by engaging with current economic and financial realities, by, respectively, showing how an informed and critical history of political economy could transform current economic practices, and by exploring the abundance of recent conceptual art addressing representation and the unpresentable in economic practice.

Richard Adelman is Senior Lecturer in English at the University of Sussex. He received his PhD in English from the Centre for Eighteenth Century Studies at the University of York and has been a visiting fellow at the Universities of Edinburgh and Freiburg. He is the author of *Idleness, Contemplation and the Aesthetic, 1750–1830*, (Cambridge University Press, 2011) and *Idleness & Aesthetic Consciousness, 1815–1900* (Cambridge University Press, 2018), as well as of a number of essays on eighteenth- and nineteenth-century literature and culture.

Catherine Packham holds a PhD in English Literature from University of Cambridge (2002). Since 2013, she has been Senior Lecturer in English at the University of Sussex, and is also Head of English Literature there. She is author of *Eighteenth-Century Vitalism: Bodies, Culture, Politics* (Palgrave Macmillan, 2012), as well as many articles on eighteenth-century literature, philosophy, and political economy. Her current monograph project, for which she was awarded a Leverhulme Research Fellowship in 2012–2013, is 'Mary Wollstonecraft and Political Economy'.

Routledge Studies in Eighteenth-Century Literature

8 **Visuality, Print, and the Body in Eighteenth-Century Satire**
"The Scope in Ev'ry Page"
Katherine Mannheimer

9 **Mary Wollstonecraft, Pedagogy, and the Practice of Feminism**
Kristin Collins Hanley

10 **Sex and Death in Eighteenth-Century Literature**
Edited by Jolene Zigarovich

11 **Women and Gift Exchange in Eighteenth-Century Fiction**
Richardson, Burney, Austen
Linda Zionkowski

12 **New Perspectives on Delarivier Manley and Eighteenth Century Literature**
Power, Sex, and Text
Edited by Aleksondra Hultquist and Elizabeth J. Mathews

13 **Daniel Defoe and the Representation of Personal Identity**
Christopher Borsing

14 **The Future of Feminist Eighteenth-Century Scholarship**
Beyond Recovery
Edited by Robin Runia

15 **Wordsworth Before Coleridge**
The Growth of the Poet's Philosophical Mind, 1785–1797
Mark Bruhn

16 **Political Economy, Literature & the Formation of Knowledge, 1720–1850**
Richard Adelman & Catherine Packham

For a full list of titles in this series, please visit www.routledge.com.

Political Economy, Literature & the Formation of Knowledge, 1720–1850

Richard Adelman &
Catherine Packham

Routledge
Taylor & Francis Group
NEW YORK AND LONDON

First published 2018
by Routledge
605 Third Avenue, New York, NY 10017

and by Routledge
2 Park Square, Milton Park, Abingdon, Oxon OX14 4RN

First issued in paperback 2021

Routledge is an imprint of the Taylor & Francis Group, an informa business

Publisher's Note
The publisher has gone to great lengths to ensure the quality of this reprint but points out that some imperfections in the original copies may be apparent.

Library of Congress Cataloging-in-Publication Data
CIP data has been applied for.

ISBN 13: 978-1-03-209568-4 (pbk)
ISBN 13: 978-1-138-54213-6 (hbk)

Typeset in Sabon
by codeMantra

Contents

List of Illustrations

List of Contributors

Richard Adelman is Senior Lecturer in English at the University of Sussex. He is the author of *Idleness, Contemplation and the Aesthetic, 1750–1830* (Cambridge University Press, 2011) and *Idleness and Aesthetic Consciousness, 1815–1900* (Cambridge University Press, 2018).

Alex Deans is based at the University of Glasgow, where he works as a research assistant on the Arts and Humanities Research Council sponsored project, *Curious Travellers: Thomas Pennant and the Welsh and Scottish Tour (1760–1820)*. He has written on eighteenth-century travel literature and the spatial humanities and on the convergences of genre and agricultural practice in the Highland tours of James Hogg. His AHRC-funded doctoral thesis, completed at the University of Glasgow in 2014, traced the dynamic between ideas of intellectual improvement and political-economic figurations of labour in Scottish Romantic literature. Deans's research interests increasingly lie in the field of ecocriticism, and particularly in the overlap between discourses of social progress, landscape description, natural history, and political economy in eighteenth-century writing.

Sarah Dredge is Senior Lecturer at Sheffield Hallam University. Her research examines intersections between nineteenth-century women's literary and political writing, particularly in the context of the mid-nineteenth-century women's movement. This has led to a more recent focus on uses of and responses to political economy in women's writing. Publications include "The Inhumanity of Political Economy: Mid-Victorian Feminism and the Politics of the Abstract," *Victorian Review* 40:1 (2014); "Negotiating 'A Woman's Work': Philanthropy to Social Science in Gaskell's North and South," *Victorian Literature and Culture* 40 (2012); and "Opportunism and Accommodation: The *English Woman's Journal* and the British Mid-Nineteenth-Century Women's Movement," *Women's Studies: An Interdisciplinary Journal* 34 (2005). She is currently working on a monograph that looks at the discursive relations between key canonical Victorian novels and the contemporary women's movement.

Joshua Gooch is an Assistant Professor of English at D'Youville College in Buffalo, New York. His research focuses on intersections of work, power, and aesthetics in literature and film, particularly in relation to cultures with financialized economies. His work in nineteenth-century literature includes *The Victorian Novel, Service Work, and the Nineteenth-Century Economy* (Palgrave Macmillan, 2015), which examines the Victorian novel's role in representing and shaping the service sector's emergence and essays about Samuel Butler, Wilkie Collins, and Joseph Conrad in *Nineteenth-Century Contexts, LIT: Literature Interpretation Theory*, and *Texas Studies in Literature and Language*. His work on film includes analyses of contemporary war film, militancy and financial crisis, and Wes Anderson, and has appeared in *The Philosophy of War Films* (University of Kentucky Press, 2014), *Widescreen, The Films of Wes Anderson* (Palgrave, 2014), and *Cinema Journal*. His current research focuses on the role of the affective in such conjunctures.

Nicky Marsh is Professor of English Studies at the University of Southampton. Her books include *Show Me the Money: The Image of Finance 1700 to the Present*, *Money, Speculation and Finance in Contemporary British Fiction*, and *Literature and Globalization: A Reader*. She is the Principal Investigator on an AHRC-funded project, "The History of Financial Advice."

John O'Brien is Professor English at the University of Virginia. He is the author of *Harlequin Britain: Pantomime and Entertainment, 1690–1760* (2004) and *Literature Incorporated: The Cultural Unconscious of the Business Corporation, 1650–1850* (2016), which won the Louis Gottschalk Prize from the American Society for Eighteenth-Century Studies. He is currently working on a book about eighteenth-century poetry and popular culture.

Catherine Packham is Senior Lecturer in English and Head of English Literature at the University of Sussex. She is author of *Eighteenth-Century Vitalism* (Palgrave, 2012) and numerous articles on eighteenth-century literature, political economy, and natural philosophy. She is currently working on a monograph exploring the work of Mary Wollstonecraft in the context of late eighteenth-century debates about political economy, a project for which she has received a Leverhulme Research Fellowship.

Mary Peace is a Senior Lecturer at Sheffield Hallam University. She has published widely on sentimental discourse, sexuality, economics, and religion in eighteenth-century culture. Her recent monograph, *Changing Sentiments and the Magdalen Hospital: Luxury, Virtue and the Senses in Eighteenth Century Culture*, was published by Routledge in 2017.

Mary Poovey is Emeritus Professor at New York University. She is the author of many articles and books on eighteenth- and nineteenth-century British culture, feminist theory, and the history of American finance. Her most recent book, co-authored with Kevin R. Brine, is *Finance in America: An Unfinished Story* (University of Chicago Press). Along with *A History of the Modern Fact* and *Genres of the Credit Economy*, *Finance in America* examines the history and epistemology of financial institutions and practices.

Lesa Scholl is Honorary Research Fellow in the School of Communication and Arts, University of Queensland. Her research interests centre on hunger, poverty, and social justice, and extend to literature as cultural history, forms of translation, sensory history, and economic fictions. Her publications include *Translation, Authorship and the Victorian Professional Woman: Charlotte Brontë, Harriet Martineau and George Eliot* (2011), *Place and Progress in the Works of Elizabeth Gaskell* (2015), and *Hunger Movements in Early Victorian Literature: Want, Riots, Migration* (2016), as well as articles and book chapters on women writers, religion and literature, poetry, and travel writing.

Elisabeth Wallmann is currently an Early Career Fellow at the Institute of Advanced Study, University of Warwick, where she is also affiliated with the School of Modern Languages (French Studies) and the History Department. She researches theories of government during the French Enlightenment, and in particular the intersections between ideas about human nature, animals, and social life. She has published in *French History* and has a forthcoming article on Noël-Antoine Pluche's (1688–1761) immensely popular bestseller of natural history in *French Studies.*

Claire Wilkinson is a postdoctoral researcher at the University of Cambridge, where she is working on an Arts Council-funded project on late capitalism and future economic structures. Her PhD thesis was completed in 2016 and is titled "Imaginative Economies: Literature and Financial Crisis." The thesis considers the history of financial crisis, and it analyses the role that literary writing has played in communicating economic catastrophe in Britain during four periods of crisis following the South Sea Bubble in 1720. Claire's research interests include the history and development of political economy, eighteenth-century intellectual history, economic criticism in literature, financial markets, and the political, economic, and ethical consequences of contemporary capitalism. Her forthcoming book is about financial crisis and the depiction of the economic market in nineteenth-century fiction.

Introduction

The Formation of Political Economy as a Knowledge Practice

Richard Adelman and Catherine Packham

To observe that an extended period of economic turmoil defines our current era is to risk stating the obvious. The indications are many, and are everywhere: from debates over debt and austerity politics; anxiety about the end of China's boom times; low, even negative interest rates; cuts, closures, retrenchments, job losses; fears about bank stability and excessive levels of consumer debt; the announcement (by Harvard economist Dani Rodrick and Princeton economic historian, Robert Gordon, for instance) of a new low-growth era.[1] Stock markets, contemporary measurers of seismic economic pressures, regularly register dramatic drops and hesitant recoveries. Newspapers run features asking when the next economic crisis will hit.[2] One feature of inhabiting a moment of economic turmoil in its current incarnation is the expectation—and anticipation—of another crunch moment like the collapse of Lehman Brothers in 2008. As a break from all this, we might relax by watching a credit crunch film: *Margin Call* (2011), *Inside Job* (2011), *The Wolf of Wall Street* (2013), *The Big Short* (2015). For one section of the culture industry, at least, economic crisis is good for business.

One consequence of this ongoing economic moment has been a marked deterioration of conditions for the arts and humanities. Within UK universities, for instance, the introduction of much-increased tuition fees was an early measure of austerity economics, and the withdrawal of direct funding for these university disciplines (and not for the so-called STEM subjects, Science, Technology, Engineering and Mathematics) has increased pressure on arts and humanities disciplines to justify themselves in the utilitarian terms whose validity they broadly question. But, rather than capitulating to a narrative in which our disciplinary expertise is threatened and diminished by difficult economic conditions, and by an increasingly pervasive market-oriented language, the present volume seeks to invert this relationship. It asks, instead, what resources do the arts and humanities have with which to respond to this moment? What can the cultural knowledge and the skills of critical and textual analysis fostered by humanities scholarship offer to this extended period of financial crisis and economic stagnation? Even a short reflection on these questions would offer many possible answers. Cultural commentators, critics, and historians have responded to the "down turn" of the past near-decade by documenting and narrativizing contemporary economic reality, critiquing economic language and models, and by theorizing the post-crash economy; cultural practitioners have responded to our current economic era with new art works, exhibits, and installations.[3] Cultural historians and critics have shown themselves ready to examine literary and other responses to the contemporary economic moment; to explore, and theorize, how financial crisis, risk, debt, and speculation structure our present; and to place that present in a longer historical perspective which often illuminates how our economic crisis is only the latest of many, going back through (to mention only some) the "stagflation" of the 1970s, the Great Depression of the 1930s, and the Long Depression of the 1870s, to the South Sea Bubble of 1720 and the Dutch Tulip Bubble of 1636–1637.[4]

Indeed, there exists within recent humanities scholarship a strong tradition of critical engagement with economic thinking, past and present, which stems back at least over the past 40 years. For ease and clarity of argument, this could be divided into three phases or areas of engagement, sometimes overlapping and co-existing, but each of which nevertheless has its own specific set of questions and concerns.

The first of these is "intellectual history," defined by Brian Young as a "supremely interdisciplinary enterprise," which explores "how ideas originate and evolve in specific historical contexts," and which traces "their histories within the broader histories of the societies and cultures which they have helped to shape, and which have also shaped them."[5] Strongly, but not exclusively associated with the University of Cambridge, both (as Young suggests) with the "Ideas in Context" series published by Cambridge University Press and with leading scholars such as Quentin Skinner, it is also linked with the University of Sussex through its long-established Centre for Intellectual History, where figures such as Donald Winch and Richard Whatmore have worked.[6] It is easy to identify the achievements of intellectual history's work on political economy: it offers a properly historical attention to economic writings; it pays attention to the rhetorical and linguistic complexity of texts and economic ideas; and it has rewritten our understanding of history of economic thought so that we can no longer think of this as a grand narrative of progress of liberal capitalism. Within literary studies, we have gained from intellectual history a sense of the complex historicity of political economy as a discourse, or a series of discourses, as well as of the intricacy of its relations with other contingent discourses, in moral, social, and political traditions of thought. Adam Smith's theorization of modern capitalism, for example, can be seen—thanks to the work of intellectual history—to have emerged out of his engagement with both the seventeenth-century natural jurisprudence of Hugo Grotius and Pufendorf, and with a long history of classical republicanism and then civic humanism.[7]

The second phase or area of scholarship on political economy might be called "Economics *and* Literature." Work in this vein might be said to envisage the fields of economics and literature as two distinct entities, which can nevertheless be brought together in order to produce fruitful interplay and exchange. These organizing principles are present, for instance, in the subtitle of *New Economic Criticism: studies at the intersection of literature and economics*, ed. Martha Woodmansee and Mark Osteen (London: Routledge, 1999). This sense of interplay between difference is also suggested in Kurt Heinzelman's *The Economics of the Imagination* (University of Massachusetts Press, 1980), which uses the phrase "imaginative economics," on the one hand, to describe economic systems as fictions founded on imaginary concepts, and "poetic economics," on the other hand, to describe how literary writers use economic discourse. Work in this area thus exploits ways in which the traditional object of one discipline might be analysed through disciplinary tools of the other, submits economic texts to rhetorical analysis, explores the economics of authorship and the literary marketplace, or investigates homologies between economic and linguistic systems as "symbolic economies."[8] It seems to us that this is a field of rich and ongoing work, but in adopting the model of "interaction" or "intersection" between two distinct entities, such an approach may risk retaining, in a relatively unquestioned way, the dual identities of the economic and the literary, and overlooking the shared but bifurcated history which produced the categories of the literary, the aesthetic, and the economic at the end of the eighteenth century.

We would suggest that we are now in a third phase, in which the critical and historical scholarship of the humanities is brought to bear on political economy in a further, newly productive way. This is one in which a concern with "economics and literature" has given way to a broader theoretical and methodological interest in the shared foundation that gives rise to—and that might justify—this supposed polarity. In this new phase, political economy is studied as part of the history of knowledge formation and discipline building, bringing into relief the relationship between discourses, knowledge, and the disciplines, but in a way which enables a return to questions of genre, literature and writing, as well as cultural and literary history. This is a field which works towards both a genealogy and a critical analysis of knowledge formation; it combines historically focused study and a close attention to the modes of representation through which economic knowledge has been produced, and through which the discipline of economics has come into being. Collectively, work in this field contributes towards a history of economics as a knowledge project, which addresses the genres, strategies, narratives, and other forms and modes through which knowledge is modelled, formed, and deployed. Mary Poovey's *Genres of the Credit Economy* (University of Chicago Press, 2008), a landmark in this field, thus builds on the achievements of her *History of the Modern Fact* (University of Chicago Press, 1998) to offer a powerful account of the shared historical emergence of modern literature and the modern credit economy.

Peter de Bolla's work on the *Architecture of Concepts* (Fordham University Press, 2013) develops this new attention to discursive domains by calling our attention to the conceptual substrata which exist below discourse. De Bolla thus examines concepts as cultural entities which structure thought, both in and beyond political economy.[9] De Bolla, Poovey, and their contemporaries thus build on the ideas and insights of both intellectual history and the work that addressed "literature and economics." But at the same time, they go beyond—and beneath—that work in order to address the building blocks of the modern disciplinary landscape and the foundations of modernity's patterns of thought and modes of organization. They enquire into the epistemological structures and cultural practices underlying and sustaining economic thinking and writing; they ask how writing, as a representational practice, teaches us to understand its object, whilst at the same time attending to how writing disturbs its object. Work in this third phase of political economy scholarship is thus especially concerned with how modes of representation (genres, concepts, narrative forms, and so on) inform and structure knowledge creation. In this way, the critical skills of textual analysis and close reading are powerfully enabled to produce detailed accounts of the emergence of political economy as a "logic of modernity" which pervasively structures our contemporary moment.[10]

Whilst much of this work is historically focused, it does not attempt to offer a history of political economy *per se*, although at times, it can be post-Foucauldian, in linking economic discourse to forms of governmentality, for instance through attention to the construction, description, and regulation of economic subjects, or populations.[11] Neither is it a philosophical critique of classical political economic thought.[12] A more helpful reference point is offered, however, by the studies in the history of science associated with figures such as Lorraine Daston and Simon Schaffer. Their work, and that of others, addresses the epistemological structures and cultural practices which have established and sustained modern science as a knowledge practice from the scientific revolution of the seventeenth century onwards. Daston, Schaffer, and others typically investigate the cultural history, social structures, and textual and rhetorical practices sustaining what Daston has described as the "epistemic genres" through which scientific knowledge is produced, whether it is the experiment, the production of evidence, the notion of scientific objectivity, or the practice of scientific observation.[13] In an analysis of the latter, for example, Daston dismantles the "great epistemological divide"[14] between subjectivity and objectivity which often structures debates over the status and nature of scientific observation, and instead offers an account of scientific observation which emphasizes how habits of perception are acquired and structured through experience, training, and gradually acquired expertise. Scientific observation thus emerges not as either "objective" or "subjective," but as historically and culturally formed through the educational and disciplinary structures and practices of its discipline.[15] It is through reference to that process of formation that both the limits of scientific sight (what it fails to see, its restrictions and boundaries) and its strengths (including the "all-at-once-ness of virtuoso perception,"[16] the expert glance which can take in immediate knowledge from an image without pause) can be understood. Daston's analysis is powerful because it illuminates how, in her terms, what "masquerades" as objective or real is a function of, or produced by, habits of perception: historically acquired modes of seeing which become embedded as transparent means of finding out about the world. In her words, "[t]here is something about the all-at-onceness of habitual perception that stamps its ontologies with the imprimatur of the really real."[17] This "all-at-once-ness" condenses "laborious, step-by-step procedures into an immediate *coup d'oeil*,"[18] so that "perceptual habit" is understood as "self-evidence."[19] That the implications of this self-evidential "coup" extend beyond the realm of visual perception is clear from Daston's own example of the use of such language of immediate understanding by Descartes, in relation to his comprehension of mathematics; we would suggest it could be extended further.

Whilst Daston's analysis, at one level, is clearly concerned with an object of investigation which falls outside our own concerns in this volume, her approach is suggestive. What would it mean to investigate the strategies by which the economy has "shored up" its ontology and produced itself as the "really real?" How might the historical formation, not of the perceptual but of the cognitive habits and virtuoso expertise which sustain it be exposed for examination? This is a question which, following Daston, could be brought to bear not only on the visualization techniques of economics (for instance, how it displays its data) but also more generally, on how it has produced and constructed the objects of its inquiry, its key terms and concepts, and itself as a knowledge practice. Its "epistemic genres" and practices (from graphs and bar charts to the modes of narrative present in its economic treatises and theories), both of the present and the past, offer themselves for interrogation and analysis. The need for this, in light not only of the pressing nature of our current economic situation, but more broadly as part of a sustained critical interrogation of economics as a form of knowledge, is clear. Timothy Mitchell, in his *Rule of Experts: Egypt, Techno-Politics, Modernity*, argues, rightly in our view, that critiques of modernity and modern forms of knowledge have addressed "the concepts of class, nation, culture, society, state, gender, race, personhood, and many others, but not the idea of the economy."[20] For Mitchell, the "territory and logic" of economics as a "systematizing form" needs interrogating. This is, not least, because the economy has become "arguably the most important set of practices for organizing what appears as the separation of the real world from its representations, of things from their values, of actions from intentions, of an object world from the realm of ideas."[21] To deploy Daston's terms, economics has produced its own "*coup d'oeil*," whereby the "really real" is produced as self-evident. According to Mitchell, the "really real" produced by modern economics includes "new forms of value, new kinds of experience, new practices of calculation, new relations between human agency and the nonhuman";[22] the practices which "form the economy operate...to establish equivalences, contain circulations, identify social actors or agents, make quantities and performances measurable, and designate relations of control and command":[23] all of which are taken as self-evident. It is the work of this book to begin to submit what constitutes the self-evidently real of the economic to interrogation, especially by tracing the moves, constructions, and representational apparatus assembled and deployed in the early formation of political economic writing from the mid-eighteenth to mid-nineteenth centuries.

This volume insists, then, in exploring the yoked problematics of economics and representation. It does so not in order to make the facile point that the economy is simply a representation, but to begin to explore the ways in which the historical construct of economics as a discourse writes itself onto the world, by structuring unexamined habits of understanding, creating objects of knowledge, and creating forms of virtuoso expertise. It explores the history and implications of the particular relations between economics and representation in light of, in Mitchell's words, the way in which "the most abstract and mathematical of the social sciences, economics" has come to claim "the task of representing what seemed the more real aspect of the social world."[24] The relationship between economics and the real, established and mediated through representation, is thus, it would seem, both peculiar and unique, compared with that of other knowledge practices. Economics is a science which has created its object—"there is nothing like an economy out there, unless and until men construct such an object"; and it has created its object through innovations in representation and writing, from the Physiocratic zigzag diagram invented by François Quesnay, through to the further conceptual, generic, epistemic, and narrative strategies which produce and sustain its knowledge.[25] At times, invention through representation involves absence and non-representation; indeed, non-representation, of various forms (including, for instance, condensation, abstraction, exclusion, occlusion, and figuration) could be said to be constitutive of economic writing. As Quesnay wrote, of his zigzag, the diagram "if properly understood, cuts out a whole number of details, and brings before your eyes certain closely interwoven ideas which the intellect alone would have a great deal of difficulty grasping, unravelling and reconciling by the method of discourse."[26] The studies collected in this volume are equally as attentive to what is "cut out" as to what is "brought before your eyes" in their explorations of the genealogy and formation of early political economic writing.

We turn, later in this essay, to the analytically suggestive presence of the absent, invisible, or non-represented in economic discourse, but first we can initially, and briefly, explore these questions regarding representation in, and of, economics, through another pervasive image in the popular cultural imaginary pertaining to the economic and the financial: that of excessive representation, or information overload. Examples of such an image might include the stock market traders' multiple computer screens filled with an ever-changing flow of digits, or the constantly updated ticker-tape display of share values. The prolixity of information in such images suggests an apparent mastery of representation: the achievement, perhaps, of a highly evolved numerical language, beyond the vagaries of mere words, capable of a precise and sensitive registering of every shift in value taking place across myriad planes of human enterprise. But such a seemingly supreme representative mode is achieved only at the cost of constantly surpassing itself. Indeed, in these examples, information produces its own excess precisely as a consequence of the very quality for which it is prized—an accuracy which, being temporally specific and therefore temporally limited, has an inbuilt obsolescence which is also a demand for regeneration: the individual "facts" represented by these numbers are short-lived, being outdated and updated in a regular, repeatable cycle. This excess of information, and of representative capacity, is in stark contrast to a global economic climate which Christine Lagarde, managing director of the International Monetary Fund, recently called the "new mediocre."[27]

But lying behind or beyond this façade of numerical facts which structures our era's economic and financial knowledge (and in a logic which we will see repeated in the notion of the graph as an occlusion as well as a communication of information) is the absence or vacuum of what remains unrepresented, or unrepresentable, in these terms. One reading of the 2008 financial crash would be as the revenge of what was excluded or repressed from high finance's complex modelling on that system itself. Certainly, the devastating effects of what has not been seen—or what lies beyond representation, knowledge, or comprehension—is conveyed effectively in J. C. Chandor's 2011 film, *Margin Call*, which narrates the collapse of a Lehman Brothers-type bank. The action turns on the discovery, by a single worker, of a huge absence of value in the bank's finances. Yet for a considerable length of the film, the exact nature of this problem is not shared with the audience; characters look at computer screens and see, but we do not: the problem, whilst being everywhere and structuring all the film's action, is never articulated or explicitly known. At one level, this may constitute the filmmakers' practical solution to the problem that the highly complex nature of economics—or, in this instance, high finance—makes it in effect unrepresentable. Less dramatically, one might say that the matter of high finance can only be manifested in highly specialized modes, or genres, of representation comprehensible only to the initiated. *Margin Call* comments astutely—and comically—on the apparently occult and specialized skills of the extreme expert, by attributing to the young banker who completes the number crunching which fully reveals the fragility of the bank's finances a former life as a rocket scientist: high finance, it is suggested, really is equally as arcane and complex (with devastating consequences both for those who should comprehend it, and for the rest of us).[28] At another level, this refracts an observation made repeatedly in the aftermath of 2008 banking crisis, that those who were supposed to be overseeing the system often had no detailed knowledge or understanding of exactly what their bankers were doing.[29] In light of all this, one way of thinking about economic crisis is as a crisis in representation or knowledge, a crisis of what economics is capable of seeing, of how it sees and knows, and of how it constructs its object of knowledge. It is as a contribution to remedying that crisis that we hope to offer our own disciplinary skills in the essays collected in this volume.[30]

* * *

Humanities disciplines thus already have significant critical tools and analytical expertise with which to address, understand, and critique the economic concerns of our time; these resources include some highly developed thinking on the history of forms, genres, and discourses in knowledge production. Despite a common perception that economics is a form of knowledge whose truths somehow transcend the often dogged problems posed by language and representation—a perception perhaps informed by its association, especially since the mid-twentieth century, with non-verbal representative modes, such as mathematical equations or the graph, of which more later—the critical expertise on representation and its role in knowledge formation which is wielded by the humanities, and especially by literary scholarship, can of course be brought to bear on the discipline of economics as well. Adam Smith, the founder of modern political economy, addressed precisely this issue in an early essay on "Principles which Lead and Direct Philosophical Inquiries; Illustrated by the History of Astronomy," written many years before the publication of his *Wealth of Nations* (1776) but not published until the 1790s.[31] Such was Smith's assessment of the importance of this essay that he saved it from destruction in the days before his death, when he allowed many of his other papers to be destroyed. In this essay, Smith portrays philosophy as "one of those arts which address themselves to the imagination," and he describes the psychological processes involved in knowledge production, whereby the mental unease of observing disconnected objects or appearances in nature is soothed by folding them into a philosophical system which is able to account for them as part of a connected and coherent explanatory whole. Setting aside "their absurdity or probability, their agreement or inconsistency with truth and reality," he offers a historical survey of different explanatory systems in the field of astronomy, assessing "how far each of them was fitted to sooth the imagination, and to render the theatre of nature a more coherent, and therefore a more magnificent spectacle, than otherwise it would have appeared to be."[32] A philosophical system, he elaborates, is "an imaginary machine invented to connect together in the fancy those different movements and effects which are already in reality performed"; philosophy "triumphs" when, "in order to connect together a few... inconsiderable objects, she has, if I may say so, created another constitution of things...such as the imagination can more easily attend to."[33] Smith's careful preservation of the difference between the theoretical status of philosophy and the reality which it seeks to explain is only threatened when, at the conclusion of his essay, he reflects that, even whilst he has "been endeavouring to represent all philosophical systems as mere inventions of the imagination, to connect together the otherwise disjointed and discordant phaenomena of nature," he has, in his account of Isaac Newton's astronomy, "insensibly been drawn in, to make use of language expressing the connecting principles of this one, as if they were the real chains which Nature makes use of to bind together her several operations."[34] Newton's system *seems* so convincing to Smith that the philosophical "machine" is almost mistakable for truth or fact, but this slip only underlines the overall import of the essay: that philosophical systems are contingent, imaginative productions, produced by postulating theoretical links in order to explain observed phenomena.[35] This conception of the theoretical and speculative nature of knowledge, as well as Smith's attention to its psychological and affective ends and origins, should be fundamental to any understanding of Smith's own economic and philosophical thought. Unfortunately, a failure to attend to Smith's own account of philosophical method—to detach the supposed findings or insights of his work from the precise philosophical and textual context which produced them—has resulted in a number of pervasive misconceptions and misreadings of Smith's work, which, given his status as founder of political economy, have also informed—or misinformed—much political economy and economic thought more generally, from the nineteenth century to the present.

The recovery of a sharper attention to the epistemological status of Smith's text, and a more precise and sensitive awareness to the processes by which he constructs his "system," could thus do much to counter established interpretations of his work. For example, in one well-established and influential (mis)reading, Smith's famous figure of the invisible hand is put at the heart of an account which understands Smith to be setting out the economy as the operation of a providential system. In Foucault's *The Birth of Biopolitics*, this reading is already conventional, to the extent that it is unattributable: "[it] is usually said that we should see the invisible hand as the remains of a theological conception of the natural order."[36] In his study of the "theological genealogy of economy and government," Giorgio Agamben evidences Smith quoting Stoic beliefs in order to support his own brief account of Smith's providentialism, but he omits both Smith's immediate characterization of Stoic belief as "speculation," and his conclusion, in his later survey of Stoic moral philosophy, that "Stoical philosophy" appears entirely divergent from latent impulses in our nature.[37] Much of the force of these interpretations of Smith is deflected if Smith's own account of philosophy as a contingent "imaginary machine" is recalled, and we understand Smith to be attempting to make postulatory connections between observed phenomena in the world, and to link them into a theoretical, explanatory system. Arguably, those who find in his work a "providentialist" or "theological" Smith are making the same error which Smith himself nearly made in his description of Newton's system: taking a postulated philosophical system as the description of (what Smith understands to be) the "really real." We offer an alternative take on the figure of the invisible hand, and what it might suggest for the discourse of political economy, below.

The issue of the epistemological status of Smith's philosophy also lies at the heart of what has come to be known as "The Adam Smith Problem." This problem is the apparent conundrum surrounding how Smith, the moral philosopher who wrote *The Theory of Moral Sentiments* in 1759, could also write *The Wealth of Nations* in 1776. The former work considers human nature as universally sympathetic, other-orientated, social, and thus moral. The latter, by contrast, treats human behaviour as almost always self-interested and calculating and addresses human activity as being almost entirely made up of profitable labour. The former follows the broad currents of classical republican thought, in other words, applying them to eighteenth-century civil society. The latter constructs and celebrates *homo œconomicus*—economic man—in his modern form.

That there even is a "problem" in the relationship between these two texts, penned 17 years apart, is a feature of the extent to which economic discourse has been retrospectively given the status of factual, empirical description. In this context, it is notable that it was not until the late nineteenth century that the phrase "The Adam Smith Problem" was coined.[38] As the disciplines hardened across the eighteenth and nineteenth centuries, and as political economic concerns became central to political debate and to a variety of cultural institutions (as Maxine Berg has demonstrated[39]), the discourse of political economy came to be understood as a science, to the extent that it apparently proceeded on knowledge derived *a posteriori*. When one looks at Smith's two most significant texts in detail, however, what one finds is a persistent deployment of a range of subjunctive modes, in both *The Theory of Moral Sentiments* and *The Wealth of Nations*, that position both projects as thought experiments and thoroughly contingent projects. In the case of *The Wealth of Nations*, furthermore, Smith's alterations to his text across the course of his lifetime render many of his key phrases more and more subjunctive, and thus more and more challengeable or relative, as the editions of the work progress. Phrases such as "may be said to be," or "some notion may be formed," or "it may be laid down as a maxim," thus eventually qualify just about all the text's beliefs and conclusions. To observe this is not to see Smith retreating from his findings, but rather to see a methodologically self-reflective and forensically precise writer striving towards an accurate expression of the epistemological status of his work.

In this context, one might describe history's decision to read *The Theory of Moral Sentiments* as a work of opinion and *The Wealth of Nations* as a work of fact as a powerful ideological distortion. Both works in fact *abstract* a string of human tendencies and consider what those qualities can show us about human interactions. This use of abstraction is shared by modern economics, which, in Mitchell's words, "depicts the rationality of social life in ideal form, proposing to understand particular cases in terms of their deviation from this unreal abstraction."[40] But neither of Smith's works claims to totally describe human capability, or to factually represent human community or society. The perspective we are taking up here, furthermore, from which long accumulative historical processes can be assessed as problematic reformulations—or even distortions—also allows for a usefully long view of current economic thought. As Nicky Marsh phrases it in her contribution to this volume, "the problem of modern economics is that it has no 'Adam Smith Problem.'" Moral, social, and psychological perspectives are frequently irrelevant to modern economics, it seems, and the reconstruction of history's partial reading of the founding texts of political economy is one step along the way to correcting such oversights.

The present-day discipline of economics is of course in many ways very different from the "system of political economy" which Smith outlined in 1776. But Smith's sense of theoretical philosophical systems being used to explain real-world phenomena can be compared to the use of "models" and "modelling" in current economics. According to Dani Rodrik, economists' models are both "abstractions and simplifications; they are incomplete maps which provide a partial guide to the peaks and troughs of human experience; they might be considered as fables, or as thought experiments."[41] Rodrik's list of comparators here is produced to answer what he calls a pervasive charge against economics: that economists apply simple frameworks to complex social phenomena, and he calls for a new disciplinary self-understanding and reflection. We would like to suggest that the humanities has much to offer to such a project, in terms of its expertise in considering what representation is, the forms it can take, the work it does, and how it might be read and understood; but also, connectedly, in terms of the history of different modes of representing, writing, or, in the economists' own word, "modelling" the economy. Indeed for a literary critic, the very proliferation of comparators (or metaphors) which Rodrik produces here to explain the nature of the economic model might be read as another instantiation of the familiar problem posed by representational forms themselves: what they appear to do, say, and be might be quite different from what their author might believe (hence Rodrik's need for multiple comparators as each in turn proves not quite right for the job in hand).[42] In many ways this observation, about the relationship between form and content, and about how representation always involves exclusion of what is not represented, is foundational in our discipline—especially in its current post-structural incarnation. Smith's sense of the contingency of his representational form—in his case, the philosophical system—could thus be seen as an epistemologically sophisticated and practical solution to this problem of method.

Alongside algebraic equations and formulae, perhaps one of the most iconic or familiar modes of representation used by present-day economists is the graph, often used to visually present the findings of a particular work of modelling. Seemingly the embodiment of incontrovertible evidence, its two-dimensional form peculiarly fitted to the flat planes of our dominant contemporary modes of communication, the computer screen and television, the graph crystallizes the authority of economics as a knowledge practice. But as Marsh's essay in this volume demonstrates, the graph can also be read as elucidating what is not shown as much as what it "officially" conveys. This striking conjunction of visibility and invisibility, of knowledge and what cannot be known, is, interestingly, also present in one of the most famous metaphors in economics, that of the "invisible hand," a figure coined by Smith to postulate that economic benefits are distributed through a population as though by an invisible force.[43] At its very moment of inception, that which can't be seen is instituted into the heart of political economic discourse through a reassuring analogy. The mistake made too often, of course, is one whereby the metaphorical "as though" is solidified into a more certain statement of truth, an error which is then—sometimes—laboriously exposed and corrected.[44] We suggest an alternative reading of the "invisible hand": as a marker of how, at its very outset, the problematic of representation, of visibility and invisibility, lay at the heart of economic discourse. From this perspective, the foregrounding of a hand which is "invisible" points to political economy's peculiar orientation, at its origins, to what can't be seen, a tendency also expressed, for instance, in its development of a series of abstractions, such as the "market," "division of labour," "value," and so on, with which its own nature as a discipline or knowledge practice are strongly identified, and which came to be fundamental to its analytical powers.[45] One history of political economy since Smith might therefore be a history of the misreadings of that figure; another might reconstruct the unstated assumptions informing the different modes of political economy practised since the eighteenth century.[46]

It is striking, in this context, that some modes of political economy have themselves addressed these issues, but that such preoccupations are frequently occluded from the official history of the discourse. John Stuart Mill's *Principles of Political Economy* of 1848, for example, exposes the "invisible hand" as a convenient and imprecise fiction by announcing that "the laws and the conditions of the production of wealth partake of the character of physical truths. There is nothing optional or arbitrary in them," but that "it is not so with the Distribution of Wealth. That is a matter of human institution solely. The things once there, mankind, individually or collectively, can do with them as they like."[47] Such statements are part of Mill's attempt to stand back from the ideologies of growth, competition, and development and identify a more considered ambition for commercial society. Mill thus embraces the "stationary state," the projected cessation of economic progress that David Ricardo had introduced into political economy in 1817, in the following terms:

> I am inclined to believe that [the stationary state] would be, on the whole, a very considerable improvement on our present condition. I confess I am not charmed with the ideal of life held out by those who think that the normal state of human beings is that of struggling to get on; that the trampling, crushing, elbowing, and treading on each other's heels, which form the existing type of social life, are the most desirable lot of human kind, or anything but the disagreeable symptoms of one of the phases on industrial progress. [...] Most fitting, indeed, is it, that while riches are power, and to grow as rich as possible the universal object of ambition, the path to its attainment should be open to all, without favour or partiality. But the best state for human nature is that in which, while no one is poor, no one desires to be richer, nor has any reason to fear being thrust back, by the efforts of others to push themselves forward.[48]

If we try and assess the status of this almost anti-economic aspect of Mill's political economy in our own day, however, we find a situation that tells us a lot about the current state of economic discourse. V. W. Bladen, the editor of Mill's *Principles* for the authoritative scholarly edition of his *Complete Works*, distinguishes between Mill the political economist and Mill "the preacher," in his *Principles*, with a passage like this one being very much in the voice of the latter persona. The point of Bladen's distinction is to delimit what is appropriate to political economy as a practical science of social mechanisms, and what belongs in a more speculative, non-empirical discourse. For Bladen, therefore, "[t]he preacher...contemplate[s] the Stationary State," when "the political economist" should be "concerned with the practical problems of contemporary society."[49] In other words, that ideologically implicated view of the "Adam Smith Problem" we encountered above, in which the *Theory of Moral Sentiments* is taken as a work of opinion and the *Wealth of Nations* is taken as a work of fact, is again deployed here. Bladen strives to render a powerful strand of Mill's economic thought irrelevant to its modern, economically enlightened reader, because it is founded on opinion-based moral "contemplation" rather than "practical," empirical facts. It is precisely this problematic opposition between opinion and fact, sentiment and science, which Smith's originary formulation of political economy as a contingent explanatory system, to be constantly measured against our empirical experiences of the world, would resist.[50]

* * *

It is these issues of political economy's purview, remit, visibility, and knowledge construction that inform the essays in the present volume. While every essay in the volume (with the exception of the final contribution) focuses its attentions on the political economic writings and concerns between 1720 and 1850, they are nevertheless all animated and inflected by a set of modern-day concerns. The final two pieces presented here, by Marsh and Poovey, draw out such latent politics by directly addressing what an informed history of political economy can teach present financial and economic practices.

The volume's first part thus begins by addressing the complex field of representations of—and representations within—political economy. Claire Wilkinson's essay on the metaphor of the financial "bubble" offers a prehistory to this consideration by introducing the practice of "abstraction," and by considering how the South Sea Bubble of 1720 was the occasion for the linguistic and conceptual naturalization of the market. Wilkinson argues that the corpus of South Sea poetry thus "rationalize[s] the idea of finance...in a manner that embraces the abstraction that is at the heart of the system." Elisabeth Wallmann's essay on "insect instinct" then explores the parallel abstractions taking place in nascent political economy and in eighteenth-century French biological thought. The essay demonstrates how the "*coup d'oeil*" of political economy is constructed upon French insect science's assertion that a "population" of creatures is above all "needs driven." The insect science that this essay attends to also forms an important link in the chain of the British tradition of political economy that was to develop from the 1760s, because Wallmann's main focus, Antoine Ferchault de Réaumur's *Mémoires pour servir à l'histoire des insectes* (1734–1742), is one of the texts Smith praises at some length in his 1756 *Letter to the* Edinburgh Review.[51]

The volume's next section then considers the status of "fictions" in relation to political economy. Lesa Scholl's essay on Harriet Martineau's *Cinnamon and Pearls* (1833) contends that this text's narrativization of political economic doctrine works to challenge—and pluralize—the assumptions it is simultaneously communicating. In this manner, Martineau's work amplifies the role allotted to the anecdote, or individualist example, in early political economy, but does so with an enhanced political agenda. Like the essay by John O'Brien in Part II of the volume, Scholl's essay brings into sharp focus the international and colonial contexts of political economy that are particularly marked in the early decades of the nineteenth century. Sarah Dredge's essay continues the exploration of political economy, fiction, and women writers by considering a broad spectrum of mid-nineteenth-century female-authored fiction engaged with economic questions and the communication of political economic knowledge. Dredge argues that political economy's attempt to present itself as a science depended on its creation of a fictional, male economic agent, and shows how this sustaining fiction is exposed and undermined in writing by Elizabeth Gaskell and others. In both this and Scholl's essay, questions of femininity seem to go hand-in-hand with narrativization and fiction, hinting at the disciplinary and generic hardenings taking place within and around early political economy.

Part II of the volume addresses political economy and its "others," and does so, to begin with, by considering the ideas of perspective, "vision" and the complex actors and groupings within an economy. John O'Brien's essay thus identifies the "master-metaphor" of sight in Thomas Malthus's *Essay on the Principle of Population* (1798) and explores how the growth of the "corporation" in the early nineteenth century works to disturb the assumptions of earlier political economy. O'Brien looks forward to the predominance of visual representation in current economics and finance addressed above by arguing that Malthus's reliance on the visual register is a strategic countering of what he takes to be an excessively narrative-based mode of historical analysis and future progress which he associates with Adam Smith and David Hume. This essay's attention to the status of the corporation also anticipates a significant feature of the current Western economic model, because according to Ha-Joon Chang, "30-50 per cent of international trade in manufactured goods is actually intra-firm trade, or transfers of inputs and outputs within the same multi-national corporation or transnational corporation, with operations in multiple countries."[52] The next essay in the volume, Alex Deans's discussion of "Economies of moral surveillance in early nineteenth-century Glasgow" also problematizes the perspectives constructed in early political economy by exposing the shared substratum between a laissez-faire economic policy and early surveillance culture. Through Deans's analysis of the writing of Thomas Chalmers and Alexander Bailey Richmond, we see the extent to which a political economy's central actor—the rational, self-maximizing man denominated *homo œconomicus*—is in fact a heavily problematic abstraction. The political intrigues within early nineteenth-century Glasgow alone demonstrate that real economic actors must be managed and understood in very different terms.

Part II's second section addresses political economy and "affect," first through Mary Peace's essay on how Smithian economics eclipsed and nullified the "marriage" of "luxury and virtue" in eighteenth-century civil society. This marriage, Peace demonstrates, was apparently embodied in the figure of William Dodd until his execution at Tyburn in 1777. By explaining the resonances of this event, Peace weaves together an intricate picture of the moral, sentimental, and primitivist currents at work within and around nascent political economy. Joshua Gooch then extends this account of the affective categories that contend with political economy to the later nineteenth century, a period in which this discourse ascends into the central mode of political and social analysis. Gooch's essay considers in detail the manner in which "love" and "anxiety" manifest the fraught politics of inheritance in the work of Charles Dickens and his contemporaries. This focus on inheritance reflects the manner in which this issue had become central to political economy's preoccupation with capital, class antagonisms, and the possibility of reform.

The volume's third part, finally, brings the concerns and ideas explored above up to the present moment by considering the current status of economics in the light of the volume's theoretical approaches. It does so through two essays: Poovey's "From the South Sea Bubble to Modern Finance: The Legacy of Two Eighteenth-Century Economic Ideas" and Marsh's "How the Market Has Been Seen." Poovey's piece draws out the political and ideological lessons that are generated by an informed and sensitive history of political economy and applies these to the current, supposedly all-powerful system of "high finance." Poovey contends that current economics needs to conceptualize the difference between "risk" and "uncertainty" with much more clarity and historical awareness, while also arguing that the current predominance of "finance" might lead us to introduce an even greater degree of scepticism into our conception of what economics is, and what it is trying to do. Like Poovey's, Marsh's essay also echoes the volume's initial concern with "abstraction," "modelling," and the unknowable, this time through detailed analysis of the meditations on abstracting and perceiving that take place in recent economic art. Marsh identifies a canon of artworks that take place simultaneously within and outside the current economic worldview. These objects thus both embody and parody the prevalence of economic modes of understanding to recent life in the West. Marsh also concludes the volume by reflecting on the value of its essays to our present intellectual moment. The essays included here, she claims, show us "forms of knowledge and knowing" that are now, slowly, infiltrating economics itself. The recent history of financial crises might now be read, in other words, as the catalyst for new possibilities, and new revisions of past knowledge.

Notes

1 See Robert Gordon, *The Rise and Fall of American Growth* (Princeton, NJ: Princeton University Press, 2016); Dani Rodrick's perspective is similar and was reflected in his Marie Jahoda Annual Lecture at the University of Sussex in February, 2016 titled "Is the Age of Growth Miracles Over?"

2 For example, Jamie Doward, Larry Elliott, Rod Ardehali and Terry Macalister, "The world has glimpsed financial crisis. But is the worst to come?" *The Observer*, 24 January 2016; Larry Elliott, "Beware the great 2016 financial crisis," *The Guardian*, 12 January 2016; Ben Marlow, "World economy stands on the cusp of another crash," *The Telegraph*, 27 February 2016.

3 The AHRC-supported project, "Show me the Money: The Image of Finance 1700 to the Present," constituting touring exhibition, website, and book is one example of work in this field. The book, of the same title, is edited by Paul Crosthwaite, Peter Knight and Nicky Marsh (Manchester: Manchester University Press, 2014).

4 Four amongst many recent critical studies of economic crisis, past and present, are Dwight Codr, *Raving At Usurers: Anti-Finance and the Ethics of Uncertainty in England 1690–1750* (Charlottesville: University of Virginia Press, 2016); Ian Klaus's *Forging Capitalism: Rogues, Swindlers, Frauds, and the Rise of Modern Finance*, (New Haven, CT: Yale University Press, 2014); Alison Shonkwiler, *The Financial Imaginary: Economic Mystification and the Limits of Realist Fiction* (Minneapolis: University of Minnesota Press, 2017); and Katy Shaw's *Crunch Lit* (London: Bloomsbury, 2015). For an illuminating collection of essays approaching financial crisis from a psychoanalytical perspective, see *Loaded Subjects: Psychoanalysis, money and the global financial crisis*, ed. David Bennett (London: Lawrence & Wishart, 2012).

5 Brian Young, "Introduction," in *Palgrave Advances in Intellectual History*, eds. Richard Whatmore and Brian Young (Basingstoke, UK: Palgrave, 2006), 1–2.

6 See John W. Burrow's survey, "Intellectual History in English Academic Life: Reflections on a Revolution," in *Palgrave Advances in Intellectual History*, eds. Whatmore and Young, 8–24. For an introduction to intellectual history, see Richard Whatmore's *What is Intellectual History?* (Cambridge: Polity, 2015) or *A Companion to Intellectual History*, eds. Richard Whatmore and Brian Young (Oxford: Wiley Blackwell, 2015); for intellectual history essays connected to the concerns and period of this volume, see *Economy, Polity and Society: British Intellectual History, 1750–1950*, eds. Stefan Collini, Richard Whatmore and Brian Young (Cambridge: Cambridge University Press, 2000). For recent work in this field, see the recently founded journal *Modern Intellectual History*, in which political economy is frequently discussed.

7 See the classic work, *Wealth and Virtue: The Shaping of Political Economy in the Scottish Enlightenment*, eds. Istvan Hont and Michael Ignatieff (Cambridge: Cambridge University Press, 1983). For the relations and differences between literary history and intellectual history, see Abigail Williams, "Literary and Intellectual History," in *Palgrave Advances in Intellectual History*, eds. Whatmore and Young, 49–65.

8 In addition to works already mentioned, see Vivienne Brown's *Adam Smith's Discourse: Canonicity, Commerce and Conscience* (London: Routledge, 1994) and the essays collected in *Adam Smith's Wealth of Nations: New Interdisciplinary Essays*, eds. Stephen Copley and Kathryn Sutherland (Manchester: Manchester University Press, 1995).

9 In addition to these works, see essays by Poovey, de Bolla and others on economic and financial concerns, in *This is Enlightenment*, eds. Clifford Siskin and William Warner (Chicago, IL: University of Chicago Press, 2010).

10 For "logic of modernity," see Timothy Mitchell, *Rule of Experts: Egypt, Techno-Politics, Modernity* (Berkeley: University of California Press, 2002), 1.

11 For Foucault's work of the history of the economy, see his *The Birth of Biopolitics* (Basingstoke, UK: Palgrave Macmillan, 2008) and "Governmentality," in *The Foucault Effect: Studies in Governmentality*, eds. Graham Burchell, Colin Gordon, and Peter Miller (London: Harvester Wheatsheaf, 1991), 87–104. Catherine Gallagher's *The Body Economic: Life, Death, and Sensation in Political Economy and the Victorian Novel* (Princeton, NJ: Princeton University Press, 2006) is one of example of work on literature and economy informed by Foucault.

12 It thus differs from, for example, Mike Hill and Warren Montag's recent study, *The Other Adam Smith* (Stanford, CA: Stanford University Press, 2015).

13 Lorraine Daston, "On Scientific Observation," *Isis* 99 (2008): 97–110 (97). Work in this field is too numerous to list but see also, classically, Steven Shapin and Simon Schaffer, *Leviathan and the Air-Pump: Hobbes, Boyle, and the Experimental Life* (Princeton, NJ: Princeton University Press, 1985), and Lorraine Daston and Peter Galison, *Objectivity* (Boston, MA: MIT Press, 2007).

14 Daston, "On Scientific Observation," 99.

15 Interestingly, this account of sight as a historically and culturally acquired practice, rather than a straightforward physical function of the body, would have been recognized by Adam Smith: see his early essay "Of the External Senses" in *Essays on Philosophical Subjects*, ed. W. P. D. Wightman and J. C. Bryce (Oxford: Clarendon Press, 1980), 135–68 and its reflection on the recovery of sight following the cataract-removal operations of the eye surgeon, William Cheselden.

16 Daston, "On Scientific Observation," 101.

17 Ibid., 107.

18 Ibid., 108.

19 Ibid., 110.

20 Timothy Mitchell, *Rule of Experts: Egypt, Techno-Politics, Modernity* (Berkeley: University of California Press, 2002), 3.

21 Ibid., 6.

22 Ibid., 5.

23 Ibid., 8–9.

24 Ibid., 82.

25 Louis Dumont, *From Mandeville to Marx: The Genesis and Triumph of Economic Ideology* (Chicago, IL: University of Chicago Press, 1977), 24. On Quesnay's zigzag, see Susan Buck-Morss, "Envisioning Capital: Political Economy on Display," *Critical Inquiry* 12:2 (1995): 434–67 (440). For other diagrammatic innovations central to the development of political economy, including Scottish political economist William Playfair's graphs and bar charts, see Edward Tufte, *The Visual Display of Quantitative Information* (Berkeley: University of California Press, 1983); on the history of visualizations of knowledge, and the innovations of eighteenth-century "political arithmetic" within that, see Anne Burdick, Johanna Drucker, Peter Lunenfeld, Todd Presner, and Jeffrey Schnapp, *Digital_Humanities* (Boston, MA: MIT Press, 2012), 43.

26 David McNally, *Political Economy and the Rise of Capitalism: A Reinterpretation* (Berkeley: University of California Press, 1988), 110; quoted in Buck-Morss, "Envisioning Capital," 440.

27 Widely reported, including in *The Financial Times*, 5 April 2016.

28 One chapter of John Lanchester's account of the 2008 crisis is indeed titled "Rocket Science"; See *Whoops! Why everyone owes everyone and no one can pay* (London: Penguin, 2010).

29 See Simon Johnson, IMF chief economist, "The Quiet Coup," *Atlantic Monthly*, May 2009, accessed 9 August 2017, www.theatlantic.com/doc/200905/imf-advice, and David Graeber, *Debt: The First 5000 Years* (London: Melville House, 2011), 401–2, n. 12.

30 Our sense of economics as a discipline in crisis is also reflected in the current student movement within the economics departments of some universities, such as Manchester, for extensive reform of a curriculum whose shortcomings have been linked to the larger failures of the economics establishment. See *Economics, Education and Unlearning: Economics Education at the University of Manchester*, Post-Crash Economics Society (PCES), April 2014, accessed 9 August 2017, www.post-crasheconomics.com/download/778r. The publication is introduced by Andrew Haldane, chief economist at the Bank of England. For essays by leading economists on the need to rethink current economic orthodoxies, see *Rethinking Capitalism*, eds. Michael Jacobs and Mariana Mazzucato (Oxford: Wiley-Blackwell, 2016).

31 Adam Smith, "The Principles which Lead and Direct Philosophical Enquiries; Illustrated by the History of Astronomy," in *Essays on Philosophical Subjects*, ed. W. P. D. Wightman (Oxford: Clarendon, 1980), 31–105.

32 Ibid., 46.

33 Ibid., 66, 75.

34 Ibid., 105.

35 For more on "The History of Astronomy," on Smith's debt to Hume's notion of the association of ideas, and for the status of the imagination in Scottish Enlightenment philosophy more generally, see Catherine Packham, "Feigning Fictions: Imagination, Hypothesis, and Philosophical Writing in the Scottish Enlightenment," *The Eighteenth Century* 48:2 (2007): 149–71; on Smith's understanding of philosophy more broadly, see Eric Schliesser, "Adam Smith's benevolent and self-interested conception of philosophy," in *New Voices on Adam Smith*, eds. Leonidas Montes and Eric Schliesser, (London: Routledge, 2006), 328–57. Dani Rodrik's revisionist account of economic methodology, offered in *Economics Rules* (Oxford: Oxford University Press, 2015), shares with Smith a stress on the contingent nature of economic thought.

36 Michel Foucault, *The Birth of Biopolitics: Lectures at the Collège de France, 1978–1979*, ed. Michel Senellart, trans. Graham Burchell (Oxford: Palgrave, 2008), 278. Foucault's note refers the reader to Jacob Viner, *The Role of Providence in Social Order* (Philadelphia, PA: Philadelphia University Press, 1972) for the theological sources of Smith's conception of the invisible hand, but Viner's brief account of Smith simply (and questionably) takes Smith's references to "nature" as self-evidently references to divine providence.

37 Giorgio Agamben, *The Kingdom and The Glory: For a Theological Genealogy of Economy and Government*, trans. Lorenzo Chiesa (Stanford, CA: Stanford University Press, 2011), 283. See Smith, *The Theory of Moral Sentiments*, eds. D. D. Raphael and A. L. Macfie (Oxford: Clarendon, 1976), 36, 292.

38 August Oncken was the originator of this phrase in 'Das Adam Smith Problem', *Zeitschrift für Sozialwissenschaft* 1 (1898): 25–33, 101–8, 267–87.

39 See Maxine Berg, *The Machinery Question and the Making of Political Economy, 1815–1848* (Cambridge: Cambridge University Press, 1980), 161–66.

40 Mitchell, *Rule of Experts*, 1; Rodrik also discusses modern economic modelling methods as abstractions or thought experiments which model the consequences of human qualities, tendencies or actions.

41 On economic models, see also Mary S. Morgan, *The World in the Model: How Economists Work and Think* (Cambridge: Cambridge University Press, 2012).

42 Rodrik's willingness to read economic models as forms of representation amongst others (such as the fable or analogy) is offset by his defense of mathematics as a supreme language for economics on the grounds of its greater claims to precision and accuracy.

43 See Emma Rothschild, *Economic Sentiments: Adam Smith, Condorcet, and the Enlightenment* (Cambridge, MA: Harvard University Press, 2001), 118–19, for the suggestion that this iconic phrase has Shakespearean origins, in *Macbeth*. For a phrase which, as Rothschild suggests, should be read as a "mildly ironic joke," it has had a remarkable afterlife. For a study of the history of organization suggested by the term, see *Invisible Hands: Self-Organization and the Eighteenth Century*, Jonathan Sheehan and Dror Wahrman (Chicago, IL: Chicago University Press, 2015); for one example of its suggestiveness for literary criticism, see Stefan Andriopoulos, "The Invisible Hand: Supernatural Agency in Political Economy and the Gothic Novel," *ELH* 66 (1999): 739–58.

44 See for instance, Warren J. Samuels, *Erasing the Invisible Hand* (Cambridge: Cambridge University Press, 2014).

45 See Mary Poovey's claim that abstraction is the stylistic key to *The Wealth of Nations*, in *Genres of the Credit Economy*, 144. For a detailed account of the formation of the abstract concept of the "division of labour," see Peter de Bolla, "Mediation and the Division of Labor," in *This is Enlightenment*, eds. Siskin and Warner.

46 Recent scholarship has indeed attempted to highlight or counter the kinds of occlusions inherent in moment of political economy's self-instantiation; see, for example, Mike Hill and Warren Montag, *The Other Adam Smith* (Stanford, CA: Stanford University Press, 2014) and Murray Millgate and Shannon C. Stimson, *After Adam Smith: A Century of Transformation in Politics and Political Economy* (Princeton, NJ: Princeton University Press, 2011).

47 John Stuart Mill, *Principles of Political Economy*, in *Collected Words of John Stuart Mill*, ed. J. M. Robson, 33 vols. (London: Routledge, 1965), 2:199.

48 Ibid., 3:754.

49 V. W. Bladen, 'Introduction', in ibid., 2:xxxix.

50 Despite such attempts to police economic orthodoxies, steady-state economics has in fact been a persistent presence in economic thinking since Mill.

51 See Adam Smith, *A Letter to the* Edinburgh Review, in *Essays on Philosophical Subjects*, eds. W. P. D Wightman and J. C. Bryce (Indianapolis, IN: Liberty Fund, 1982), 242–54 (248–49).

52 Ha-Joon Chang, *Economics: The User's Guide* (London: Penguin, 2004), 177.

Part I

Representation and Political Economy

Section 1

Abstractions

1 "The Visionary Scene Was Lost in Air"[1]

Conceptualizing Finance after the South Sea Bubble

Claire Wilkinson

Currunt scilicet Omnia
Sphærâ, non vitreâ quidem,
(Ut quondam siculus globus)
Sed vitro nitidâ magis,
Sed vitro fragili magis,
Et vitro vitreâ magis.

Obviously all things run in a
sphere, indeed not glassy
(as once the Sicilian globe)
but more shining than glass,
more brittle than glass, more
glassy than glass.[2]

Richard Crashaw's "Bulla" was first published in 1646, appended to an edition of Daniel Heinsius's *Crepundia Siliana*. The poem conducts a metaphysical examination of the empirical world, which is found to be as fleeting and unstable as a bubble, before conflating both life and poetry with the bubble's ephemeral physical manifestation: "Vixit ad huc. Cur Vixit? Adhuc tu nempe legebas" ("Still it lived. Why did it live? Indeed [because] you read this far.")[3] The poem exists in being read, and then, like a bubble, it bursts—ends—and becomes nothing, its substance shown in retrospect to be sustained only by the reader's attention. The bubble becomes a representation of the emptiness of language, but the poem is provocatively aware of its own paradoxical status: as spoken words, it is intangible, but in its inscribed form, it has a substantivity that exists beyond any singular instance of being read. It is this playfulness that makes it a particularly suitable postscript for Heinsius's *Crepundia*, which was initially published in 1600 and argues that writing is an enduring form and is worthy of sustained critical attention.[4] With its interest in the mutable substance of language, Crashaw's poem at once endorses and unsettles this belief: the poem is something and nothing, and is itself implicated by the conceit that everything observable is transient.

Although "Bulla" was written nearly 50 years before the establishment of the Bank of England and the first issue of a bank note in 1694, the poem resonates with several of the key structural economic changes that would come to define the Financial Revolution in Great Britain.[5] The Revolution of 1688 is distinctive for its introduction of public credit to the English economy. As P. G. M. Dickson describes in *The Financial Revolution in England*, when King William III faced the urgent question of increasing national wealth to enable developments in agriculture and commerce, and—critically—to finance war with France, he developed a system of long-term government borrowing. This system allowed funds to be raised without tax rates being increased, and it also set a precedent for a new type of investment in the state, whereby private individuals could receive a guaranteed income on money lent to the country.[6] The new credit economy had reached a point of almost intractable crisis by 1720: The South Sea Company, which had been created in 1711 to reduce government debt, was facing disaster. Stock prices had steadily risen since the company's inception, but the decision to issue more shares in 1720 to further alleviate the National Debt proved catastrophic.[7] Public interest in the new stock was unprecedented, and prices rose rapidly before crashing in the late summer. Swift, who would later criticize the grounds for the Company's operation, was supportive of the project in its early years and argued that it was "likely to prove the greatest Restoration and Establishment of the kingdom's Credit" in 1711.[8] The opposite proved to be true, and as the promises of new finance came crashing down, the task of analysing the Bubble's social and political ramifications fell to the economic commentators, journalists, and literary writers of the day. There are many reasons why the South Sea Bubble offers a compelling moment in financial history to reflect upon the structural changes that the economy underwent after the accession of King William to the throne in 1688: the Bubble was the first stock market crisis in England, and in its aftermath, various assumptions that had kept South Sea shares afloat were exposed. As Christine Gerrard explains, "the South Sea crisis marked the culmination of the process begun with the creation of the National Debt under William."[9] In addition, the cultural accounts of the crisis that emerged in the wake of the Bubble are remarkable and span visual art, literary writing, journalism, private letters, and theatre. The crisis prompted a widespread process of reconceptualization, during which the implications of the new economic structure were reflected upon, debated, and finally integrated into an understanding of what the financial market might represent. The structural changes that were beginning to become manifest in the early 1720s provide the framework for how Britain's economy functions to this day.

Crashaw's "Bulla" predates the South Sea Bubble by almost a century; however, the poem's interest in interconnection pre-empts one of the most significant imaginative shifts that took place during the Financial

Revolution, a shift which began to be consolidated in the months and years following the South Sea Bubble. Crashaw writes "*Currunt scilicet Omnia / Sphærâ*" ("Obviously all things run in a / sphere") and, earlier in the poem, "*Orbes orbibus obvii*" ("the spheres meet the spheres"). He is interested in interconnection, in how these connections are intrinsic but nevertheless fragile, and in how observing these networks in some way changes, or obscures, their substance. The appearance of the Bubble in 1720 was a symptom of the increasing connection and interdependence of all sorts of economic market players. As J. G. A. Pocock observes, by selling state debt to private investors, the government created a class of investors with a specific financial interest in the country's economic success.[10] One of the prevailing interests of authors writing about the Bubble after its rupture is the speciousness of value represented by South Sea Company shares. A letter written to the *Weekly Journal or Saturdays-Post* in March 1721 asked "how could it be [...] that such Numbers of people should lay out *substantial Fortunes* for a Thing which has *no Being* but in *Imagination*?"[11] The theme is alighted upon too in poetry by Swift, Gay, and Pope. In "The Bubble" (1720), Swift writes about the folly of investors:

> While some build Castles in the Air,
> Directors build 'em in the Seas;
> Subscribers plainly see 'um there,
> For Fools will see as Wise men please.[12]

Gay is equally acerbic in 1721's *A Panegerical Epistle to Mr. Thomas Snow*, lamenting the loss of "Millions of imaginary Gold."[13] Pope's most substantial comment on the crisis did not follow until 1733, when he wrote in the *Epistle to Bathurst*:[14]

> Blest paper-credit! last and best supply!
> That lends Corruption lighter wings to fly!
> Gold imp'd by thee, can compass hardest things,
> Can pocket States, can fetch or carry Kings.[15]

The preoccupation of each poem is the role of the imaginary in the crisis, and how value had become ascribed to entirely fictitious tokens. The authors question the significance of perspective, with Swift's watery South Sea offering a strange refraction of a directors' promise, and Pope's contracted "imp'd" at once signifying "implied," "enlarged," and "stolen."[16] It becomes clear that the substantivity of South Sea value is a matter of projection, and that the illusions of wealth are subject to modulations, depending upon who is looking, and how. It is the subscribers to the shares who see phantom castles and gold, whilst the Company's directors experience the materialization of these objects in reality, as they reap the profits of widespread investment. Crashaw's poem comments upon how objects in the empirical world exist when observed, but vanish as the subject's attention turns away. This fragility of substance is transmuted to metaphor in the South Sea Bubble work: the wealth is always an illusion, and the Bubble serves to show that the financial innovation represented by early eighteenth-century credit instruments has the potential to unsettle all established modes of representation.

In *Genres of the Credit Economy*, Mary Poovey explores how "the credit economy in which we still live came to be naturalized and understood," and it is the formative stage of this process of naturalization that I take as my topic in this paper.[17] Public credit was new in the early eighteenth century, and it reshaped not only how the economy could function, but also demanded that existing ideas about economic structure and operation were reconceptualized. The South Sea Bubble represented both the zenith and the nadir of this new potential, and the crisis exposed the connections between the imaginative and actual systems that underpin economic function. If we take the dominant historical argument, which is set out by Pocock and P.G.M. Dickson before it is taken up by a later generation of critics, that the South Sea Bubble provided space—in intellectual thought and market function—for a consolidation of the terms of the post-1688 credit economy, then what actually *happens* during this period of consolidation is of fundamental importance to understanding today's economy, precisely because it is formative.[18] The highs and lows of 1720 show enthusiasm for the inflationary properties of credit being tempered by the reality of absolute loss, triggering a phase in which cultural concepts of the economy were redefined. Speaking about this process in broad terms has a certain allure, not least because there is something intriguing about the idea of a formative reconceptualization that is evidenced in cultural output without being overtly aspired to, but it is the contention of this chapter that the language of a small group of literary writers working in the post-Bubble years demonstrates the integration of the rhetoric of credit in popular culture. I want to make a series of small and interconnected arguments relating to this process. The first is that Swift and Gay—to differing extents—attempt to understand the new economic world by way of the vocabulary of the old. The second is that this mode of representation eventually fails, and it is in failing that it is, perhaps paradoxically, most successful. The final turn of my argument is that the language employed by these three writers in a series of poems performs a variety of microtransaction, which more fully exposes the extent of establishment of the new system that was shaped around credit at the turn of the eighteenth century. Central to this point is the idea that the economic metaphors used in a set of poetic examples of South Sea Bubble writing are encoded at a systemic level, and thereby do not belong to the author, but are a distinctive facet of a system which is being integrated by the very writing in which it is observed.

Before I come to rely upon the word "system," some explanation is needed about my use of the term. In *System: The Shaping of Modern Knowledge*, Clifford Siskin argues that "system is a genre—a form that works physically in the world to mediate our efforts to know it," and he aims to "illuminate system's role in the shaping and reshaping of modern knowledge."[19] "System" is a form of organizing practice, in which interacting processes complement one another in operation, and provide a framework within which activities and actions both happen and can be understood. Siskin describes literature as a "cultural form," itself involved in systemic practice, but simultaneously a medium through which the shape of other contemporaneous systems is made manifest.[20] System-related words begin to be used more frequently during the eighteenth century, and Siskin comments:

> What these variations of *system* at the century's end — *systematise, systematising, systemization* — signal is not just the presence or increasing number of things called "system," but the spread of a social practice: of using system's scalability to provide order within and across more things. As those things were put into the form of system — their parts reordered into new wholes — those wholes became parts of a larger whole. The reordering, that is, replicated itself at a larger and larger scale, producing a historically specific effect: that extraordinary sense of the social — of the totalizing of the social — that we now call "The System."[21]

What matters here is the system's ability to "provide order within and across more things": viewed as a system, state finance in the eighteenth century becomes an operational *thing*, which is more than the sum of discrete parts: indeed, its systemic function dictates that its parts cannot be discrete. The South Sea Bubble provides a moment in cultural history when an epistemic reconceptualization of the (new) market in finance was necessitated in the wake of crisis. This new variety of crisis is defined by the functionality of the changing financial system, and after the 1720 Bubble, assumptions which had become unexceptional *within* the system demanded integration in social understanding.

Siskin's earlier work on systems is developed by Robert Mitchell in his *Sympathy and the State in the Romantic Era*, which claims that theories of sympathy and identification develop in periods of financial crisis, because the system that governs state finance becomes observable at these moments:

> It was no coincidence, I suggest, that theories of sympathy and identification emerged around periods of financial crisis (1720s, early 1750s, late 1780s, final years of the 1790s, and 1815-21), for it was precisely during periods of financial panic that state finance became

> visible *as* a "system" that connected people to one another through affective bonds of belief, "Opinion," and desire. During these periods of crisis, the system of state finance appeared both totalizing and contingent: totalizing in the sense that the other systems of society seemed to depend upon it; contingent in the sense that the system of state finance appeared on the verge of collapse.[22]

Mitchell creates this line of argument to assert that the defining features of Romanticism grow out of an emerging awareness of systems which remain hidden when they operate smoothly, and when this perspective is looked at in conjunction with Siskin's, it becomes clear that it is the exposure of the system's mechanisms that defines the drive towards social identification with systemic structures more generally. This idea of "social identification" depends upon a further concept which is discussed by Mitchell, that of the "collective imagination," which forms in the late seventeenth and early eighteenth centuries, and behaves as a vehicle for "the sort of change [...] capable of encouraging conceptual transformations."[23] What Mitchell means by this is that the nature of social relations was reconfigured in the years after the Financial Revolution, and that this reconfiguration allowed for certain ideas connected to finance and the economy to become dominant in discourse; effectively, "public understanding" was born.[24] The idea emerges from observation of the different varieties of social systems that connect individuals in their understanding of the separate, institutional, systems that they must, by necessity, interact with. The nascent financial institutions that represented and propagated "state finance," for example, are discrete but contributory elements to the overarching systemic phenomenon of "state finance"; the system cannot be located in any one particular place, but yet it provides a governing hierarchy, and, critically, a place of imaginative recourse. As Siskin writes in "Novels and Systems":

> The power—political and discursive—of The System is indexed by our capacity to make it both ubiquitous and culpable, for invoking The System has become a primary modern means of totalizing and rationalizing our experience of the social.[25]

In some ways, the modern system that Siskin invokes (his commentary, here, applies the principles of the post-1780 novel to contemporary life) represents a reification of abstract processes into a definable object, whilst, with an unerringly precise simultaneity, representing the exact opposite of this: a specific identification of the separate social components that come to behave as systems. The examples of South Sea Bubble literature that I look at here are starting to understand—or to naturalize, to use Poovey's vocabulary—the foundations of a financial system that was already operational by 1720, but which only started to become manifest in the aftermath of the crisis. That language performs awareness of this regardless of the rhetorical grain of a piece of writing stands as further evidence for the extensiveness and penetration of the systemic in early eighteenth-century finance.

* * *

It is difficult to cut a clear path through existing criticism of the South Sea Bubble, in part because the work spans several disciplines and theoretical inclinations, and in part because of the multifocal lens through which the crisis has been viewed. Different studies have stressed the role of gambling, cheating, hysteria, manipulation, rationality and irrationality, market fundamentals, continental share markets, and political alliances, in the period leading up to and following the Bubble, and it is a fair assumption that some permutation of the elements above influenced the market conditions of 1720.[26] As Crashaw argued in 1646, a physical bubble is by its nature isolated, but yet the South Sea Bubble arose not as an aberration in the financial market, but as a species of connection; the culmination of a series of political, social, and economic factors that were beginning to define the structure of the national economy after the introduction of state finance.[27] As South Sea writers attempt to explain the manifestation and consequences of the Bubble, they demonstrate an early, but fascinating, comprehension of the new shape of the market. This work represents a naturalization of the credit economy, and the permanent entrenchment of inflationary capital in public discourse. In *Writing and the Rise of Finance*, the most comprehensive literary study of this period, Colin Nicholson describes how "the paper money systems of public credit and the commodities thereby circulated seemed to be assuming sole and overwhelming command of all social valuation."[28] Nicholson argues that the shift in the economic system after the introduction of public credit was mirrored in society as the country experienced a movement away from a traditional understanding of the domestic economy, to a new and more abstract mode founded upon the tenets of modern finance. This difference between the "traditional" and the "new" forms the basis of Nicholson's comparison, which he centres around political differences between the Tories and the Whigs: the post-1688 Financial Revolution is seen to create a new class of "moneyed men," to use Swift's phrase, who are separate from the landed gentry, and have different economic interests.[29] The divide is at least partly political: the Tories represent the interests of "old" money and land, and the Whigs the "new" financial capital, their voices circulated by publications including Addison and Steele's *Spectator*.[30] The poetry that Gay and Swift wrote about the South Sea Bubble in the months and years after its rupture reveals an underlying systemic shift away from the Tory terms of land and inherited wealth; however, the conceptual shift that would subsequently naturalize the precedence of state finance remains incomplete in the rhetoric of these works, which discuss the rise of the credit economy using the language of old, inherited economic structures. The writing thereby provides an imaginative resistance to the consequences of the newly embedded abstraction in the financial system.

John Gay's pre-1720 poetry adheres to an understanding of the pre-credit economy, despite being written after the beginning of state finance and public credit. The work sits, historically, in the interstitial period between the introduction of the various instruments that would come to define the new shape of the economy and their naturalization after the South Sea Bubble. Gay's writing, even before the 1720 crisis, is often heavily interested in financial matters, and in a series of epistles written for three different patrons in 1720, the fiscal relationship between subjects, and between poet and patron, is represented according to the principles of material exchange. David Nokes writes that "Gay is the poet of money [...] His emphasis is simple and consistently ironic," an observation which holds true in relation to Gay's pre-Bubble writing, in which the structure of a marketplace in which all things can be reduced to commodities and exchanged for one another is manifest.[31] A letter written in 1720 to Jacob Tonson, Gay's publisher, demonstrates this preoccupation:

> To go to the strictness of the matter, I own my note engages me to make the whole payment in the beginning of September, had it been in my power, I had not given you occasion to send to me, for I can assure you I am as impatient & uneasy to pay the money I owe, as some men are to receive it, and tis no small mortification to refuse you so reasonable a request, which is, that I may no longer be obliged to you.[32]

The note was written in the immediate aftermath of the South Sea Bubble, after Gay had lost a substantial amount of money held in shares—of which a more detailed discussion follows below. The letter conflates personal and financial commitment: the debt is figured as a possession, which changes hand in the opposite direction to the money that forms the substance of the loan. Whilst Gay holds Tonson's money, Tonson holds Gay's obligation, which is immaterial but nevertheless a retrievable form of collateral. Gay's inability to repay the loan according to the terms of the agreement places him in a position of debt which is not exclusively financial: Tonson, in possession of Gay's figurative obligation, will retain this moral currency until his money is returned. The dialogue between moral and physical ownership informs the entirety of the letter, and when Gay writes "I own my note engages me," he juxtaposes the nuance of "I own" meaning "I admit" with the more literal sense of physical ownership. This crafts a complicated relationship between the material and the immaterial. Gay is in receipt of a sum from Tonson which is physical, whilst Tonson temporarily possesses the figurative "obligation" named by Gay in his apology. Gay's personal obligation is written as a physical thing here, and by rendering the loan as an exchange of two substantive materials, a straightforward debit / credit equation is formed. Gay's "note," invoked in the first line, represents the loan and is itself a tangible item which can be purchased, owned, and exchanged—much like the considerably less tangible credit that it signifies. The contract behaves in the same manner as a bank note: it is a signifier for value deferred, but it does not attain the level of abstract signification that bank notes represent because the debt can only be expressed between the two men. The "note" indicating the terms of the loan thereby behaves *almost* as a bank note, but the value is never truly abstract because the debt is strictly personal. Though Gay's language quite clearly commoditizes the obligation, it will not be sold on, and the market frame that the token exists within is strictly delineated.

It is this honour-based understanding of financial relationships that Gay pursues in his Epistles to Burlington, Pulteney, and Methuen, all published before the South Sea Bubble burst, in 1720. Each piece was written under patronage, an employment model Gay frequently relied upon for income, and the poems are quite explicit about the terms of their composition.[33] The irony that Nokes observes in Gay's writing is particularly explicit in this group of poems; the pieces perform a dual service, behaving as purchased commodity and as medium for sardonic praise. In the "Epistle to Burlington" and the "Epistle to Pulteney," the act of patronage is further compounded: Gay makes a journey on behalf of his patron and also writes a poem to commemorate both the grandeur of the trip and the act of patronage itself. The opening six lines to "Burlington" set this scene:

> While you, my Lord, bid stately Piles ascend,
> Or in your *Chiswick* Bow'rs enjoy your Friend;
> Where *Pope* unloads the Bough within his reach,
> Of purple Grape, blue Plumb, or blushing Peach;
> I journey far.—You knew fat Bards might tire,
> And, mounted, sent me forth your trusty Squire.[34]

Gay, as speaker, does not appear in the poem until the fifth line, after an opulent west London house has been described. The opening two lines serve to elevate Burlington, whilst the next two mock Pope—who, as a rather more wealthy contemporary of Gay, is seen lounging and eating ripe fruit in Burlington's house. The opening is densely allusive: the implication that Burlington might "enjoy [his] Friend" has an explicit sexual nuance, which is complemented by the "blushing Peach" consumed by Pope, who is himself criticized for his short stature and excessive weight; he is likely the "fat Bard" of line four. The poem's uninterrupted iambic rhythm is sustained into line five, when the dash separating the first two feet from the following three forces a pause after four relatively flat syllables. The poem slows, the idyllic scene is interrupted, and just as the *clip-clop* of the regular opening fades, Gay is introduced, mounted on a horse, in a position of servitude that is juxtaposed to the excessive luxury of Burlington's home building and Pope's indulgence. The act described in the poem is work to Gay, and he positions himself rhetorically as the best-suited man for the job: Burlington is too busy, Pope too lethargic and gorged with money and food. In the "Epistle to Pulteney," patronage and commission are handled less explicitly, but nevertheless are manifest in both the texture and language of the poem. The exclamation "What! cannot Paris one poor page afford?" (l. 2) makes a pun on page, referring to a page of written poetry and Gay's employment. The poem opens with this and a direct address to "*Pult'ney*," so there is no sense that Gay is trying to obscure the origins of composition of the piece, but patronage is addressed indirectly, as opposed to being explicitly discussed:

> Trav'lers should ever fit expression chuse,
> Nor with low phrase the lofty theme abuse.
> When they describe the state of eastern Lords,
> Pomp and magnificence should swell their words;
> And when they paint the serpent's scaly pride,
> Their lines should hiss, their numbers smoothly slide;
> But they, unmindful of Poetick rules,
> Describe alike Mockaws and great *Moguls*.[35]

In the description of upper class Paris, Gay criticizes travellers who cannot speak in the appropriate register when describing "Lords," on one hand, and "serpents" on the other. In error, and unaware of both poetic and courtly conventions, these unversed visitors describe macaws—known for their imitation of the human voice—and moguls using the same words. The poem owes part of its effect to its ironically straight-laced approach; the poet writing under patronage must prioritize the reputation of the Lord, rather than the truth, and he must seek to perpetuate the "lofty theme." In this passage of the poem, Gay exhibits his own claims to high culture, and assures Pulteney that he will be treated according to the poetic convention surrounding patrons, if not explicitly honestly. Pulteney has purchased a service, and Gay's writing is figured as a commodity—a material—that can be exchanged in return for money.

In "Burlington" and "Pulteney," Gay is concerned with the presentation of material exchange, both in the context of the poem's commodity status and in terms of the transactions represented within the writing.

Assets and services are given prices, and are situated in a framework of relative value. This creates a distinct dialogue of commodity exchange, as found in this example from "Burlington":

> The Morning rose; the Supper Reck'ning paid,
> And our due Fees discharg'd to Man and Maid,
> The ready Ostler near the Stirrup stands,
> And as we mount, our Half-pence load his Hands.[36]

The payment for a night's lodging and the inn's services is repeated three times across four lines: "the Supper Reck'ning paid," "our due Fees discharg'd," and "our Half-pence load his Hands." The first two payments are described once they are complete, and the money that settles the bills is not seen. The final payment is different: the ostler, or innkeeper, waits by the party's horses, and the final settlement of the balance is conducted as the transfer of a "Half-pence," witnessed by the reader, as it passes from the travelling party to the attendant. The value of services rendered is expressed materially with the object coin, and the action of loading the worker's hands makes reference to the job carried out on behalf of the party, and the acceptance of payment in return. A similar instance is found later in the poem:

> The Maid, subdu'd by Fees, her Trunk unlocks,
> And gives the cleanly Aid of Dowlas Smocks.[37]

The maid's action is directly governed by payment, and she is subordinate to the financial value of her task. The *OED* traces subdued, which commonly means "to be toned down or quiet," to 1785, and in Johnson's *Dictionary*, an earlier definition of "subdue," "to crush; to oppress; to sink; to overpower" is given.[38] The verb is more active, and Gay contrasts a relatively unexceptional task—removing linen from a trunk—with its effect. The maid is obliged to carry out the work, and her "Fee" purchases her service, ultimately commoditizing her time, and oppressing her. "Load," in the previous quotation, and "subdud'd," here, reveal a complicated interaction between material and abstract values. The verbs point to the physical weight of money and the material nature of the exchange described, as well as the manner in which this materiality is experienced by, or registered on, each individual's own material embodiment. Gay seems to describe a simple dialectic relationship between goods and services, and the money that pays for them: a quantifiable task is performed, and the worker is reimbursed in return for their efforts. The individual—and his or her time—is thereby directly commoditized, and the act of payment resolves a simple equation.

The straightforward exchange of services for money gestures towards a material accountability which admits no abstraction, yet whilst the system Gay sketches appears to behave in this way, ultimately it cannot be reduced to such rudimentary terms. Payment, as "Fees" which are "discharg'd" in cash in the poem, depends upon the established monetary system. Money operates as a signifier—or token—of material value which defers or blurs the presence of any substantive material value, even before the development of the credit economy. The concern is demonstrably contemporary: Locke, in a 1691 pamphlet which describes money in circulation, writes:

> Now Money is necessary to all these sorts of Men [landowners, labourers, brokers, shopkeepers], as serving both for Counters and for Pledges, and so carrying with it even Reckoning and Security, that he, that receives it, shall have the same value for it again, of other things that he wants, whenever he pleases.[39]

Locke describes the abstraction that must be accepted for money to function within a financial system; the token must retain a consistent value, and it must be a *universal equivalent*. The token, or coin, that represents this value, is by nature a representation of an abstraction. Gay's choice of words in the "Epistle to Burlington" emphasizes the materiality of the coins transferred, which "load" and "subdue" their recipients with a physical presence that is surely non-abstract. Whether we are dealing with denial, irony, nostalgia, or misunderstanding on the level of Gay's conceptualization of the deferred value signified by money remains in question. The note to Tonson visualizes money in a similarly absolute manner; the moral debt to the publisher is incurred in an inability to pay the monetary debt, and Gay does not seek to deconstruct the substantivity of the financial commitment itself. It is a fixed quantity, the most pure form in which Gay's obligation can be expressed.

The apparent disjunction in Gay's understanding of money, between its physical and symbolic properties, cannot be resolved by way of reference to the fundamentally abstract qualities of the monetary system. Locke's writing from the 1690s explains a historic assumption that must be accepted for abstract monetary systems to function under any circumstances, and it seems that Gay neglects this, preferring instead to describe trade relationships in tangible and immediately accountable terms, without considering the abstraction built into the heart of the system. Writing off Gay's representation of payment systems as dysfunctional or poorly substantiated might resolve the matter of the opposition between materiality and abstraction, but it does not allow us to consider the other relations that inform the exchanges that Gay describes. Hume's *Treatise of Human Nature* (1738) offers a social framework alongside which Gay's poetic transactions are much more clearly intelligible. For Hume, the credit instruments introduced in the late seventeenth century by the state are only the latest incarnation of the essentially speculative or imaginative nature of "social essence," an intrinsically speculative force which emerges from a collective investment in the future.[40] Hume writes: "the actions of each of us [...] are perform'd upon the supposition, that something is to be perform'd on the other part."[41] This equation takes away the problem of money's difficult relationship with materiality, and reduces the commitment recounted in Gay's "Burlington" to the action of payment in exchange for the action of service. Robert Mitchell argues that Hume's intervention is important precisely because it "suggests that late seventeenth-century financial instruments such as annuities and joint-stock companies should not be understood as displacing the purportedly true foundation of wealth in hereditary land; rather, they simply harnessed the speculative social essence in new forms."[42] This disrupts the idea that the introduction of new, credit-based financial instruments caused a rupture in the social fabric of the country. If we read Gay according to Hume, he is already describing a speculative economy which depends not upon tangible transactions, but a universal—and non-financial—investment in futurity. Money behaves primarily as a social relation, and the relationship between its substance and its signification is already accountable to a higher ordering system.

Whether Gay's representation of money is interpreted as simplistic or sophisticated, the different epistles considered here certainly show a reluctance to embrace an increasingly financialized monetary economy, which is finally realized in 1721's "Epistle to Snow." The dialogue of commodification and exchange persists in "Burlington" and "Pulteney," and the poems repeatedly make the case for a material understanding of financial worth, in which the attributes of wealth are rendered physically, and seen in animation. In describing wealth as a decoration that ornaments affluent members of society, Gay creates an order in which wealth is manifested as material but also removable, and simultaneously subject to a set of social relations that exert power within the economic system. In the "Epistle to Pulteney," Gay contrasts the power that a rich man commands over women, with the powerless position of the impoverished poet:

> How happy lives the man, how sure to charm,
> Whose knot embroider'd flutters down his arm!
> On him the Ladies cast the yielding glance,
> Sigh in his songs, and languish in his dance;
> While wretched is the Wit, contemn'd, folorn,
> Whose gummy hat no scarlet plumes adorn;
> No broider'd flowers his worsted ankle grace,
> Nor cane emboss'd with gold directs his pace;
> No Lady's favour on his sword is hung.[43]

The financial assets of the wealthy man purchase adornments that in turn seduce the women around him, whilst the poet, too poor to buy embellishments, is unable to attract attention. Gay once again creates a simple equation—money buys advantage, and can be exchanged for "favour." Though this "favour" is by nature intangible, it is made material, and is "hung" on a sword. The passage's irony is inescapable: Gay is describing the purchase, direct or indirect, of sex, from women who are at once mercenary and at once commodities available for purchase. There is little sense that the poem's "Ladies" have any autonomy; they are driven away from the "Wit" (which stands as proper noun and adjective), towards the extravagantly adorned gentleman. This sense of wealth as material, as embodied in objects and ornamentation, is anachronistic, and deliberately so; the simplification of all social relations, including sexual power and exchange, to a monetary equation is provocative, and it seems to act as a rejection of an increasingly financialized monetary economy, in which the directness of financial relationships between individuals is obscured. Gay exhibits a nostalgia for a simplicity that has, perhaps, never existed, and all social tokens are taken into the orbit of directly exchangeable materiality.

This wealth, represented resolutely materially, is figured similarly in "Burlington," in which it bridges the gap between the town and the country:

> 'Twas here the Stage-coach'd Lass resign'd her Gold;
> That Gold which had in *London* purchas'd Gowns,
> And sent her home a *Belle* to Country Towns.[44]

"Gold" is animated in exchange; it is owned and exchanged, and possesses a residual transformative quality even after it has been swapped for goods. Gay's representation of materiality here moves away from the exchange of thing-for-thing seen in the "Half-pence" exchange for services elsewhere: gold is cast as the catalyst that enables movement up, or down, the social ladder, and its expenditure has a lingering magical effect. The "Stage-coach'd Lass" is robbed of her gold, but the very same material has *already* purchased gowns and transformed her into a "Belle." The material narrative and the metaphorical narrative cannot be consolidated with one another, and gold already expended is given substance again. The material is used like money in the way that it can purchase commodities—showing that it operates as a token of value—but its resistance to being spent (and even stolen—the dresses and status are not taken with the gold) marks it as different. The gold can be expended again and again, which perhaps represents a variant of credit, extended on reputation, against the perceived value of the original material.

Jameson discusses money becoming abstract in "Culture and Finance Capital," in the context of a much later historical moment (his focus is upon the formation of global capitalist connections in the early twentieth century):

> Capital itself becomes free-floating. It separates from the concrete context of its productive geography. Money becomes in a second sense and to a second degree abstract (it always was abstract in the first and basic sense), as though somehow in the national moment money still had a content. It was cotton money, or wheat money, textile money, railroad money, and the like. Now, like the butterfly stirring within the chrysalis, it separates itself from that concrete breeding ground and prepares to take flight.[45]

So many of Jameson's terms have no application in the late seventeenth and early eighteenth centuries: the empires that would grow around cotton grown by slaves in the Caribbean were still forming (one of the founding promises of the South Sea Company was that it would capitalize on the lucrative slave trade between Europe and America), the first intercity railway did not open until 1830, and in a world before industrialization, connecting money to commodities generated by specific industries is anachronistic. What Jameson detects is a second-degree abstraction in the monetary signification system, such that it becomes untethered in its representative capacity, and free to signify itself before any other relation. The South Sea Bubble shows that this "becoming abstract" happens much earlier, as a consequence of the integration of credit systems in both the national economy and the national psyche. The lines in "Burlington" demonstrate a simultaneous resistance to, and acceptance of, the principle of abstraction: Gay, who will not admit to the "first and basic sense" of money's abstract form in the payment of the ostler and maid, here embraces a wholly immaterial and abstracted account of financial worth, which links monetary tokens and commodities without rendering the former in the shape of the latter.

Gay's account of material exchange is not simplistic before the South Sea Bubble, but it does exhibit nostalgia for a straightforward relationship connecting work and worth. The multiply substantive gold in "Burlington" is a participant in this material understanding of exchange, though its characteristics extend beyond the model in which it is spent, and firmly connect the imagined material to a more nebulous credit system which is resisted by the poem's various narrative accounts of expenditure. The final element of Gay's pre-Bubble financial rhetoric to take into account is how patronage, and writing poetry on commission, interacts with this economy of incremental gains made in clearly conceptualized transactions. Whilst "Burlington" and "Pulteney" make reference to the patronage that has paid for their composition, the "Epistle to Methuen" concentrates upon the restrictions that patronage enforces. The relationship between patron and poet is described in the terms of a purchase, with the poet indebted to the patron until the piece is complete. In "Methuen," the exchange is complicated by an incomplete commodity-token swap, and Gay suggests that though poetry can be purchased, the transaction fundamentally compromises the integrity of the work produced. "Praise" is repeated three times in the poem, initially regarding the flattery of the subjects selected by the patron, but then subsequently in relation to the poet's own reputation in light of his work:

> Or if you chuse more sure and ready ways,
> Spatter a Minister with fulsome praise;[46]
> [...]
> Though let not me of grievances complain
> Who (though the meanest of the Muse's train)
> Can boast subscriptions to my humble lays,
> And mingle profit with my little praise.[47]
> [...]
> He who would free from malice pass his days,
> Must live obscure and never merit praise.[48]

The meaning of "praise" gradually modulates as the epistle progresses. The first example refers to the purchased pen, to the need for the poet to write according to his benefactor's demands. The praise is false, and the tone set here influences the subsequent uses of the word. Gay's second claim, that he is content with the money that patronage brings him, plays on patronage and recognition, and "praise" operates as both a reference to the praise within the work, and to the acclaim that Gay might receive, like a non-monetary value token, in recognition of his work. The final instance is sarcastic, and implies that praise is received in inverse proportion to merit. Gay comments upon the falsely complementary content of poems written for patrons, and also on the conflation of the poem as economic commodity and piece of art. "Praise" thereby becomes a form of payment given in numerous incarnations of exchange for the poem.

Without patronage, Gay would no longer need to write false praise, but equally he would not be able to gather the "little praise" that he is granted by the audiences of the work he produces by subscription and sponsorship. Poetry, according to this model, is complicit in the world of commodity exchange. In 1725, Defoe noted the rise of writing in English business, and commented that writing

> is becoming a very considerable Branch of the English Commerce. The Booksellers are the Master Manufacturers or Employers. The several Writers, Authors, Copyers, Sub-Writers and all other

operators with Pen and Ink are the workmen employed by the said Master-Manufacturers.[49]

Gay undermines this trade relationship as he profits from it, and though he engages with poetry in its most commoditized form, he resists the final collapse of the boundary between "poem" and "commodity." The aesthetic behaves as a site of potential resistance to material and transactional exchange. Gay uses the form of the poem to narrate transactions, and to describe the transactional history of his own commissioned work; however, despite the rising "business" of English writing that Defoe comments upon only five years later, and his own involvement in the market for commissioned poetry, Gay envisions poetic form as a site for representation rather than participation, first in the terms of simple material transaction, and then in the terms of credit. Though this resistance is consistently maintained, it is not consistently substantiated, and the imaginative system does not correspond to the financial system that was being shaped around the growing structures of credit. We see Gay dealing with a new financial mode before its naturalization in the collective imagination.[50] As Gay's writing employs the language of old and inherited economic structures and assumptions, metaphors belonging to the new system begin to appear in language before they are digested and crystallized in economic thought. It is to this phenomenon that we can attribute the unease, and the incomplete consolidation of abstract value forms in Gay's pre-Bubble writing.

Gay was the only of the Scriblerus writers who was not independently wealthy, and alongside writing poems for patronage and by subscription, he pursued several other avenues to improve his financial situation.[51] The investment opportunity offered by the South Sea Company in 1720 proved irresistible, and Gay's plight was later described by Johnson in *Lives of the English Poets*:

> Being now generally known, he published (1720) his Poems by subscription with such success, that he raised a thousand pounds; and called his friends to a consultation, what use might be best made of it. Lewis, the steward of Lord Oxford, advised him to entrust it to the funds, and live upon the interest; Arbuthnot bade him entrust it to Providence, and live upon the principal; Pope directed him, and was seconded by Swift, to purchase an annuity.
>
> Gay in that disastrous year had a present from young Craggs of some South sea-stock, and once supposed himself to be master of twenty thousand pounds. His friends persuaded him to sell his share; but he dreamed of dignity and splendour, and could not bear to obstruct his own fortune. He was then importuned to sell as much as would purchase an hundred a year for life, *which*, says Fenton, *will make you sure of a clean shirt and a shoulder of mutton every day.*

> This counsel was rejected; the profit and principal were lost, and Gay sunk under the calamity so low that his life became in danger.[52]

The 1720 "Poems by subscription" to which Johnson refers is the collection *Poems on Several Occasions*, which included the "Epistle to Pulteney" and the "Epistle to Methuen" (the "Epistle to Burlington" appeared in *Two Epistles*, several months earlier).[53] The publication had earned Gay a substantial profit, and he invested the money in South Sea shares before the Bubble's rapid ascendancy began in the summer of 1720. Both Swift and Pope encouraged Gay to sell a portion of his shares to purchase an annuity, which would provide a guaranteed income, but he refused, and eventually lost almost the entire investment when the market crashed. Johnson's compelling two-paragraph version of the story has made Gay's losses the stuff of biographical anecdote, but the impact of this period on his work stretches beyond a brief aside. *The Beggar's Opera*, written and first performed in 1728, satirizes the fabric of a society in which every relationship and motivation is understood through money, but poetry written almost immediately after the event articulates a moment of social cognition in which the redundancy of dated concepts begins to become clear.[54] Studying Gay's earlier work next to some examples of poetry from after the South Sea Bubble reveals a formative change in his understanding of the economic market, as the crisis and its aftermath began to force a naturalization of the increasingly abstract terms of the economy. What is expressed is a movement from the solid and the concrete, towards abstraction and metaphor, and this de-substantialization is expressed in words, but also by the nature of words, as Crashaw's "Bulla" poem demonstrates. Gay's *A Panegyrical Epistle to Mr Thomas Snow* (1721) and Swift's "The Bubble" (1720) both express this movement, but not necessarily *as* a movement. This finding helps to explain some of the intricacies of poetry contemporary with the event, but it also has a wider implication for how language understood and articulated the first moment of credit-induced panic in the global economic market. The poems by Gay and Swift begin to contextualize the credit economy, a process which is shown most clearly by the application of old market assumptions to the new financial world. It is in the places where this system of representation fails that a new imaginative version of the financial system arises, and the bubble is seen as a metaphor that transcends its metaphorical framework.

Swift's "The Bubble" closes with the line "South Sea, at best, a mighty Bubble."[55] The poem's 55 stanzas appeared in various forms throughout the 1720s, including in Thomas Bowles's *The Bubblers Medley*, a collage of illustrations and verses memorializing the crisis. Like Crashaw's "Bulla," Swift's 'mighty Bubble' suggests that the object at stake manifests only fleetingly, but unlike the manner in which an empirically observed bubble disappears when it bursts, the failure of the financial scheme has a tangible reverberation. The specious thing gains a litotic substantivity; its effects outlast its presence, and in no longer being there, the consequences of its one-time presence are all the more marked. The poem attempts to rationalize the Bubble by approaching it from three different angles: transfiguration, alchemy, and political cheating, and it views these processes in a connected fashion, as parts of the overall manifestation of the crisis. Swift does not prioritize the import of any one of these elements in favour of another, and instead looks at the social conditions which contributed to the Bubble's formation and ascendancy. Pat Rogers claims that the poem "belongs to the huge array of satire (graphic as well as literary) provoked by the collapse of the South Sea Bubble."[56] Like the poems by Gay and Pope, "The Bubble" is engaged in direct political criticism, but the texture of the piece's language, as well as its manipulation of modes of presentation, reveal a conceptual engagement with the terms of finance which is striking for its newness. The poem's opening address to "Philosophers" emphasizes the irresolvable tension between trickery, magic, and manipulation, and begins the piece with a resolutely satirical focus:

> YE wise Philosophers explain
> What Magick makes out Money rise,
> When dropt into the *Southern* Main;
> Or do these Juglers cheat our Eyes?[57]

The "wise Philosophers" are made unwise in the face of the Bubble's inexplicable loftiness, and are called upon to make sense of the strangely paradoxical magic that sees the value of money increase as it is "dropt" in to the South Sea investment. The poem's "Juglers" at once orchestrate this supernatural ascendency, whilst simultaneously making it appear an ascendancy when it is really an illusion. Swift explores a rhetorical tension, but he also reveals a mechanical tension in the movement of the share price; money's value rises as monetary tokens fall, in an equation which is fundamentally irresolvable. This logical incompleteness lies in an inability to convincingly attribute either side of the phrase to metaphor. When invested in the South Sea Company, money's value *does* rise, and the original sum remains "dropt" in South Sea funds. The upward action is dependent upon an opposite, downward movements: money perpetually falls, and money (significantly not "profits," but the money originally invested) perpetually rises. Swift's equation is a mimesis of the seemingly contradictory economic market, and the difficulty in conceptualizing the abstract financial substance of the Bubble is made material.

This difficulty is written into the poem as reification, and the abstract is treated as if it were concrete. Swift discusses the money physically rising and falling, and the boundary between what is metaphorical and what is reified is challenged: the Bubble itself can never me more than metaphor, but it is a metaphorical vehicle for an evidenced effect, a sort of catalyst for financial gain and loss. The poem attempts to resolve these material traces by inverting the process of reification, and it questions what happens when an abstraction is turned back on itself, and considered in terms of the fundamentals it collapses:

Thus in a Basin drop a Shilling,
Then fill the Vessel to the Brim;
You shall observe, as you are filling,
The Pond'rous Metal seems to swim:

It rises both in Bulk and Height,
Behold it swelling like a Sop!
The liquid Medium cheats your Sight,
Behold it mounting to the Top![58]

Trickery provides a filter through which the supposed physical binaries of "rise" and "fall" can coexist, and Swift begins to offer a material consolidation. A trick of the light makes the coin appear to rise, mirroring the process by which South Sea investors were seduced: the observer is cheated, but the tone of the fourth stanza in comparison to the third integrates the excitement experienced as the metal appears to rise. In the third stanza, the metal is "Pond'rous," and retains its weight as it "seems" to swim. This seeming is removed in the fourth stanza, where the movement of the coin is as if it were real—it expands, and is transfigured into a porous material, "swelling like a Sop," as it rises in the basin. Swift contrasts the acceptance of the coin's elevation with the reminder that the movement is not physically possible: "cheats," in the third line, is a pun upon the visual trick, and the implied widespread fraud committed by politicians as they promoted the South Sea Company despite its tenuous grounds for trading. The "liquid Medium" is held responsible for the optical illusion, and though "liquidity" is not linked to the interchangeability of assets and money until 1923, Swift's poem is so densely allusive that the "liquid Medium" is as much the market as it is water.

The transformation of the coin is only imagined, within the imaginary structure of the poem, and the token remains on the basin's floor. It only appears to expand and rise as the water is added, a line of enquiry continued in stanzas 29, 30, and 31:

A Shilling in the *Bath* you fling
The Silver takes a nobler Hue,
By Magick Virtue in the Spring,
And seems a Guinea to your View:

But as a Guinea will not pass
At Market for a Farthing more,

Shewn thro a multiplying Glass,
Than what it always did before;

So cast it in the *Southern* Seas,
And view it through a *Jobber's* Bill;
Put on what Spectacles you please,
Your Guinea's but a Guinea still.[59]

Magic sees the silver alchemically changed into gold, but the actual substance of the metal is not transfigured. The shilling seems a guinea, but is not, and neither the "*Southern* Seas" or the "Jobber's Bill" can effect the fantastical transformations they promise. The satirical measure of this poem is straightforward, and consistently maintained, but something much more interesting is happening in its account of materiality. For Swift, like Gay in the pre-Bubble epistles, the materiality of currency acts as the final guarantee of worth, and in "The Bubble," the coin is absolute. In terms of its potential for exchange, the transfigured shilling cannot be passed off as anything else. This reading is undercut, gently, by the poem in two different ways, which in turn demonstrate that Swift's materially focused reading is perhaps engaged in a satire of its own. The first of these is the claim, in the final line of the 31 stanza, that "Your Guinea's but a Guinea still." The description is tautological, and the coin is defined in terms of itself, which certainly doesn't admit any of the second inference of abstraction that Jameson applied to free-floating capital in the mid nineteenth century, but equally does not register the first sense, that money is always abstract anyway. Swift seems to rely on the substantivity of the coin to assert the argument that inflationary capital cannot work; however, he seeks conceptual solidity where there is none. The argument is thereby true: the guinea, regardless of its role in a complex system of signification, is still a guinea, even if it signifies nothing. The second, and more brilliant, destabilization lies in a rhetorical reading of the guinea line in the context of the other three stanzas. Swift's addressee possesses a shilling at the beginning of stanza 29, and the coin cannot be changed by investment in the South Sea Company. By the final line of stanza 31, "your" coin, originally a shilling, is a guinea. It becomes swept up in the inflationary rhetoric of finance, and language is seen to be doing what the market can: transfiguring one thing into something else. Swift's choice is deliberate—both "shilling" and "guinea" are trochaic, and, when coupled with the opening "Your," create an iambic line with the word divided between the first and second feet in the first instance, and the third and fourth in the second:

Your Gui / nea's but / a Gui / nea still.
Your Shi / lling's but / a Shi / lling still.

Either option works metrically, and when breaking the line down into its constituent feet, Swift's most subtle imposition becomes clear: the presence of the coin in each foot shows that the poem, and by extension the market, is saturated in money. Maintaining the irony, of course, is the fact that this money is revealed to be only "air" and "wind" when the bubble is exposed. Rogers writes that "to depict the South Sea as actual water, and the Bubble as actual gas, is to call in the cash loans of metaphor," and Swift recalls these loans to great effect.[60] The poem at once draws attention to the inflationary and abstract promises of credit, but it simultaneously acknowledges that linguistic representation is engaged in these strategies too. The system of finance is connected to the system of language, and conceptualizing one by reference to the function of the other allows a new conceptualization of the credit economy to take shape in literary structure, as well as in the social imagination.

Gay's *Panegyrical Epistle to Mr. Thomas Snow* crafts a similarly complex picture of the post-Bubble financial landscape. The poem was published on 8 February 1721, when Gay still held the—now relatively valueless—South Sea shares he'd purchased eight months before.[61] Snow was a banker at Goldsmiths, responsible, as the epithet describes, for "Buying and Selling the THIRD *SOUTH-SEA* SUBSCRIPTIONS, taken in by the DIRECTORS at a Thousand *per Cent.*"[62] Snow was part of a secondary trade in South Sea shares, which had been so popular upon 1720's third release that a booming market in officially purchased shares was quickly formed in the City. The panegyric attacks Snow for his immoral financial trades, and chronicles the manner in which City bankers and politicians sold the South Sea "dream" to naïve "Fools," "Poets," and "Madmen"—investors who were "taken in" metaphorically, just as their money was "taken in" to the investment. The *Epistle to Snow* refigures dreams of wealth into depictions of loss, and it narrates a version of the economy in which there is no tangible relationship between economic tokens and the things they signify. Gay's previously commodity-focused rhetoric is markedly absent. Like Swift's "The Bubble," the poem is engaged in representing a process of metaphorical, but ultimately never realized, transformation. The investment Bubble is described as an "empty Dream" (l. 34), a "fleeting Vision" (l. 35), shrouded in "Mist" (l. 60), a "Visionary Scene" (l. 61), and a "vanish'd Prospect" (l. 62). These ephemeral descriptions are juxtaposed with the images of the substantive wealth that Snow has procured in the course of the crisis: his hand "grow[s] black with Gold" (l. 4), in contrast to the "imaginary Gold" (l. 24) purchased by the subscribers to the South Sea Company's stock. Gay is as interested in the problematic substantivity of financial tokens as Swift, and he narrates the untethering of financial systems from a perceived position of security to a referential system of abstract tokens. Finance becomes fantastic; however, the concepts that Gay narrates are not exclusively metaphorical, and money's taking to air occupies a territory between metaphor and lateralization. The disappearance of material assets from the market as economic tokens is orchestrated as a removal which is almost metaphorical—subscriptions and shares take the place of physical money—and, simultaneously, this abstraction demands from language a system of representation that is at once metaphorical, and at once a mimetic rendering of the increasingly less-centric position of material tokens within the financial system.

The poem considers the transformative properties of finance, and like "The Bubble," considers these modulations in the context of alchemy and trickery:

> Why did 'Change-Alley waste thy precious Hours,
> Among the Fools who gap'd for golden Show'rs?
> No wonder, if we found some *Poets* there,
> Who live on Fancy, and can feed on Air;
> No wonder, *they* were caught by *South-Sea* Schemes,
> Who ne'er enjoy'd a Guinea, but in Dreams;
> No wonder, *they* their Third Subscriptions sold,
> For Millions of imaginary Gold:
> No wonder, that *their* Fancies wild could frame
> Strange Reasons, that a Thing is still the same,
> Though chang'd throughout in Substance and in Name.
> But *you* (whose Judgement scorns Poetick Flights)
> With Contracts furnish Boys for Paper Kites.[63]

The South Sea shares are seen as a scam here, and investors ("*Poets*") are described purchasing a dream of wealth that will never materialize. The old commodity-exchange binary is exposed once again: the subscribers to the shares, and those who purchase them in the secondary market, are being tricked, and they exchange something for nothing—"Paper Kites," or playthings, for hard-earned money. The art of poetry, and by extension, the property of language, is conflated with the business of finance, and the very trade of writers—who live by recording imagined scenarios—is compared to the poetry of investment, which sells the same promise. That poets "live on Fancy, and can feed on Air" therefore refers to the poverty of the profession, but also to the nature of poetic labour. Writing a poem and arranging an investment become extensions of the same faculty: metaphorical transformation. It is

> No wonder that *their* Fancies wild could frame
> Strange reasons, that a Thing is still the same,
> Though chang'd throughout in Substance and in Name.[64]

Literature is party to the process of conceptualizing finance, and financial systems are seen not only as profoundly poetic, but more significantly, the very texture of language moderates this understanding. Economic tokens retreat into metaphor, and it is deeply ironic that bankers—who, according to Gay, scorn poetry—orchestrate it by selling share certificates whose advertised values are so divorced from their actual values, and from the substantive purchases they put in reach of subscribers, that they may as well be used as toys. Even the base materiality of money as signifier is dispatched, and finance takes root alongside the metaphorical, as opposed to the substantial, token.

Swift and Gay's South Sea poetry (Swift's "The Bank Thrown Down," 1721, should be counted in this corpus) show the workings of a conceptual movement that rationalized the idea of finance, and the monetary tokens that represent it, in a manner that embraces the abstraction that is at the heart of the system. Though both poets seem to be engaged in the process of representing the South Sea Bubble as the consequence of financial trickery, their language pulls towards a representation of the economy in which interconnection is becoming more established. There is a tradition in criticism to ascribe this to a division between the fixed value represented by land and substance, and the floating value associated with shares and paper money in writing about South Sea Bubble literature: as old assumptions about money's referential system break down, so too must assumptions about language's referential system.[65] If, instead, we place the work within a phase of critical economic reconceptualization, during which the consequences of crisis inform how finance is understood, the structure of the system that drives this change begins to emerge.

The—deliberately—unconvincing retreat into the abstract is a stylistic and rhetorical property of Swift's and Gay's Bubble poems, and their ironic recourse to substance signifies an awareness of the plurality of the financial system. The linguistic microtransactions of "The Bubble" and *A Panegyrical Epistle to Mr. Thomas Snow* perform an understanding which moves against the more manifest irony of either poem's rhetoric. These transactions, which are non-financial exchanges themselves, demonstrate the redundancy of applying archaic terms to the post-credit world. When Crashaw describes a bubble in 1646, he alights upon the apparently contradictory features of the physical instantiation of its form: the bubble is ethereal, temporary, and subject to rupture, but yet it is also like language—a variety of connection, no more or less fragile than anything else. If, as Mitchell argues, the crisis of 1720 is understood as the moment in which the intricate connections that form the system of the market—hitherto unconceptualized—were laid bare, then the significance of South Sea Bubble writing within a wider history of crisis in capitalism is that it animates an epoch in which the fundamental units of economic thought were challenged.[66] The eventual collapse of the Bubble represented the failure of an investment scheme that was wholly reliant upon *fictitious capital*, manipulated by the introduction of capitalist credit instruments—a phrase that first appears in Volume III of *Capital*, in 1894.[67] Marx discusses the fundamentally superficial nature of money generated as interest upon a base sum:

> In the form of interest-bearing capital [...], capital appears as a mysterious and self-creating source of interest, of its own increase. The thing (money, commodity, value) is now already capital simply as a thing; the result of the overall reproduction process appears as a property devolving on a thing in itself.[68]

This variety of capital is financial capital in "its most superficial and fetishized form," a product which is wholly divorced from labour, and inextricably bound to laws of irrational propagation (compound interest being the most corrupt form of this self-perpetuation).[69] Marx continues:

> For vulgar economics, which seeks to present capital as an independent source of wealth, of value creation, this form is of course a godsend, a form in which the source of profit is no longer recognizable and in which the result of the capitalist production process—separate from the process itself—obtains an autonomous existence.[70]

Money begets money. The illusion (fantasy), perpetuated by the generation of interest, subsumes the true relation between "thing" and "capital" (reality), to such an extent that global financial systems can be built on the unstable foundations of its premise. Of course, it is anachronistic to call upon Marx to explain the 1720 crisis; however, the process observed as "abstraction" in relation to the South Sea Bubble is, in fact, the entrenchment of this concept as a fundamental component of a growing financial system. Marx's "fictitious capital" is as good as axiomatic today, but this has not always been the case. What Swift and Gay's 1720 and 1721 South Sea poems communicate is the beginning of this phase of finance taking to air. As Marx writes in relation to the failed German revolution in 1848:

> All that is solid melts into air, all that is holy is profaned, and man is at last compelled to face with sober senses, his real conditions of life, and his relations with his kind.[71]

Marx describes the disintegration of one system of reference, and the establishment of another, where abstract connections take precedence over concrete ones. The processes of consolidation that we detect in the work of South Sea authors do more than simply represent the economic market in verse and prose. They are part of a phase of cognition, in which the consequences of crisis reshape how the structure of the market is understood. In a mimesis of its true form, then, the bubble's adequacy as South Sea metaphor simultaneously endures and bursts: the forms that Swift and Gay see taking to air, both metaphorically and literally, did not find solidity after 1720. Instead, the progressively expanding—and expansively connecting—economic market began to settle within the realm of the abstract, and within the terms of public credit.

Notes

1 John Gay, "A Panegyrical Epistle to Mr. Thomas Snow," in *Poetry and Prose*, eds. Vinton A. Dearing and Charles E. Beckwith, 2 vols. (Oxford: Oxford University Press, 1974), 1:280–82 (l. 61).

2 Richard Crashaw, "Bulla," in *The Complete Poetry of Richard Crashaw*, ed. George Walton Williams, trans. Phyllis S. Bowman (New York: New York University Press, 1972), 612–21 (ll. 115–20).

3 Ibid., l. 156.

4 Stephen Guy-Bray, "'Pulchrum Spargitur Hic Chaos:' Crashaw's Meta-Commentary," *Journal for Early Modern Cultural Studies* 9 (2009): 147–59 (152).

5 See P. G. M. Dickson, *The Financial Revolution in England: A Study in the Development of Public Credit, 1688–1756* (London: Macmillan, 1967), 39–46.

6 Ibid., 11.

7 Adam Anderson, *An Historical and Chronological Deduction of the Origin of Commerce, From the Earliest Accounts*, 4 vols. (London: J. Walter, 1787), 3:103–7.

8 Jonathan Swift, *The Examiner* 45 (7 June 1711), in *The Prose Works of Jonathan Swift*, ed. Temple Scott, 12 vols. (London: George Bell, 1902), 9:291–97 (295).

9 Christine Gerrard, "Political Passions," in *The Cambridge Companion to Eighteenth Century Poetry*, ed. John Sitter (Cambridge: Cambridge University Press, 2001), 37–62 (43).

10 J. G. A. Pocock, *The Machiavellian Moment: Florentine Political Thought and the Atlantic Republican Tradition* (Princeton, NJ: Princeton University Press, 1975), 425.

11 Cited in Robert Mitchell, *Sympathy and the State in the Romantic Era: Systems, State Finance, and the Shadows of Futurity* (New York: Routledge, 2007), 37.

12 Jonathan Swift, "The Bubble," in *The Poems of Jonathan Swift*, ed. Harold Williams, 3 vols. (Oxford: Clarendon, 1958), 1:248–59 (ll. 165–68).

13 Gay, *A Pangerical Epistle to Mr. Thomas Snow*, l. 24.

14 For readings of Pope's *Epistle to Bathurst* in relation to finance, see Earl R. Wasserman, *Pope's Epistle to Bathurst: A Critical Reading with an Edition of the Poem* (Baltimore, MD: Johns Hopkins University Press, 1960); James Engell, "Wealth and Words: Pope's *Epistle to Bathurst*," *Modern Philology* 85 (1988): 433–46; and Colin Nicholson, *Writing and the Rise of Finance* (Cambridge: Cambridge University Press, 1994), 141–57.

15 Alexander Pope, *Epistle to Bathurst*, in *The Poems of Alexander Pope*, ed. John Butt, 11 vols. (London: Methuen, 1939–1967), 3.ii:83–125 (ll. 69–72).

16 Samuel Johnson, *A Dictionary of the English Language*, 2 vols. (London: J. Knapton, 1755), vol. 1 [n. page refs].

17 Mary Poovey, *Genres of the Credit Economy: Mediating Value in Eighteenth- and Nineteenth-Century Britain* (Chicago, IL: University of Chicago Press, 2008), 24.

18 See Pocock, *The Machiavellian Moment*, 423–27; Dickson, *The Financial Revolution*, 54–56; and Charles H. Wilson, *Anglo-Dutch Commerce and Finance in the Eighteenth Century* (Cambridge: Cambridge University Press, 1941), 18–24.
19 Clifford Siskin, *System: The Shaping of Modern Knowledge* (Cambridge, MA: MIT Press, 2016), 1.
20 Ibid., 173–74.
21 Ibid., 150–51.
22 Mitchell, *Sympathy and the State*, 5.
23 Ibid., 39.
24 Ibid., 27–30.
25 Clifford Siskin, "Novels and Systems," *Novel* 34 (2001): 202–15 (202).
26 Bubble histories fall into several broad categories: those which practice archival reconstruction of the events of 1720, including Dickson's account in *The Financial Revolution*, as well as John Carswell's *The South Sea Bubble* (London: Cresset, 1960), John G. Sperling's *The South Sea Company* (Boston, MA: Harvard Graduate School of Business Administration, 1962), and William R. Scott's *The Constitution and Finance of English, Scottish, and Irish Joint-Stock Companies to 1720* (Cambridge: Cambridge University Press, 1910). More recent studies have integrated recent economic studies into narratives of historical reconstruction, for example, Helen J. Paul, *The South Sea Bubble: An Economic History of Its Origins and Consequences* (New York: Routledge, 2011), and Richard Kleer, "Riding a Wave: The Company's Role in the South Sea Bubble," *Economic History Review* 68 (2015): 264–85.
27 In "Myths of the South Sea Bubble," Julian Hoppit argues that the Bubble was retrospectively named in 1771. Hoppit's theory has been debunked by Pat Rogers, in a *TLS* article titled "South Sea Bubble Myths." It should be noted that there is ample evidence linking the "bubble" as a word and as a concept to writing about the South Sea crisis in the 1720s, and I follow Rogers's conclusion. See Julian Hoppit, "Myths of the South Sea Bubble," *Transactions of the Royal Historical Society* 12 (2002): 141–65 (163), and Pat Rogers, "South Sea Bubble Myths," *TLS*, 9 April 2014, accessed 19 June 2017, http://the-tls.co.uk/tls/public/article1397751.
28 Nicholson, *Writing and the Rise of Finance*, 9.
29 Ibid., 71.
30 Ibid.
31 David Nokes, *John Gay: A Profession of Friendship* (Oxford: Oxford University Press, 1995), 297.
32 John Gay to Jacob Tonson, October 1720, in *The Letters of John Gay*, ed. C. F. Burgess (Oxford: Clarendon, 1966), 37–38. Burgess notes that the date of this letter is uncertain: "[t]he dating is, at best, a guess based on the fact that Fay was known to be in financial difficulties in the autumn of 1720, following the collapse of the South Sea Company."
33 Brean S. Hammond, "'A Poet, and a Patron, and Ten Pound:' John Gay and Patronage," in *John Gay and the Scriblerians*, eds. Peter Lewis and Nigel Wood (London: Vision Press, 1989), 23–43 (26).
34 Gay, "Epistle to Burlington," in *Poetry and Prose*, 1:203–7 (ll. 1–6).
35 Gay, "Epistle to Pulteney," in *Poetry and Prose*, 1:208–14 (ll. 21–28).
36 Gay, "Epistle to Burlington," ll. 79–82.
37 Ibid., ll. 103–4.
38 *Oxford English Dictionary*, 3rd ed.; Johnson, *A Dictionary of the English Language*, vol. 1 [n. page refs].

39 Nicholson, *Writing and the Rise of Finance*, 135–36.
40 Mitchell, *Sympathy and the State*, 54.
41 Cited in Mitchell, 54.
42 Ibid.
43 Gay, "Epistle to Pulteney," ll. 43–51.
44 Ibid., "Epistle to Burlington," ll. 36–38.
45 Fredric Jameson, "Culture and Finance Capital," *Critical Inquiry* 24 (1997): 246–65 (251).
46 Gay, "Epistle to Methuen," in *Poetry and Prose*, 1:215–17, ll. 21–22.
47 Ibid., ll. 43–46.
48 Ibid., ll. 81–82.
49 Cited in Nicholson, *Writing and the Rise of Finance*, 9.
50 For a full discussion of the origins of the "collective imagination," see Mitchell, *Sympathy and the State*, 27–60.
51 Gay was offered the role of "Gentleman Usher" to the daughter of Queen Caroline, two-year-old Princess Louisa, in 1727. The offer offended him, and he refused to take up the position. Swift's poem "To Mr Gay" comments upon the appointment: "How cheaply had thy liberty been sold, / To squire a royal girl of two years old!"); see *Jonathan Swift: The Complete Poems*, ed. Pat Rogers (New Haven: Yale University Press, 1983), 466–70 (ll. 9–10).
52 Samuel Johnson, *Lives of the English Poets*, 2 vols. (London: Oxford University Press, 1906), 2:63.
53 Gay, *Poetry and Prose*, 1:vi.
54 Colin Nicholson gives a thorough analysis of *The Beggar's Opera*'s post-South Sea context in *Writing and the Rise of Finance*, 123–38.
55 Jonathan Swift, "Upon the South Sea Project," in *Jonathan Swift: The Complete Poems*, 207–14 (l. 228). The poem was likely named by Swift's friend Ford, rather than Swift himself. The piece had been sent to him to forward to the printer, with no title. In Rogers's Yale edition, the piece is titled "Upon the South Sea Project." Harold Williams discusses this naming at length in *The Poems of Jonathan Swift,* 3 vols. (Oxford, Clarendon, 1937), 1:248.
56 Pat Rogers, "Plunging in the Southern Waves: Swift's Poem on The Bubble," *Yearbook of English Studies* 18 (1988): 41–50 (41).
57 Swift, "Upon the South Sea Project," ll. 1–4.
58 Ibid., ll. 9–16.
59 Ibid., ll. 121–32.
60 Rogers, "Plunging in the Southern Waves," 50.
61 Nokes, *A Profession of Friendship*, 314.
62 Gay, *A Pangerical Epistle to Mr. Thomas Snow*, Preface.
63 Ibid., ll. 17–29.
64 Ibid., ll. 25–27.
65 Tom Jones, "Pope's *Epistle to Bathurst* and the Meaning of Finance," *Studies in English Literature* 44 (2004): 487–504 (487).
66 Mitchell, *Sympathy and the State*, 5–6.
67 Karl Marx, *Capital*, trans. David Fernbach, 3 vols. (London: Penguin, 1981), 3:515–42, 594–606.
68 Ibid., 3:516.
69 Ibid., 3:515.
70 Ibid., 3:517.
71 Cited in Nicholson, *Writing and the Rise of Finance*, 14.

2 Insect Nature and Human Political Economy

The Notion of the Population across Natural History and Physiocracy in Enlightenment France

Elisabeth Wallmann

> Insects cause astonishing damage: these animals search for a home and for food, deep inside the leaves, rind and fruits of plants. People have seen armies of grasshoppers reap entire fields, legions of crickets, of snails and of cockchafers gnaw on everything in a province, & etc. [...] Midgets attach themselves to the rind and leaves of plants and lay millions of eggs there, the irritation they cause makes the rind peel off and the leaf roll up, and the plant, sacrificing its own tissue to feed the insects, finally dies of exhaustion; this loss brings about the partial or even the total destruction of the plant, even in the case of trees.[1]

Historians tend to read passages like this extract from a 1766 article in the *Journal oeconomique* as evidence for the "anxiety" felt by early modern men and women in the face of swarms of insects eating the grains on which their livelihoods depended.[2] While such a reading is certainly justified if we consider the very real threat posed by insect pests in the pre-industrial era, there is, perhaps, also more than an element of projection back onto earlier epochs of our own modern attitudes towards the "uncanny" creatures that haunt our (post-Freudian) imaginations.[3] The author of this passage was not, after all, expressing his "anxiety about maintaining humankind's privileged position in creation."[4] On the contrary, his list of the damage done by hungry insects serves merely as a reminder of the importance and success of the new methods for pest control developed with the help of natural historical observation and with the aim of contributing to the field the author terms "science économique." He acknowledged that the risk of outbreaks of insect infestations was impossible to eliminate completely, but provided his readers with means for controlling the extent of the risk developed through the observation of insect bodies, both individual and in groups. Instead of traditional theological explanations or methods aimed at killing individual specimens, that is, he proposed systematic techniques for controlling insect "populations." Natural historical knowledge of food sources, birth rates, and illnesses of various kinds of insects, the author (like other eighteenth-century writers interested in pest control) claimed, would reduce the damage to crops to a minimum.

This essay argues that eighteenth-century investigations of insects—whether for the purposes of natural history or for its concrete application in pest management—provided a site for the construction of the new abstraction that would come to structure the as yet nascent field of political economy: the "population." It reads writings on pest control alongside the oeuvre of the Physiocrats (the most famous and innovative French writers in political economy) to show that both need to be understood as important contributions to one of the most fundamental discussions of the eighteenth century: the question of how to govern so as to increase the wealth of the state as a whole. At the centre of this discussion, which formed the basis for political economy, stood the population, which Foucault has called a new "economic personage."[5] The term itself was not new; until roughly the seventeenth century, however, it referred above all to the action of populating a territory.[6] Subsequently, over the course of the eighteenth century, it acquired new meanings and, as I shall argue, was filled with "life" and made visible through the observation of animals. Earlier theorists had tended to see the population as a collection of subjects to be ruled by laws, whose purpose was to increase the wealth of the sovereign. Increasingly "the population" was believed to be a "natural" and thus a potentially manageable entity. Its material well-being—and therefore its "care" by the enlightened sovereign and its officials—was coming to be seen as central to the prosperity of a country as a whole. "Population" thus came to be considered not simply as the totality of individuals, but rather as a "natural" body—a "species"—with its own laws, such as those regarding mortality, natality, migration, or the occurrence of epidemics. The population's laws were, in turn, constantly interacting with the variables of the territory it inhabited; population could thus only be understood and governed in relation to its territory.[7]

This investigation of the "birth" of the "population" relies on the framework provided by Foucault's late work on biopolitics, particularly his lectures at the Collège de France published in English as *Security, Territory, Population* (2007). Foucault analysed the emergence of this concept of the "population" as it was created through (human) medicine on the one hand and population statistics (or what was then called political arithmetic) on the other. Several scholars have noted that Foucault himself was not interested in examining the role of animals, nor in broaching the question of what it means to be "animal" as opposed to "human."[8] However, as the present essay seeks to show, the emergence of "biopower"—and the concomitant creation of a new kind of human subject as both an individual and part of the population—as conceptualized by Foucault is not thinkable without the re-conceptualization of animality that took place at the same time. Both naturalists and political economists explored ways of governing bodies driven by physical needs rather than rational souls; in so doing, they could share concepts as well as methods for observation and abstraction for the construction of the "population." This essay argues, then, that observations of animals imagined the population as a "natural" body.

In order to demonstrate that the new field of political economy and observers of animals pursued the same question of government, I first highlight the changing understanding of the two inseparable concepts of the species and the population. This is followed by a discussion of the physiocratic understanding of population, and in particular the question of how to govern the Crown's rural subjects. This then allows me to draw out the strong parallels between discussion of government of humans and the increasingly scientific methods for pest control. This discussion suggests that in addition to the role played by literary, sentimental, and rhetorical discourses in the formation of political economy—as discussed by the contributors to this volume—we need to take into account the study of animals, which in itself should be understood as a political economic endeavour. Just as political economists shaped their theories of government on the basis of a conception of the human as, fundamentally, a need-driven animal, observers of animals began to conceive of their objects of study in political economic terms. At the heart of eighteenth-century political economic discourse, we thus find the question of the distinction between the human and the animal, a distinction that we, in the age of the Anthropocene, continue to recognize as central to our understandings of the natural as well as the social.

The Eighteenth-Century Concept of the "Population" across the Human and Animal Realms

The idea that human (and, in natural historical research, animal) individuals can be understood as part of a population was, in the eighteenth century, relatively new; indeed, the author of one of the first dictionary entries on the topic in French claims that population and populateur are both "new words" (his dictionary was published 1788).[9] While population was not, strictly speaking, a neologism, this article in the *Dictionnaire critique* points to the fact that the word and the concept became crucial units of analysis for thinking about government only in the second half of the eighteenth century.[10] In France, the popularity and redefinition of the term owed much to future Physiocrat Victor Riquetti, marquis de Mirabeau's (1715–1789) bestseller *L'ami des homme ou traité de la population* (1756–1758), which elaborated on the idea that France's prosperity—and thus the prosperity of its sovereign—depended directly on the well-being and physical health of the population.[11] Together with the founder and leader of the physiocratic movement, the court medic François Quesnay (1694–1774), Mirabeau promoted the idea that population should form both the target and the method of government. Following his "conversion"—the conversation with Quesnay that swayed him over to physiocracy and made him the doctor's principal collaborator—Mirabeau reversed the traditional assumption that high population numbers both indicated and constituted prosperity, arguing instead that government should focus on maximizing the means of subsistence.[12] By the end of the century, thanks in part to the Physiocrats' efforts, state officials as well as political thinkers in France had generally come to accept that it was the state's responsibility to ensure that the population, in its new meaning, could flourish.[13]

The fact that knowledge of the human body and knowledge of its government were closely connected to the eighteenth-century discussions of animals can be gleaned, for example, from another eighteenth-century definition, Étienne-Noël Damilaville's *Encycopédie* article "Population":

> This word is abstract; taken in its most general sense, it refers to the product of all beings multiplied by generation; for the earth is populated not only by men, but also by animals of all species which inhabit it with them. [...] But this expression is particularly used for the human species: and in this sense, it describes the relation between men and the territory they occupy, in direct relation to their number and in inverse relation to space.[14]

Population thus referred to a group of individuals as members of a natural (animal or human) "species" in relation to a given territory. Closely tied to the concept of the population, definitions of the concept of the species were narrowed down over the course of the eighteenth century. Species did not yet, of course, refer to its post-Darwinian sense of a class of beings with hereditary and changeable traits, but was used more broadly to describe a category of animals (or plants, humans, and even objects) with similar natural properties.[15] Increasingly, natural philosophers limited use of the term to "beings multiplied by generation," working to make visible their unchangeable traits and laws of reproduction, mortality, and subsistence.

Antoine Ferchault de Réaumur (1683–1757), the most famous and influential eighteenth-century naturalist to observe insects, did much to define what was meant by the laws of animal species. Although he did not, to my knowledge, employ the term population in his descriptions of insects, many of what would soon become the key elements of the population discourse in the field of political economy are clearly present in his *Mémoires pour servir à l'histoire des insectes* (1734–1742). Réaumur has recently been studied as the exemplary eighteenth-century observer of nature.[16] His attentive observations, however, need to be considered in the light of his role as one of the most influential members of the Paris Académie des sciences, founded in 1666 by the minister

Jean-Baptiste Colbert (1619–1683) in order to increase France's financial and natural resources.[17] Réaumur was certainly not a disinterested and curious observer, but working from the perspective of the state. This is manifest also in his volumes and articles on insects, produced over the course of almost his entire career at the Académie. Modern entomologists concerned with insect pest control have claimed Réaumur as forefather to their discipline, given that he "probably gave the earliest published recommendation for biological pest suppression" on the basis of the "dynamics of natural population."[18] For Réaumur, that is, insects could only be understood in relation to the dynamic variables of the territory they inhabited. Studying caterpillars that attack fruits and grains, for example, Réaumur described issues such as the insects' natural enemies, the probable effects of climate on their population numbers, what they eat, and during which season and how manipulation of these food sources could affect the birth and death rates of a species.

As Brian Ogilvie has discussed, Réaumur was not particularly interested in offering a comprehensive system of classification that would enable naturalists to identify all classes of insects.[19] The sheer variety of insects, Réaumur argued, made this an impossible project. He instead proposed that observers focus on those that they encounter on a daily basis:

> It has seemed to me that the insects which most often appear before our eyes are those we should seek the most to know; they are those, so to speak, with which we have to live;[20]

Ogilvie argues that Réaumur chose his "anthropocentric ordering of insects" because it enabled both naturalist and his readers to enjoy "the pleasures of seeing insects" in their daily lives and thus to study the "beautiful pattern of change that was imbued in them by the Creator."[21] For our purposes, however, we need to push this point further, for what matters to Réaumur are not only the beauties of insects (though these mattered too), but also their geographical appearance. The observer, that is, should study the insects that he (or perhaps she) encounters in the territory that matters to him or her. By emphasizing the appearance of the insect not in abstract classificatory tables, as the Swedish naturalist Linnaeus had done, but in relation to their territory, Réaumur had begun to study insect species in the way that political economists were beginning to study humans: as a population.

The Naturalness of the "Population" Reproduction and Subsistence in Physiocracy

The Physiocrats, a group of thinkers gathered around the court physician François Quesnay, are often considered to have formulated the first coherent theory of political economy.[22] While Quesnay himself published very little during his lifetime, he was able to recruit a number of skilled disciples, including the bestselling author Mirabeau, who disseminated physiocratic ideas in a series of works and journals appearing between the late 1750s and 1780s. As their name (meaning "rule of nature") indicated, the Physiocrats wanted to found a system of government anchored in the laws of nature, and thus also in a theory of the human as a need-driven animal. According to the core principle of their doctrine, agriculture was the sole source of all wealth and, as a consequence, should, first, be the only source of tax income for the state and, second, be allowed to circulate unencumbered by state regulation. If the grain trade was freed, they argued, agricultural wealth would flow to other branches of the economy, as farmers would, for example, invest their surplus in manufactured goods and pay rent to the landowners. With more wealth circulating, farmers and labourers would be encouraged to marry early and increase the population. The wealth flowing from agriculture thus determined the living conditions, territorial distribution, and numbers of the population. At the same time as emphasizing the physical nature of humans, the Physiocrats stressed their capacity to behave reasonably, which seemed to distinguish them from all other animals. However, once we shift our focus from the level of the individual and his or her decisions to the population as a whole, it is the physical body considered in the light of his or her animal needs (food, reproduction, and rest) that becomes important in the physiocratic analysis.[23] At a time when new theories of government depended on a conception the human body as defined and driven by animal needs which had been fixed by nature, naturalists' methods and findings on animal bodies and their needs contributed to thinking through how to observe and control all living bodies. Insects were particularly useful for this endeavour because they could only be understood—just like the Crown's human subjects—as they appeared on a specific territory and, crucially, in the aggregate. This distinguished them from, for example, the exotic, "noble" beasts favoured by the court's anatomists in the seventeenth century, at the height of the Sun King's reign.[24]

I am not arguing that the Physiocrats and other political economists concerned with population later in the century had necessarily read naturalists' texts on insect pests. We might add however, that the *Journal oeconomique*, one of the first (printing began in January 1751) and most important periodicals concerned with political economy, published a host of articles on pest control that took up methods and concerns found in Réaumur's *Mémoires*.[25] This suggests that political economists were most probably aware of natural historical ideas about insect population control, even if they had not studied them in detail. Instead, what I am proposing is that, first, natural historians like Réaumur were trying to answer political economical questions and, second, that natural historical reflections on insect populations formed part of the same discourse on the question of how to govern. Observations of the control and management of insect populations that could not, or rather should not, be eradicated thus provided an important arena for making visible the new, still abstract idea of the "population."

Before the Physiocrats, "the population question," though vigorously debated, had referred above all to the issue of France's supposed depopulation. The idea that more men meant more labouring hands and thus more wealth and prosperity for the crown was rarely, if ever, questioned.[26] The reasons for decreasing numbers were sought above all in the moral, and much less in the material realm. The Physiocrats, on the contrary, argued that men, like all other animals, were fundamentally driven by their sensations and their needs, most crucially their need for subsistence. Even religious freedom became a material issue, as it increased men's ability to work for their subsistence unencumbered by fear of prosecution. They also severed the assumed link between high population numbers and good government, insisting instead that the "natural" and thus right number of subjects depended on the territory and the subsistence it offered. As historians remind us, the main innovation of the Physiocrats was to make population dependent on the available means of subsistence—and thus on variables such as the fertility of the soil, the kinds of products one could grow or the climate—rather than vice versa.[27] If governmental policies ensured a blockage-free framework, the number of citizens would "naturally" increase (this is the doctrine associated with the famous phrase "laissez-faire, laissez-passer," though it was, in fact, Quesnay's contemporary Vincent Gournay, and not the Physiocrats who coined it).[28] Agricultural growth, in other words, preceded population growth:

> men gather and multiply where they can acquire riches, live comfortably, possess securely and properly the riches that their labor and their industry can procure them.[29]

This view of the anteriority of wealth to population growth differed from the ideas of most of Quesnay's and Mirabeau's predecessors, who argued that population growth would lead to increased wealth.[30] Even Mirabeau, before his conversion, had sometimes asserted that the wealth of a nation lay in the number of its citizens.[31] For Quesnay and the later Physiocrats, however, such measures could not be effective, no more than trying to force bees or silkworms to multiply without increasing their food supply. As Mirabeau put it somewhat crudely with the help of an animal analogy: "Men multiply like rats in a barn, if they have the means to subsist."[32] The sovereign's (or his political economic advisors') task, in other words, was not to formulate a plan for increasing the population and then inducing his citizens to follow it, whether by force or by appeals to their self-interest.[33] Instead, the sovereign, guided by the enlightened *économiste*, had to work on the elements of the territory in order to ensure nothing stood in the way of increases in the productivity (though not necessarily the numbers) of the population.

Mirabeau, the more "literary" writer in the collaborative pair he formed with Quesnay,[34] made the link between the concepts of population and species, and their dependence on a territory, explicit. Famous for his flowery language, Mirabeau frequently employed metaphors from the animal realm; in one famous passage of his immensely successful bestseller *L'ami des homme*, for example, he writes:

> If the multiplication of a species depended on its fecundity, then certainly there would be in this world a hundred times more wolves than sheep. The wolves' litters are large, & as frequent as those of sheep, which give birth to only one lamb. Man condemns whole armies of sheep to celibacy, & and I haven't heard that he commits the same injustice to wolves. He kills a lot more sheep than wolves: & nevertheless the earth is covered by the first race, while the other is very rare. Why? Because food is scarce for wolves, and plentiful for sheep.[35]

These animal metaphors, if we take them seriously, highlight the Physiocrats' understanding of the human population as a natural entity. Even though economic actors seem to act rationally, the observer is interested not in inner motivations, but in broad patterns visible only at the level of the group. Discovering these patterns would, of course, provide the basis for Malthus and his followers, who elaborated on the notion of population theorized by the Physiocrats to argue that they had been mistaken in their optimistic faith in the balance between human needs and the means to fulfil them once the "rule of nature" would be established.[36] In the eighteenth century, naturalists and agronomists insisted on the interconnectedness of all aspects of nature's oeconomy; tackling an insect plague, for instance, required knowledge not only of the reproductive mechanism of the species in question but also of the external factors that influenced the number of individuals. The same principles hold true for the physiocratic theory of population.[37] As Mirabeau and Quesnay put it in their collectively written primer on physiocracy, the *Philosphie rurale* (1763):

> Since everything is subject to the needs of common subsistence, the expansion of a species is an invasion of the territory claimed by another. Hence all devours all on this earth. This inviolable law of nature means that in principle propagation is boundless, & that in reality it is constrained by the limits of subsistence.[38]

Bodies pertaining to a species, whether animal or human, are infinitely fertile in principle, but limited in reality by the available means for subsistence. Just as the number of crop-devouring caterpillars, for instance, depends on the number of its enemies and on available food sources, human populations depend on the amount of territory and the food they can find and grow within it.

Given the primacy of subsistence and, as a consequence, of agriculture, within the physiocratic system, one effect of the supposedly misguided treatment of the "population question" on the part of the French monarchy particularly troubled the *philosophes économistes*: the migration of the rural population to the cities. Quesnay frequently lamented the desertion of the countryside by farmworkers and particularly by their children who took on "sterile" jobs in towns and cities.[39] He insisted that no amount of legal pressure would be able to halt the process, as workers were "naturally" drawn to environments that promised to fulfil their needs and thus provide for their well-being. For Quesnay, attempts to force the rural population to stay through the implementation of laws or directives were based on a misunderstanding of human nature:

> It has been thought that politicians regarded the poverty of countryside dwellers as a necessary spur to excite them to work, but there is no one who does not know that riches are agriculture's great resource, and that a lot are needed in order to cultivate well. [...] men are not excited to work, when they have no hopes for their good fortune; their activity always corresponds to their success.[40]

The workers cannot be expected to work the land if doing so cannot fulfil their material needs. Rather than punishing "lazy" peasants, the Physiocrats argued, governors should ensure that the territory—its rivers and canals, the kinds of crops planted—is arranged in such a way as to allow them to be as productive as their "nature" allowed. Governing the population as a species meant not giving orders but respecting the natural relation between bodily needs and the elements of the territory destined to fulfil them.

Insect Pests as "Populations"

The abstract debate on the relation between population and territory was made visible and concrete in writings on insect pest control. One aspect of the natural history of insects that made (and makes) it particularly plausible to think of them in terms of a population were the high fertility rates of most species, and particularly of those feeding on human crops. They thus allowed their observers to find an example in nature of an aggregation of large numbers of individuals and to test methods for controlling their numbers and their movements across the territory. In a nation as dependent on agricultural produce as eighteenth-century France, savants at the Académie des sciences—working for the state—were alert to the effects of insect fertility. In the introduction to the second volume of his insect memoirs, for example, Réaumur announced detailed observations on a particularly ravenous insect:

> a singular event which has caused us damage, & which in itself would merit a whole article on these caterpillars, is that although they have always seemed quite rare to me, they multiplied prodigiously in 1735. They caused extraordinary ravages to great parts of the kingdom, & above all around Paris, where they have devoured entire fields of crops.[41]

The case of crop-devouring caterpillars thus seemed a particularly apt field of exploration for an observer as intent on contributing to national prosperity as Réaumur: knowledge of the reasons for increases in fertility and techniques for manipulating them promised higher yields for human farmers. He recognized, however, that there was never just one factor involved, but that the number of insects depended on a whole range of external factors such as temperature, humidity, the number of enemy specimens, or the availability of an insect's preferred food. Even as the insect body could not change in our post-Darwinian evolutionary sense, the regularities produced by the behaviours of the collective of insects on a given territory—the population—were not static and inflexible, but constantly fluctuating as the insects moved: their mating patterns, fertility, mortality, and migration depended, most crucially, on the available means of subsistence provided by a given territory as the caterpillars satisfied their needs by eating crops planted by humans.[42]

The plague of 1735 was caused, Réaumur argued, by particularly unfortunate weather patterns favourable to the pests and hostile to their diseases and enemies. This represents a shift from earlier considerations of insect plagues, even by Réaumur's immediate predecessors. Sheila Wille, in an article on British writings on the ichneumon fly, argues that it was not until the late 1790s that naturalists began to advocate intervention in the balance of nature on the grounds that insect populations would self-equilibrate.[43] The English natural theologian William Derham (1657–1735), for instance, in his efforts to explain every detail in nature as created by God for the benefit of mankind, considered the sudden proliferation of harmful insects, a punishment for man's sinful infraction of God's laws:

> That as to Man, those Creatures are not without their great Uses, particularly in the Cure of some of the most stubborn and sinful Men. And I am apt to think that the Nations which know not God, are the most annoy'd with those noxious Reptiles, and other pernicious Creatures.[44]

As a consequence, for Derham there was little man could do to prevent such scourges. In France, on the other hand, observers were, at least from the early century onwards, proposing methods for managing, if not eliminating, insect pests. In doing so, they echoed the greater emphasis on state control on the part of French political economist in comparison to their English counterparts.[45]As naturalists purged their views of nature from God's intervention beyond the establishment of fixed laws, they retained Derhams's insistence on natural balances. Nature, they argued, constituted a self-regulating system with checks and balances, such as the relationship between prey and predator. Nevertheless, they admitted that this balance was fragile and that its hospitality to humans fluctuated.[46] Both abundance and scarcity occurred naturally, not because of God's direct interventions but because of the laws of correlation between different variables.

Some 20 years after Réaumur's experiments with caterpillars, as the physiocratic movement was in full swing, the academicians Duhamel de Monceau and Mathieu Tillet were commissioned by the Academy of Sciences to carry out investigations on the cause of a particularly devastating insect plague in the region of Angoumois (today's Charente).[47] The region's provincial intendant had called for help from experts in natural history from the Capital since a species of moth—still today called the "Angoumois grain moth"—had become so widespread in the region as to threaten entire harvests of grain.[48] Using a whole battery of experimental and observational techniques, the two Parisian naturalists set out to determine the causes of the increase in the moth's population and to find methods for controlling the damage done by the insects. Methods for controlling harmful insects contributed to thinking about and practicing government in two related ways. First of all, the observations of naturalists helped produce new ways of managing the insect bodies via the manipulation of the variables determining their lives; the term "government" is particularly appropriate here because observers admitted that even scientifically informed pest control could never eliminate, only ever reduce crop-devouring insect populations. To turn to our case study, in one experiment described in Duhamel's and Tillet's treatise, a local helper and "zealous citizen" planted seven wheat grains in crystal containers; a mere 27 days later he had observed the butterflies hatch. The Parisian naturalists, treating the local as a mere provider of observational facts rather than as a naturalist in his own right, used his observations to calculate the insect's fertility rate. They estimated that out of the seven insects (each grain could only house one insect) three would be female, which could in turn give birth to 180 new caterpillars; if temperatures would remain high until the end of September, this meant that the approximately 90 new females could give birth to a staggering 5400 caterpillars.[49] Studying the insects' body temperature, the weather in the months before they bred, and the temperature inside the granary, the men could thus determine the conditions that allowed the caterpillars to breed at particularly high rates. Although they could not, of course, influence the weather, knowledge of the conditions best suited to meet the insect's needs did help them determine when attempts to eliminate them would be most favourable. Clearly, it made little sense trying to kill insects on one's small plot of land, and Duhamel and Tillet admitted that their enlightened method for preserving the grain from hungry insects could not completely prevent the loss of grains, but only cut them down to about one-fifth.[50] The pests, in other words, could not be fully controlled, but they could be managed.[51] Only by thinking of them as a population—a body with its own natural laws spread over a territory—could the inhabitants of the Angoumois region hope to combat the plague.

Duhamel and Tillet knew that their attempts at "governing" the insects depended on their ability to "govern" the farmers who suffered because of them. They conceived of both the insect pests and the farmers as part of a circulatory system—the natural "oeconomy"—that required their supervision as savants in order to continue to function. They thus considered both insects and farmers as natural entities, driven by their needs rather than moral or intellectual considerations. Just as the naturalists extrapolated the general laws of insect behaviour from their experiments on individual bodies, they considered the mechanics of self-interest in their farmers to be generalizable.

As a solution to the problem of the moths' enormous fecundity, Duhamel and Tillet proposed ovens in which the insects would be killed but the grains preserved. Hard-working farmers could do much to reduce the damage by using these ovens, while lazy ones would suffer the consequences of neglecting these measures through significantly diminished harvests and would thus ultimately accept that using the ovens was in their self-interest. However, given that it was in the interest of the common good that the neglectful farmers acted in their own best interest immediately rather than once the damage was done, Duhamel argued that the state's "police" should force neglectful farmers to exterminate the moths in their fields and granaries so that they wouldn't attack those of their more conscientious neighbours.[52] Self-interest was a powerful motivation for most farmers, but they required the help and supervision of savants for controlling those citizens who neglected both their own, and the commonwealth's, interests.

These descriptions of crop-devouring insects rendered visible, and thus supposedly showed to be "true," the idea that bodies could be more easily managed when considered as a population with its own natural laws of vitality and mortality. This idea, perhaps, was unacceptable to the peasants who refused to have their methods controlled by Parisian observers. As we saw in the last section, the Physiocrats' reflections on government paralleled writings on insects, as they further naturalized the concept of the human population. As naturalists demonstrated that the quantity of insects depended on factors such as the availability of their chosen foodstuff, the climate, or the quantity of their enemies, they had, essentially, shown how to think of the collective—whether of insects or of humans—as a natural entity, with its own natural laws of fertility, mortality, health, or life expectancy. It is thus because of the efforts of Enlightenment savants to persuade their governments to adopt populationist thinking that twenty-first-century citizens and politicians find it "natural" to, in the words of one population scientist, "creat[e] causal and actionable knowledge via the transmutation of data from unique individuals into population distributions, dynamics, and rates" and then use this knowledge as the basis for political intervention.[53] Naturalists had also pointed out that insect populations could never be fully eliminated, only managed; this idea that to govern a population meant to manage it as a natural body with its own needs, rather than to completely control it was central also to the doctrines on the government of humans put forward by the Physiocrats.

* * *

The close connection between observing and governing humans and observing and governing animals that I have begun to tease out in this essay did not go unnoticed in the eighteenth century. Indeed, some of the Physiocrats' contemporaries were appalled by the alignment they had made between subjects and need-driven animals. The abbé de Mably, for instance, passionately decried physiocracy as a crime against morality.[54] Famous as one of the most revolutionary thinkers of the Old Regime,[55] the abbé based his rejection of the group's theories on their attempt to ground human politics in the physical need for subsistence:

> Isn't it evident, they say, that it is physically impossible to live without subsistence? Yes; but isn't equally impossible to live in society without social qualities? Who could deny, Monsieur, that moral qualities have contributed more to the establishment of Society than the need for subsistence?[56]

Like the Physiocrats, the abbé was engaged in a redefinition of government that steered away from the central importance of the will of the ruler. Unlike the Physiocrats, however, the abbé wrote in order to subvert rather than strengthen the absolutist state.[57] The measures he proposed for reforming the French state were thus diametrically opposed to the physiocratic principles and strikingly similar to the measures endorsed by earlier, mercantilist thinkers. He recommended, for example, intervention by the state in order to prevent poverty, strict regulations of the people's "*mœurs*" (roughly translatable as customs and behaviours), and censorship.[58] The crucial difference, of course, was that for Mably the sovereign was now constituted by the people instead of the absolutist monarch. As a consequence, despite their differences, Mably and Quesnay's disciples agreed on the fundamental idea that government should target not the sovereign's wealth, but the happiness of what for Mably was not the "population," but the "people." Humans, for Mably, should not be understood as an animal species (and thus as a population); they were fundamentally different from animals.[59]

The abbé insisted that human decisions were grounded in men's double nature (physical as well as moral, that is, in possession of a rational soul). Once basic bodily needs were fulfilled, choices based on reason and with the common good of mankind in mind, not the pursuit of self-interest, should form the basis of government. Keith Baker has argued that Mably's goal was to construe "a definition of situation in which public order in France was perceived not as the expression of tradition or prescription, custom or law, but as the outcome of willful action."[60] Mably agreed with the Physiocrats that the aim of government should be the happiness of all. Unlike the Physiocrats, however, Mably wanted to ground this order in what made humans different from, rather than similar to, animals. Instead of the formers' insistence on the importance of agriculture and hence private property, Mably proposed that man's capacity for moral behaviour explained the institution of the first society:

> Our game, I should say, our fish, the fruits we have gathered, everything will be shared. If fortune hasn't looked favorably upon my search, others will provide my subsistence; & I will console them in turn when their labor has been in vain, I will share with them the fruits I have collected or the animals I have hunted.[61]

Government should not encourage the pursuit of self-interest. For Mably, the Physiocrats had confused the misguided self-interests of the property owners, who benefited from a workforce considered only as animals in search of subsistence, with the law of nature. Mably, instead, exhorted his contemporaries: "Let us not merely occupy ourselves with our food, like vile animals."[62]

In sum, what was at stake in Mably's critique of the Physiocrats were two different conceptions of the human, based on differing notions of the relationship between animals and humans. While for Mably, the differences between humans, capable of moral bonds that went beyond need fulfilment, far outweighed the communalities, the Physiocrats argued that from the point of view of the governor at least, humans could indeed be viewed as instinctive, need-driven animals responding to sensual and physical stimuli. As I hope to have shown in this chapter, observations of animals played their own distinctive role in the emergence of both the abstract, complex notion of the "population" and the ideas of those who contested the normative power of this new category. This tension between a political theory based on the analysis of populations as the aggregate of generic, need-driven, self-interested men, and a theory of society based on moral choices of individuals capable of acting with the common good firmly in view, did not resolve with the end of the Enlightenment era. This opposition between humans as moral agents and, in the aggregate, as self-interested and driven by natural laws is familiar to us now, as it continues to inform the status of the discipline of economics today.

Notes

1 Anonymous, *Journal Oeconomique, ou Memoires, notes et avis sur l'Agriculture, les Arts, le Commerce, & tout ce qui peut avoir rapport à la santé, ainsi qu'à la conservation & à l'augmentation des biens des Familles, & c* (Paris: chez Antoine Boudet, 1766), 78. All translations are my own unless otherwise stated.
2 Janelle A. Schwartz, *Worm Work: Recasting Romanticism* (Minneapolis: University of Minnesota Press, 2012), xxi; Lucinda Cole, *Imperfect Creatures: Vermin, Literature, and the Sciences of Life 1600–1740* (Ann Arbor: University of Michigan Press, 2016). Historian of medicine Mary Fissell warns against assuming such continuity in our emotions towards verminous animals: Mary Fissell, "Imagining Vermin in Early Modern England," *History Workshop Journal*, 47 (1999), 1–29.
3 On the coming-into-being of this modern attitude, see Charlotte Sleigh, "Inside Out: The Unsettling Nature of Insects," in *Insect Poetics*, ed. Eric C. Brown (Minneapolis: University of Minnesota Press, 2006): 281–97.
4 Cole, *Imperfect Creatures*, 91.
5 Michel Foucault, *Security, Territory, Population: Lectures at the Collège de France, 1977–78* (Basingstoke; New York: Palgrave Macmillan, 2007), 67.
6 Jean F. Féraud, *Dictionnaire critique da la langue française: O-Z*, 3 vols (Marseille: Chez Jean Mossy, Père et fils, 1788), vol. 3, 209.
7 Foucault, *Security, Territory, Population*, 44–48.
8 Clare Palmer, "'Taming the Wild Profusion of Existing Things'?," *Environmental Ethics*, 23.4 (2001), 339–58; Peter Singer, 'Preface', in *Animal Philosophy: Ethics and Identity: Essential Readings in Continental Thought*, eds. Matthew Calarco and Peter Atterton (New York: Continuum, 2004): xi–xiii; Paola Cavalieri, 'A Missed Opportunity: Humanism, Anti-Humanism, and the Animal Question', in *Animal Subjects: An Ethical Reader in a Posthuman World*, ed. Jodey Castricano (Waterloo, ON: Wilfrid Laurier University Press, 2008): 97–124.
9 Féraud, *Dictionnaire critique*, vol. 3, 209.
10 Christine Théré and Jean-Marc Rohrbasser, "L'emploi du terme «population» dans l'Encyclopédie," *Recherches sur Diderot et sur l'Encyclopédie*, 31–32 (2002), 103–22.
11 Michael Kwass, "Consumption and the World of Ideas: Consumer Revolution and the Moral Economy of the Marquis de Mirabeau," *Eighteenth-Century Studies*, 37.2 (2004), 187–213.
12 On the 'conversion', see Michael Sonenscher, *Before the Deluge: Public Debt, Inequality, and the Intellectual Origins of the French Revolution*

(Princeton, NJ: Princeton University Press, 2007), 200; Liana Vardi, The Physiocrats and the World of the Enlightenment (Cambridge: Cambridge University Press, 2012), 47.

13 For nineteenth-century developments, see Joshua Cole, *The Power of Large Numbers: Population, Politics, and Gender in Nineteenth-Century France* (Ithaca, NY and London: Cornell University Press, 2000).

14 Étienne-Noël Damilaville, 'Population, (Physique, Morale, Politique)', eds. by Jean le Rond d'Alembert and Denis Diderot (University of Chicago: ARTFL Encyclopédie Project (Spring 2016 Edition), Robert Morrissey and Glenn Roe (eds.), 2016) http://encyclopedie.uchicago.edu; note also the three categories under which population is classified, indicating that it was understood both as a physical and a political entity.

15 For a recent discussion, see Marc J. Ratcliff, 'Duchesne's Strawberries: Between Growers' Practices and Academic Knowledge', in *Heredity Produced: At the Crossroads of Biology, Politics, and Culture, 1500–1870*, eds. Staffan Müller-Wille and Hans-Jörg Rheinberger (Cambridge Massachusetts ; London: MIT Press, 2007), 205–28.

16 Mary Terrall, *Catching Nature in the Act: Réaumur and the Practice of Natural History in the Eighteenth Century* (Chicago, IL: The University of Chicago Press, 2014).

17 Alice Stroup, *A Company of Scientists: Botany, Patronage, and Community at the Seventeenth-Century Parisian Royal Academy of Sciences* (Berkeley: University of California Press, 1990).

18 Harry C. Coppel and James W. Mertins, *Biological Insect Pest Suppression* (Berlin, Heidelberg: Springer, 1977), 17.

19 Brian W. Ogilvie, "Order of Insects," in *The Life Sciences in Early Modern Philosophy*, eds. Ohad Nachtomy and Justin E. H. Smith (Oxford University Press, 2014), 222–45.

20 René Antoine Ferchault de Réaumur, *Mémoire pour servir à l'histoire des insectes: Sur les chenilles & sur les papillons* (Paris: Imprimerie royale, 1734), vol. 1, 17.

21 Ogilvie, "Order of Insects," 15; 17.

22 Useful overviews of the physiocratic movement and thought can be found in T.J. Hochstrasser,"Physiocracy and the Politics of Laissez-Faire, " in *The Cambridge History of Eighteenth-Century Political Thought*, eds. Mark Goldie and Robert Wokler (Cambridge: Cambridge UP, 2006): 419–42; Sonenscher, *Before the Deluge,* 161–184; Vardi, *The Physiocrats.*

23 Philippe Steiner, *La 'science nouvelle' de l'économie politique* (Presses universitaires de France, 1998), 45–48. On needs in Mirabeau's thought, see Michael Sonenscher, "Physiocracy as Theodicy," *History of Political Thought*, 23.2 (2002), 326–39 (329).

24 Peter Sahlins, "The Royal Menageries of Louis XIV and the Civilizing Process Revisited," *French Historical Studies*, 35.2 (2012), 237–67.

25 On 'oeconomic' journals, see John Shovlin, *The Political Economy of Virtue: Luxury, Patriotism, and the Origins of the French Revolution* (Ithaca, NY: Cornell University Press, 2007), 52, fn. 10.

26 Carol Blum analyses depopulation discourses in her *Strength in Numbers: Population, Reproduction, and Power in Eighteenth-Century France* (Baltimore, MD and London: The Johns Hopkins UP, 2012).

27 Though dated, the following essay by Landry provides a very useful overview: Adolphe Landry, "Idées de Quesnay Sur La Population", *Revue d'Histoire Des Doctrines Économiques et Sociales*, 2 (1909), 41–87.

28 See Hochstrasser, "Physiocracy and the Politics of *Laissez-Faire*," 422.

29 François Quesnay, "Hommes", in *Oeuvres économiques complètes et autres textes: Textes polémiques, Documents associés*, eds. Christine Théré, Loïc Charles and Jean-Claude Perrot (Paris: INED, 2005), 257–323 (284).

30 Although Quesnay had important predecessors, such as Richard Cantillon. See Landry, "Idées de Quesnay," 44.

31 Vardi, *The Physiocrats*, 47.

32 Mirabeau, *L'ami des hommes ou traité de la population, nouvelle édition corrigée*, vol. 1 (Avignon: 1758), 16. This formulation appeared also in Cantillon's *Essai sur le commerce*, written around 1730 but unpublished until 1755: 'Les hommes se multiplient comme des Souris dans une grange, s'ils ont le moïen de subsister sans limitation;' Richard Cantillon, *Essai sur la Nature du Commerce en général. Traduit de l'Anglois* (Londres: Chez Fletcher Gyles, 1755), 110.

33 As Ann Firth explains with reference to James Steuart's theory of government; see Ann Firth, "From Oeconomy to `the Economy': Population and Self-Interest in Discourses on Government," *History of the Human Sciences*, 11.3 (1998), 19–35 (25–26).

34 As Vardi argues; see Vardi, *The Physiocrats*, 91.

35 Mirabeau, *L'ami des hommes*, 16.

36 Sonenscher explains the Physiocrats' optimism as a consequence of their Malebranchian theology, according to which God had given men both evil and the ability to remedy it; see Sonenscher, "Physiocracy as Theodicy". See also Deans' essay in this volume on how observation of populations became 'surveillance' of individuals' behaviours.

37 Indeed, one economic historian defines their concept of population as a 'dependent variable'. Yves Charbit, *The Classical Foundations of Population Thought: From Plato to Quesnay* (Dordrecht: Springer, 2010), 124.

38 Victor Riquetti Mirabeau marquis de and François Quesnay, *Philosophie rurale, ou économie générale et politique de l'agriculture*, 3 vols (Amsterdam: chez Les Libraires associés, 1763), vol. 2, 3.

39 See, for example, Quesnay's reflections in his unpublished article "Hommes".

40 François Quesnay, "Fermiers, (Econ. polit.)", in *L'Encyclopédie*, eds. Jean le Rond d'Alembert and Denis Diderot, ARTFL Encyclopédie Project, eds. Robert Morrissey and Glenn Roe (University of Chicago: (Spring 2016 Edition)), http://encyclopedie.uchicago.edu.

41 René Antoine Ferchault de Réaumur, *Mémoires pour servir a l'histoire des insectes. Suite de l'histoire des chenilles & des papillons; & l'histoire des insectes ennemis des chenilles* (Paris: chez Pierre Mortier, 1737), vol. 2, viii.

42 These are the criteria listed as essential for reflections on 'population' in Charbit, "Population," 3.

43 Sheila Wille, "The Ichneumon Fly and the Equilibration of British Natural Economies in the Eighteenth Century," *The British Journal for the History of Science*, 48.4 (2015), 639–60. Wille, accordingly, focuses on the notions of 'stability' and 'just equilibrium' in her analysis of the fly.

44 William Derham, *Physico-Theology, or, A Demonstration of the Being and Attributes of God from His Works of Creation: Being the Substance of Sixteen Sermons Preached in St. Mary-Le-Bow Church, London, at the Honourable Mr. Boyle's Lectures, in the Years 1711, and 1712 : With Large Notes, and Many Curious Observations* (W. and J. Innys, 1720), 398–99.

45 This emphasis on the social framework as existing prior to economic activity distinguishes the Physiocratic theory from Smith's political economy. As David McNally puts it: 'The Physiocrats anticipate Adam Smith's doctrine of the "invisible hand." Unlike Smith, however, they specify the social context

which is an indispensable precondition to the operation of the invisible hand.' David McNally, *Political Economy and the Rise of Capitalism* (Berkeley: University of California Press, 1988), 123.

46 See also Fredrik Albritton Jonsson, 'Rival Ecologies of Global Commerce: Adam Smith and the Natural Historians', *The American Historical Review*, 115.5 (2010), 1342–63, who argues that Smith's optimistic view of the balance of nature contrasted with the darker view of naturalists, particularly of those who had observed the rough conditions in the colonies. On scarcity as a natural phenomenon, see also Foucault, *Security, Territory, Population*, 60.

47 Henri-Louis Duhamel Du Monceau and Matthieu Tillet, *Histoire d'un Insecte, qui devore les grains de l'angoumois. Avec les moyens que l'on peut employer pour le détruire.* (Paris: H.L. Guerin & L. F. Delatour, 1762); For a different take on this text, see Etienne Stockland, ""La Guerre Aux Insectes": Pest Control and Agricultural Reform in the French Enlightenment," *Annals of Science*, 70.4 (2013), 435–60. Stockland uses the text to trace the construction of networks of observers, landlords, and amateurs and analyses the role of patriotic discourse in natural historical practice, particularly for recruiting helpers. On the Angoumois grain moth, which continues to ravage human fields, see Steve Jacobs and Dennis Calvin, "Angoumois Grain Moth (Department of Entomology)," *Department of Entomology (Penn State University)*, 1990, accessed 14 September 2016, http://ento.psu.edu/extension/factsheets/angoumois-grain-moth.

48 Monceau and Tillet, *Histoire d'un insecte*, 5–7.

49 Monceau and Tillet, *Histoire d'un insecte*, 138.

50 Monceau and Tillet, *Histoire d'un insecte*, 243.

51 Monceau and Tillet, *Histoire d'un insecte*, 75; 133–34.

52 Monceau and Tillet, *Histoire d'un insecte*, 299–300.

53 Nancy Krieger, "Who and What Is a "population"? Historical Debates, Current Controversies, and Implications for Understanding "Population Health" and Rectifying Health Inequities," *Milbank Quarterly*, 90.4 (2012), 634–81.

54 For a brief overview of the Physiocrat's reception, see Hochstrasser, "Physiocracy and the Politics of *Laissez-Faire*."

55 Keith Michael Baker, "A Script for a French Revolution: The Political Consciousness of the Abbé Mably," *Eighteenth-Century Studies*, 14.3 (1981), 235–63.

56 Gabriel Bonnot de Mably, *Doutes proposés aux philosophes économistes, sur l'ordre naturel et essentiel des sociétés politiques* (La Haye; Paris: chez Nyon et Veuve Durand, 1768), 29.

57 Baker, "A Script for a French Revolution", 237.

58 Johnson Kent Wright, *A Classical Republican in Eighteenth-Century France: The Political Thought of Mably* (Stanford, CA: Stanford University Press, 1997), 106.

59 On Mably as a natural rights theorists with regards to the question of property, see Wright, *A Classical Republican*, 96–99.

60 Keith Michael Baker, *Inventing the French Revolution: Essays on French Political Culture in the Eighteenth Century* (Cambridge: Cambridge UP, 1990), 87.

61 Mably, *Doutes proposés*, 39.

62 Mably, *Doutes proposés*, 34.

Section 2
Fictions

3 "Pilfering, and Burning, and Studious Waste"

Food Security and Political Economy in Harriet Martineau's *Cinnamon and Pearls*

Lesa Scholl

> A delicious scent pervaded the region as the fire spread, like airs from heaven finding their way among blasts from hell.[1]

At the climax of Harriet Martineau's *Cinnamon and Pearls* (1833), Volume 20 of her *Illustrations of Political Economy* series, Rayo, a poor Cingalese pearl diver, who has been dismissed for attempting to steal a pearl on his very first day of diving, sets fire to the East India Company's cinnamon crop as a wilful act of destruction designed to cripple the Company's harvest. The juxtaposition of the pervasive "airs from heaven" with the reference to 'hell' gestures towards the complexities of political economy in the colonial context. Paul Manning borrows from Hegel to define political economy broadly as a "system of needs";[2] and while his essay focuses on Wales, the way he draws on the linguistic understanding of ownership, property, and belonging across the English and Welsh languages speaks to the layering of political economy in a colonized arena. Belonging can be *a* belonging—a possession—or a sense of belonging, in a moral sense, to a community or a social organization, and both meanings, Manning argues, contribute to an individual's understanding of identity.[3] This understanding, however, is also informed by the individual's needs and wants, the access that they have to them, and what constitutes a right to such access. In a colonial setting, in which the most basic needs (food, clothing, shelter) are appropriated through imperialism, food security becomes central to the understanding of political economy. Access to food, or types of food, becomes as much about physical or biological survival for the colonized as it is about maintaining a distinct cultural identity through a discrete system of needs. Amartya Sen observes that one's relationship to food—one's position of ownership and access towards it in terms of economic power—is what determines whether or not one will starve:

> Food supply statements say things about a commodity...considered on its own. Starvation statements are about the *relationship* of persons to the commodity... Leaving out cases in which a person

> may deliberately starve, starvation statements translate readily into statements of ownership of food by persons. In order to understand starvation, it is, therefore, necessary to go into the structure of ownership.[4]

Sen goes on to write, "Indeed, some of the worst famines have taken place with no significant decline in food availability per head."[5]

In Martineau's Cingalese tale, the lateness of the monsoon season exposes, through the natural disasters of drought and flood, the inequity of distribution and access in the colonial context. As Helga Leitner et al. point out, ecological security, including food security, is heavily politicized, recognizing that the level to which an individual or community is affected by adverse environmental or economic circumstances is, to a degree, determined by their existing socioeconomic capital: "not all bodies and places are equally affected, nor are they endowed with equal capacities."[6] In the early nineteenth-century imperialist context, Martineau, in her mission to demonstrate what political economic theory would look like in practice, exposes the flaws and loopholes of a system that struggled with this uneven socioeconomic playing field. From its inception, the discipline of political economy has intervened in these questions through the tension between private and public interests. Adam Smith sought to reconcile this tension through his metaphor of the "invisible hand," which he endowed with a certain level of providential power. Although criticizing the rich for being driven by their "luxury and caprice" instead of their sense of "humanity and justice" in *The Theory of Moral Sentiments* (1759), Smith suggests that "in spite of their natural selfishness and rapacity, though [what] they mean only their own conveniency...be the gratification of their own vain and insatiable desires," they are nevertheless

> led by an invisible hand to make nearly the same distribution of the necessaries of life, which would have been made, had the earth been divided into equal portions among all its inhabitants; and thus, without intending it, without knowing it, advance the interest of the society.[7]

Smith's contemporary Adam Ferguson similarly argued in 1767 that such providential order is "the result of human action, but not the execution of any human design," a perspective that has contributed to economic theories of spontaneous order.[8] Michelle Schwarze and John Scott suggest that Smith's invisible hand in *The Theory of Moral Sentiments* differs from the later rendition in *Wealth of Nations* (1776); in that it is more concerned with

> a moral philosophy in which individuals sympathize with others in efforts to achieve psychic harmony, modifying their emotional

> expressions and moral judgements...When successful, this process produces the psychological harmony central to the happiness of individuals as well as moral and political order.[9]

While I appreciate the way in which Schwarze and Scott go on to challenge this sense of order, the way that Smith positions the invisible hand in his earlier text is not so removed from his perspective in *Wealth of Nations*, in which, as Joseph Persky argues, "owners of capital, when left to themselves, would inadvertently promote the public interest by pursing their own private interests."[10] In Persky's reading of both renditions, neither invisible hand is truly endowed with a proximate moral imperative that will benefit individuals; rather they both suggest a distant assumption that through providential accident, pursuing self-interest will ultimately benefit the broader society. Smith's theory depends, furthermore, on an assumption of a "natural sense of fellow-feeling":[11] *The Theory of Moral Sentiments* opens with the statement that

> How selfish soever man may be supposed, there are evidently some principles in his nature, which interest him in the fortune of others, and render their happiness necessary to him, though he derives nothing from it, except the pleasure of seeing it.[12]

It is, perhaps, this kind of unmitigated optimism alongside his engagement with the tensions between capitalism and community in Smith's work that leads scholars such as Mark White to see ethical contradictions in Smith's economic philosophy.[13] John Dwyer maintains that "Smith's economics were subservient to his ethics";[14] however, his ethics are called into question in relation to the limits of community responsibility. Within ideas of "fellow-feeling," where do ideas of one's community responsibilities begin and end? While Smith focuses on sympathy, particularly in his earlier work, the interpretation of his ethics is malleable precisely because of the subjectivity of the limits of community, sympathy, and the scope of social responsibility. Within the colonial context, in which the colonial other is seen as *not* one's neighbour, this kind of limitation becomes much more pronounced. In Martineau's tale, ideas of community and neighbourliness—and therefore ideas of sympathy—are inherently vexed; and in this way, Schwarze and Scott's argument that communal resentment of injustice disrupts the possibility of Smithean spontaneous order becomes increasingly relevant to the vision of political economy.[15]

Although often read as lauding the way in which political economy was appropriated by the imperialist agenda (also labelled by some as the civilizing mission), Martineau actually uses early political economy to turn imperial conquest on its head. Rather than celebrating Britain's appropriation of colonial wealth, Martineau gives voice to the starved and desperate dispossessed "natural" owners, as she repeatedly refers to the Cingalese natives, not just of the land, but of its produce. Indeed, she uses arguments founded in political economy of individual ownership and investment in labour increasing productivity to call for removing the East India Company's monopoly on Ceylon's trade. In this way, rather than "subordinating her fiction explicitly to the 'truths' of political economy,"[16] Martineau in fact complicates political economy through the colonial context. Like Smith, who disparaged the East India Company in *Wealth of Nations*, describing the monopolistic company as "a national cancer,"[17] Martineau similarly saw the work of such organizations as misappropriating the laws of political economy, even depicting its employees as former men of character being reduced to "moral corruption."[18] While Eleanor Courtemanche's claim that "Martineau's stories gain authority from access to the abstract laws of economic theory" seems to simplify Martineau's agenda, her observation of Martineau's "insist[ence] that theory cannot be realized in social life without fiction" provides a useful entry into understanding the way Martineau uses the relatively new form of literary realism to subvert the practicability of political economy.[19] While, as Courtemanche suggests, the pervasive "invisible hand" metaphor "displace[s] to some indefinite spatial and temporal distance" the "moral causality" of political economy,[20] Martineau's tale problematizes this kind of convenient distancing, particularly through the character of Mr. Carr, who, while able to articulate the damage done by the East India Company, is blind to his own hand in the matter as the agent of the "Honourable Company," and is, in fact, no more palatable a figure than his comically lazy wife who bemoans the laziness of the Cingalese.[21]

In this essay, I seek to draw out Martineau's complex relationship to political economy, capitalism, and imperialism, as well as the way in which she privileges the voices of the dispossessed and disenfranchised. By the time she had published *Cinnamon and Pearls*, she had already used her political economy series to critique French and Russian imperialism (*French Wines and Politics* and *The Charmed Sea*), as well as Britain's colonization of Ireland and Van Diemen's Land (*Ireland* and *Homes Abroad*). Therefore, her setting of Ceylon under the reign of the East India Company engages with a narrative Martineau had already established of colonial dispossession and unrest. While Martineau was known for her appreciation of industrial and educative progress, she found dispossession and waste problematic aspects of imperialism. As Deborah Logan observes, "Martineau's faith in culturally transcendent values…undergoes serious scrutiny and restructuring as the disparities between imperial principles and practices and the realities of globalization became increasingly apparent."[22] Indeed, while Martineau believed in the "benefits of civilized, industrial society" in theory, she struggled to "reconcile the lofty principles of imperialism [that is, of the civilizing mission] with its dubious practices."[23] Martineau would go on to formalize her critique of England's imperialism in an 1854 article for the *Westminster Review* entitled "England's Foreign Policy," in which she states that England has lost its "vital idea" and its "national conscience";[24] yet her disaffection is evident in her earlier tales. While some critics prefer to look at the critique of *Cinnamon and Pearls* through the very narrow definition of Martineau's views of economic monopolies, which fits with her faith in free trade and allows the critic to uphold the belief in Martineau's imperial idealism, it is my conviction that her critique is broader in the way she addresses ownership and legitimacy, and individual and institutional responsibility for dispossession, through the experiences and actions of her characters, both the imperialists and the dispossessed. She satirically plays on the commodification of human life alongside produce, and deplores the waste of both. The tensions are revealed most powerfully through the voices she contrives to give the dispossessed; for, it must be acknowledged, apart from fiction, those voices would not be heard.

Ownership, Legitimacy, and the Value of Labour

Rayo's theft of the pearl is not a one-off lapse due to unprecedented temptation. For Rayo, theft—if it is to be defined as such—is a political act. Martineau's novella opens as Rayo, with his fiancée Marana accompanying him, surreptitiously dives for conch shells in the middle of the night. The shells are a crucial commodity for this scene because not only have the conch beds been appropriated by the East India Company, the shells had been a specific item of trade for the Cingalese, both domestically and with India, and this trade was embedded in ritual practices surrounding marriage and burial. To a degree, the conch shell in Martineau's tale responds to Adam Smith's discussion of fashion, ornament, and utility in *Wealth of Nations*. Smith, in his critique of industrialization and manufacturing over agrarian values, argues that

> Manufactures for which the demand rises altogether from fashion and fancy, are continually changing, and seldom last long enough to be considered as old established manufactures. Those, on the contrary, for which the demand arises chiefly from use or necessity, are less liable to change, and the same form or fabric may continue in demand for whole centuries together.[25]

Yet while for the imperialists the conch shell is an object of fashion, for the Cingalese is it more of an object of utility because of its cultural significance. By using this object, Martineau conjures a dispossession that goes beyond economic property or capital, invading cultural and historical practices that are a part of two of the most vulnerable rites of human passage. The utility of the conch shell for the Cingalese is significant to Martineau: it is not as if without the imperial appropriation the shells would go to waste. The colonists are thus positioned as thieves, taking livelihood and life from the Cingalese, and putting a guard on duty each night to protect the stolen fare, or "treasure," as the narrator puts it, alluding to piracy.[26]

Writing about *Cinnamon and Pearls*, Logan observes that "Ceylon... offers a wealth of natural resources, literally there for the harvesting... Yet, while the Civilizing Mission had made some progress toward introducing literacy and religion, most Cingalese (Singhalese) suffered from disease, malnutrition, and premature death."[27] Martineau reveals from the start of the novella that the forced exchange of "literacy and religion" for Ceylon's natural resources is a poor one for the colonized. Instead of education idealistically removing superstition, Marana, for example, is doubly crippled by the combination of ancient religion and the Catholicism introduced by Father Anthony, the priest who is also their teacher. As she fears for Rayo in his quest for conch shells, she "finger[s] her ebony beads meanwhile, and her lips moved as she murmured some aspirations compounded of a catholic prayer and a native charm."[28] However, Marana is also able to claim that the rare right-handed shell Rayo finds is proof of God's favour when the pair are confronted by the priest, and although she ends up afraid of curses from both directions, she holds onto that one shell while dangerously returning the others—against Rayo's will.

Rayo is much more willing than Marana to confront Father Anthony's definitions of theft, legitimacy, and ownership, appropriating the language of early political economy for his argument, and he is also willing to defy the priest by not confessing to the colonial "owners." When the priest says "These chanks [conch shells] cannot be yours," and goes on to ask, "Rayo, why did you steal these chanks? Do not you know that God punishes theft?" Rayo replies with his own question: "Is it theft to get chanks for my bride, when I have worked long for them, and can get no chanks by working?"[29] Father Anthony argues that "God gave them into the hands of those who possess them; and He will be angry with any who take them away by fraud or violence," meaning to scare Rayo with God's judgement while legitimizing the East India Company's ownership as delivered to the Company by God;[30] yet, ironically, the conches are literally in Rayo's hands, and Martineau shows throughout the tale the violence of imperial conquest, which overturns the priest's argument. Martineau moves the dialogue into indirect speech in order to lend Rayo the authority and alignment of the omniscient narrator's voice: "Rayo was very much in want of his friend's guidance. In the school, it was taught as a duty that a just reward should be given for toil. Was it was a duty out of school to toil without reward?"[31]

Martineau confronts directly the hypocrisy of teaching an idealized form of political economy, partly attributable to Adam Smith's *The Theory of Moral Sentiments*, in which Smith suggests that through "look[ing] around and admir[ing] the condition of the rich," man is compelled to change his situation—that seeing the wealth of others encourages the poor man to work harder to achieve the same standards.[32] Regenia Gagnier has referred to this moment in Smith's theory as one of "manifold irony," not the least because "the great system of wealth and social order is a delusion for most of society."[33] E. P. Thompson, in his seminal essay on "The Moral Economy," writes of the way in which early political economists like Adam Smith, David Ricardo, and even Thomas Malthus, sought to "disinfest" their economic theories of "intrusive moral imperatives" by deferring to the science of the market.[34] This reading, however, fails to note the anger and displeasure with which Smith invests the poor man's son, who, in his ultimate sense of hopelessness, "feels himself naturally indolent, and willing to serve himself with his own hands as little as possible."[35] Martineau recognizes the moral economy through the voices of the dispossessed; yet it could also be argued that Rayo's arguments regarding labour and reward also pre-empt Karl Marx's alienated labour in *Capital* (1867), by challenging how far economic thought had travelled away from the initial idea of political economy—perhaps, in Martineau's terms, its "vital idea"—of community connection and economic/trade diversity. Instead, the worker (Rayo) is distanced and alienated from the reward of his labour through the imperialism of the East India Company, and as a result, his prosperity is rendered impossible:

> Great pains had been taken to civilize Rayo. He had been schooled and watched over—he could read, and he respected the religion of his priest; he was willing to toil, and had a taste for comfort. But, beyond the hope of acquiring a hut and a mat or two, there was little stimulus to toil, and as little to conduct himself with a view towards any future circumstances. Strangers not only carried away the wealth of the land, *but they prevented that wealth from growing*, and therefore the labour of the inhabitants from obtaining a wider field.[36]

The flaw of political economy within the colonial setting is that it prevents the development of ambition and desire because there is no possibility of the colonized being able to repossess their land and its resources. Instead, they exemplify the disaffection of alienated labour, made even more unpalatable by being labelled as thieves of their own land.

Martineau's tale is distanced from discourses of hunger to a degree because it focuses on non-edible commodities (conch shells and pearls) and spices, rather than staple foodstuffs, and all of these commodities are treated as items to trade, rather than food items that could directly combat the starvation of the Cingalese population. However, the Cingalese lack of access to the market is what prevents them from being able to buy sufficient food, and therefore signals their lack of freedom. It is in this context that Sen's theories of exchange entitlement are most useful. Sen explains that:

> An entitlement relation applied to ownership connects one set of ownerships to another through certain rules of legitimacy...Each link in this chain of entitlement relations "legitimizes" one set of ownership by reference to another, or some basic entitlement in the form of enjoying the fruits of one's own labour.[37]

This web of entitlement, or what Sen refers to as "exchange entitlement mapping,"[38] is precisely that which entangles Rayo and Marana, and their lack of market entitlement caused by imperialism means that they are at risk of starvation. Gagnier refers to this kind of lack of freedom in the opening of *The Insatiability of Human Wants* (2000): "Is freedom in market society anything more than the capacity to exercise choice in the marketplace?"[39] Yet where Gagnier's work goes on to discuss the development of wants as needs, for Rayo and Marana, their extreme lack of entitlement in the colonial context leaves them unable even to hope for the barest of necessities. As Sen states, "[s]tarvation is the characteristic of some people not *having* enough food to eat. It is not the characteristic of there not *being* enough to eat";[40] but the statistics of quantity turn sour when those with entitlement legitimacy (economic capital) destroy quantities of produce in order to push up prices, even though those who would go without would go without regardless because of the exchange entitlement structure. Hence, the profound simplicity of the statement, "[the] history of hunger is interwoven with the history of plenty."[41]

Civilizing Myths and Crop Destruction

Waste for commercial gain was one of Martineau's most crucial concerns, one she addressed in terms of the disempowerment and delegitimizing of rightful owners alongside vexed understandings of indolence and non-utility of resources. As her tale moves into the beginning of the pearl-diving season, Martineau's narrative engages with David Ricardo's concerns regarding indolence and its possible solutions. In his *Principles of Political Economy*, Ricardo writes:

> In those countries where there is abundance of fertile land, but where, from the ignorance, indolence, and barbarism of the inhabitants, they are exposed to all the evils of want and famine, and where it has been said that population presses against the means

> of subsistence...the evil proceeds from bad government, from the insecurity of property, and from a want of education in all ranks of the people.[42]

The problem for Martineau, however, is that in the colonial setting, the colonized people themselves become commodities as much as the pearls, through their provision of labour. The "various merchants" are given the "gracious permission...to make what they could of the natives of the land as well as of the sea," which provocatively renders the oysters on the same level of sentient agency as the Cingalese.[43] The merchants are further given the authority "not only to appropriate the natural wealth of the region, but to bring its inhabitants as near to the brink of starvation as they pleased in their methods of employing their toil."[44] Martineau goes on to describe the Cingalese as "hungry and half naked...being, all the while, the natural owners of the native wealth of their region. And why is all this injustice and tyranny? That a few, a very few, may engross a resource which should enrich the many."[45] Perhaps one of the most perverse results of colonization is that the food of those who have laboured is positioned almost as a gift bestowed upon them by the colonizers, for which they should be grateful. Furthermore, to be allowed to labour for the East India Company, or other imperial agent, is something for which they should be thankful: "hundreds and thousands of their families and neighbours stand on the shore envying them as they depart, and preparing to be jealous of them on their return."[46] Those who can labour are the lucky ones, and the scrutiny is moved away from the colonizers who have enacted the dispossession.

Yuki Masami has written recently on the concept of food as gift, and the way in which it reifies the provision:

> Food as gift refers to food that is perceived as given, rather than produced by humans. In other words, it is food that is not entirely appropriated by human management or control....The perception of food as gift evokes a sense of human smallness in an interrelated and interdependent more-than-human world.[47]

While Masami's essay addresses people growing and eating food in areas contaminated by nuclear waste disasters, strong correlations can be drawn between her understanding of the "more-than-human world" and food bestowal, and the ways in which the imperial mission reified Adam Smith's "invisible hand." In relation to the dispossession of the Cingalese of Martineau's text, instead of literal contamination, there is economic and cultural contamination caused by the East India Company and, while the effects are indirect, this contamination is precisely what leads to the starvation and disease that is rife in the Cingalese population. While Masami's essay addresses consequences of the nuclear revolution, Martineau's tale essentially contends with the ramifications of the industrial revolution; and in both contexts, the questions that arise are not just in regard to the effects of human intervention on the natural world, but also the effects of changes in labour and agricultural practices, economic and imperial policy, and the negotiation (or lack thereof) between humans, nature, and each other. The crop destruction that takes place in *Cinnamon and Pearls* is an extreme version of this, expressed in terms that are chaotic, irrational, and ultimately impotent, but also crucially mirrors the economically "rational" crop destruction that routinely takes place in an ordered fashion under the instructions of the East India Company to push up prices. Both examples speak to the economic and social ramifications of trying to control nature.

When Rayo sets fire to the cinnamon crop, he intends on it being an act of protest against the East India Company for not allowing the Cingalese to grow their own cinnamon crops to sell, and therefore earn an income. This motivation is assumed, however, rather than articulated directly—a narrative move that reinforces the idea that Rayo's act is irrational rather than considered. It seems intended to be read parallel to the food riots that plagued Britain and Continental Europe throughout the late eighteenth century, driven by the starving who could not afford to buy the food they themselves produced. More important to this scene, however, and to the scene directly after, in which Rayo overhears the effect of his actions, is his lack of control both over his message as well as its material results, manifested through his inability to control the fire itself:

> The fire he kindled did not catch the green shrubs; but some flakes were carried off by the wind, and fell among the parched grass near the outskirts of the plantation. There were in an instant rivulets of fire running beneath the stems, joining and parting, according to the quantity of fuel which lay in their way.[48]

That his fire misses its target is reflective of the fact that setting the fire itself misses the target of hurting the Company, while the "rivulets of fire" evoke the monsoonal storm that inadvertently protects Rayo from prosecution, but also silences his protest. Because the monsoon hits as Rayo is lighting his fire, the fire is blamed on a lightning strike, rather than on wilful destruction. However, what is most defeating for Rayo is that by lighting the fire, he actually plays into the Company's hands, because it means that they do not have to burn the crop because it was too abundant, which would have angered the Cingalese. They are therefore gifted with social as well as economic capital:

> "The lightning has saved the Company from the curses of the people," he heard Captain Cinnamon whisper to a modelier of the

> garden. "There was too good a crop this year; and if some of it must be burned, it was very well that accident should do it."
>
> And that accident should have burned more than the Company would have dared to destroy in the face of the natives. Now they may put their own price on the bark; and a pretty price it will be, to judge by Mr. Carr's pleased face.[49]

From a humanist perspective, and arguably from Martineau's, it would seem irrational to destroy crops in order to push up prices when people are starving, even though she recognizes the mathematical logic of supply and demand. However, where Martineau sees this as irrational is where the rationale becomes severed from human society and human feeling. Martineau exposes the corruption of political economy by juxtaposing imperial rationality with the harshness of human suffering.

Mr. Carr, as the East India Company's agent, is Martineau's key spokesperson for the imperialist corruption of political economy. His character is highly contrived, displaying the narrative contortions required for him to hold onto his economic views, yet unlike his wife, his character does not become comedic. Mr. Carr exemplifies the patriarchal nature of imperialism, as well as the need to justify the failures of imperialism through displacing blame onto the dispossessed. Throughout the novella, Mr. Carr presents himself as a rational, just, ethical man; yet this position requires selective denial. It is through holes and absences, and in particular his deferral of his own hand onto the invisible, faceless authority of the Company, that he is able to maintain his "rational" perspective. Instead of seeing his own human agency, he positions himself as a good servant of the Company, only working diligently towards his employers' goals; however, his ideological contortions and justifications, expressed in a conversation with his young daughter, Alice, are followed by his supercilious treatment of the Cingalese working in his crops, also in front of his daughter. He accuses the Cingalese of stealing the cinnamon—an ironic accusation, since he knows there is too much and that some must be burned—and demands that the workers go into the shrubs to intimidate and frighten the perceived thief, while encouraging his daughter to expect, perhaps demand, obsequious treatment from the workers. Mr. Carr's actions seem a performance of power, following his seemingly rational comments to Alice that "the natives would have little scruple; for, like all people who are cruelly pinched, they are apt to take what they can get without caring to whom it belongs."[50] But he suggests that the problem is that once they have stolen the cinnamon, they have no means to sell it. Even though he knows that they may steal in order to eat, and even though he knows that the crop is "too good," he still exerts his authority in an extreme manner by having the workers stop their peeling to chase the thief: "a grand show of zeal they made in beating amongst the shrubs, and uttering cries."[51] What is more disturbing than this kind of psychological brutalization, however, which affects the thief as well as the Cingalese who are expected to find him, is that in the passage that goes before, Mr. Carr sounds rational, articulate, and even thoughtful and concerned about the plight of the very people he abuses. His response is selective: he is able to see the connection between the East India Company's cinnamon trade and the West Indian slave trade and sugar plantations,[52] yet he cannot see the correlation between his own treatment of the Cingalese workers and the treatment of slaves.

As a counterpoint to Mr. Carr's blindness, the extended conversation he has with Alice on imperial economics occurs because Alice observes the number of diseased and emaciated bodies of the Cingalese. Martineau often uses children's voices to cut through the justifying contortions of adults, yet Alice, as a colonist's child, has already absorbed strong patriarchal attitudes at the foundation of the civilizing myth of British imperialism. She says to her father: "But if there was not enough, I would rather make the king of Candy[53] go without than these poor people *who belong to us*. We ought to take care of them first."[54] Alice's sense of ownership over the dispossessed people reveals the embedded slavery narrative, and reinforces the disempowerment of the Cingalese in ideological and cultural terms as well as their economic dispossession. This disempowerment is also written through their lack of access to nutritional food, which Mr. Carr recognizes, but for which he does not believe himself accountable or responsible. He tells Alice: "There would be few such swollen or emaciated bodies as these if the people had flesh to eat, or good bread, or even the seasoning which was necessary to make their vegetable food agree with them."[55]

This attitude recalls Masami's discussion of contamination, in which "the act of eating contaminated food and perceiving it as a gift—that is, the act of eating life—challenges our complacent norms of food safety and thereby opens up a conceptual realm of human interactions with the environment."[56] Having to eat toxic food in order to survive is not far removed from Martineau's Cingalese, who are diseased because of the quality, as well as quantity, of the food available to them. Mr. Carr matter-of-factly lists three things that could improve the health of the Cingalese: meat for protein, quality bread, and seasoning—which, importantly, does not just improve the flavour of food, but also assists in preserving it. Sen writes that "the translation of minimum *nutritional* requirements into minimum *food* requirements depends on the choice of commodities,"[57] and in a very material sense it needs to be recognized that access to quality food is not merely a sign of economic capital, but an imperative for base-level health.[58]

Given the dual role of taste and preservation, it is important to note that of the four seasonings that Mr. Carr references—salt, pepper, cardamom, and cinnamon—he spends the most time talking to Alice about salt. All four he speaks of as commodities that the Cingalese could sell if they had access to them, but it is salt in particular that he seems to recognize as something that they need to consume themselves, rather than trade, noting the irony that there is plenty of salt, but that the people are not allowed to access it. Alice at first expresses her mother's opinion of the laziness of the Cingalese as an excuse for their not being able to consume it:

> Salt, papa! They must be very lazy if they do not get salt enough. There is the sea all round Ceylon; and I have seen several ponds where the water was so salt[y] I could not drink it. There was a crust of salt all about the edge, papa.[59]

However, her father explains the way in which the imperial relationship works:

> Very true, my dear; but the people are not allowed to take it. The king of Candy lives in the middle of this island; and the kings of Candy have sometimes been troublesome people to the English, as they were to the Dutch before them. Now, as the king of Candy cannot get to the sea, or to any salt lake, without our king's leave, he and his people depend upon us for salt; and our government likes to keep him quiet, and get a great price for its salt at the same time by selling it to the Candians very dear, and by letting nobody else sell any. So the people of the country are not allowed to help themselves to salt.[60]

Mr. Carr goes on to say:

> There is salt enough for every body here, and for half India besides; and large quantities are destroyed every year, to keep up the price, while many are dying for want of it, and those who live can get nothing better than coarse dirty salt which the beasts in your grandmama's farm-yard would turn away from. If we could count the numbers of Hindoos who die in India for want of the salt which their own country produces, we should find that a fearful reckoning awaits the Company there, as there does the government here; a fearful balance of human life against the price of salt.[61]

There is little to disagree with from Martineau's perspective on the detail of how the imperial economy operates; however, there is the unspoken consternation that while being able to articulate the effects of dispossession, even down to recognizing that human life is essentially sacrificed in order to push up prices for the East India Company, Mr. Carr is unable or unwilling to accept his own role in bringing about such a sacrifice. He is merely the agent of the company; and in this way, he can conveniently ignore his own responsibility, instead deferring to the faceless Company.

In this way, Mr. Carr exemplifies the moral corruption that Adam Smith saw in the employees of the East India Company, and as the head of his household, this corruption filters down through his family. While Mr. Carr is positioned as a problematic voice of imperialism's rationale, and his daughter provides a counternarrative that expresses a naïve, innocent response—a simple reason from a child's perspective—they are triangulated by Mrs. Carr, a figure who demonstrates the imperial vision in the basest (to the point of comedic) terms. Although Mrs. Carr is a caricature, her imperial blindness powerfully reflects her husband's capacity to distance himself from his actions in dispossession, as well as the plight of the Cingalese. As her husband and daughter ride off, Mrs. Carr "closed her eyes on the dewy radiance of a morning in paradise, and was glad that she had nothing more to do with cinnamon than to be tired of hearing of it, and to taste it when she pleased."[62]

Conclusion: Individual and Institutional Responsibility

When Martineau's narrative turns conveniently without explanation to enable a conclusion in which the Cingalese are suddenly allowed to plant and sell their own cinnamon, Mr. Carr is disturbingly positioned as a type of hero. This positioning is not unlike the role of Alice as a type of economic heroine, in that she buys Marana's precious charmed conch shell from her, which gives Marana enough money to buy food, although the narrative makes it clear that these do not last very long. Marana gains a few meals, but at the price of her culture and her beliefs, and, although the amount given is not clear, it can be assumed that it was not the full value that such a shell could have purchased, given Marana's desperation. In this way, Alice becomes the imperial capitalist, who is able to justify her actions in that she sees herself as providing for Marana and Rayo. It is also at a moment of acute fear for Marana, as her husband is returning, and he does not know that she still has the shell, so when Marana signals to Mr. Carr to hide the shell, he takes that as an indication that he is to keep it. Marana, then, in her vulnerable position, is taken advantage of, but momentarily appreciates the exchange: "the idea of the hag vanished for the instant before the image of a basket of steaming rice, stewed with cardamoms or peppercorns."[63]

James Vernon suggests that

> However much we might like to think of hunger as happening elsewhere, to strangers in far-off lands ravaged by famine, it is always just around the corner...It connects us in elemental ways to others, because we believe that in the modern world no one deserves to live with hunger, let alone die of it.[64]

In the colonial context, however, the colonists must find other ways to justify their position, given that the starvation and disease is on their doorstep. This challenge recalls the question of the limits and extent of sympathy and community in Smith's political economy, and the need to justify where the lines of responsibility are drawn. For the Carrs, it is the faults of the Cingalese—their laziness, their governance, their poor dietary choices—that lead to their demise, rather than any action on the colonists' part. Martineau uses the voices of the Serles, who are American missionaries, to counter the Carrs: "When we find starving men in paradise, our next business is to find out whose fault it is that they are starving."[65] While Mrs. Carr's immediate response is to charge the Cingalese with extreme laziness, the reality of dispossession hovers over the scene. Even more powerfully, though, Martineau lends the Cingalese women an almost biblical rhetoric, in the tone of a catechism, when they respond to Father Anthony's chastisement of their ungratefulness for the education and protection that imperialism has afforded them. They use their education to speak back to the colonist:

> "Who is it that robs us, not only of our spice and our pearls, but of all that many another country would give us for our spice and our pearls, if it be not the English?" cried one.
>
> "Are we the happier for their wisdom and skill?" cried another. "And as for the arts of life, do we need strangers to teach us to lie beneath the fig-tree, and sleep away our hunger?"
>
> "From what do they protect us?" asked a third. "If they will go away, we will protect ourselves against their returning: and our own expenses we can bear as soon as ships from every land may come to trade on our shores."[66]

Through these rhetorical questions, Martineau reveals the desire of the Cingalese to take responsibility for, and ownership of, their own land and resources, thus emphasizing the criminality of imperialism. While Father Anthony tries to reinforce the benefits of imperialism, "his pupils were obstinate in the opinion that slavery could not be said to be abolished while labourers were dependent for daily bread on the arbitrary will of a monopolizing party."[67]

The frustration of the Cingalese women gestures towards rebellion, as much as Rayo's act of burning the cinnamon was potentially self-destructive. Both moments in the novella are political as well as personal. Self-destruction, or potential self-destruction, evokes suicide, which is important in this context as "committing suicide was seen by the British colonial state as a sign of disaffection with its policies, and a statement about its inability to provide order."[68] In this context, the irrationality of self-destruction is no longer clear because it holds a political purpose, and therefore there is no distinct binary between rational and irrational. While Mr. Carr states that "property is sacred in the eye of God and man," Mrs. Serle points out, "therefore, whenever that which is called property is extensively desecrated, the inevitable conclusion is that it is not really property."[69] She goes on to observe to Mr. Carr,

> Rayo's property will be sacred in the eyes of his country. But the whole island has long risen against your monopoly gardens. There have been not only curses breathed within its shade, and beyond its bounds, but pilfering, and burning, and studious waste.[70]

Ending powerfully on a note of moral economy, while Mr. Carr's misappropriation of political economy is rendered impotent, Martineau ends with a hopeful possibility in which Rayo is given the means to build a life for himself that is not fearfully dependent on the imperialists for benefits, but ultimately self-supporting. There is a slight sinister twist, though, as it is suggested that Rayo would thus first be able to "supply his simple wants, and then to afford to let them become more complex,"[71] which hints towards Rayo being trapped within the liberal capitalist market. The narrative thus returns to Thomas Malthus's view in *Principles of Political Economy* (1820) that a flowing market requires a given society to believe itself perpetually in a state of want: "[n]o country with a very confined market, internal as well as external, has even been able to accumulate a large capital, because such a market prevents the formation of those wants and tastes."[72] For the pragmatic Martineau, once this market is established, it is difficult to escape; however, she emphasizes the importance that such a market should not be at the expense of humanity, and that there is space, and indeed the necessity, through the recognition of the moral economy, to build community and benefit the hungry.

Notes

1 Harriet Martineau, *Cinnamon and Pearls* (London: Charles Fox, 1833), 70.
2 Paul Manning, "Owning and Belonging: A Semiotic Investigations of the Affective Categories of a Bourgeois Society," *Comparative Studies in Society and History* 46:2 (2004): 300–25 (304).
3 Ibid., 301.
4 Amartya Sen, *Poverty and Famines: An Essay on Entitlement and Deprivation* (Oxford: Clarendon, 1981), 1.
5 Ibid., 7.
6 Helga Leitner, Emma Colven and Eric Sheppard, "Ecological Security for Whom? The Politics of Flood Alleviation and Urban Environmental Justice in Jakarta, Indonesia," in *The Routledge Companion to the Environmental Humanities*, eds. Ursula K. Heise et al. (London: Routledge, 2017), 194–205, (195).
7 Adam Smith, *An Inquiry into the Nature and Causes of the Wealth of Nations*, eds. R. H. Campbell, A. S. Skinner, and W. B. Todd (Oxford: Oxford University Press, 1976), 296.
8 Quoted in Michelle A. Schwarze and John T. Scott, "Spontaneous Disorder in Adam Smith's *Theory of Moral Sentiments*: Resentment, Injustice, and the Appeal to Providence," *The Journal of Politics* 77:2 (2015): 463–76 (463).

9 Schwarze and Scott, "Spontaneous Disorder," 464.
10 Joseph Persky, "Retrospectives: Adam Smith's Invisible Hands," *The Journal of Economic Perspectives* 3:4 (1989): 195–201 (197).
11 Jerry Evensky, "Adam Smith's *Theory of Moral Sentiments*: On Morals and Why They Matter to a Liberal Society of Free People and Free Markets," *The Journal of Economic Perspectives* 19:3 (2005): 109–30 (113).
12 Adam Smith, *The Theory of Moral Sentiments* (Philadelphia, PA: Anthony Finley, 1817), 1.
13 Mark D. White, "Adam Smith and Immanuel Kant: On Markets, Duties, and Moral Sentiments," *Social Economics* 39 (2010): 53–60 (53).
14 John Dwyer, "Ethics and Economics: Bridging Adam Smith's *Theory of Moral Sentiments* and *Wealth of Nations*," *Journal of British Studies* 44:4 (2005): 662–87 (662).
15 Schwarze and Scott, "Spontaneous Disorder," 464.
16 Eleanor Courtemanche, *The "Invisible Hand" and British Fiction, 1818–1860: Adam Smith, Political Economy, and the Genre of Realism* (Basingstoke, UK: Palgrave, 2011), 122.
17 Quoted in Dwyer, "Ethics and Economics," 674–75.
18 Ibid., 675.
19 Courtemanche, *The "Invisible Hand,"* 126.
20 Ibid., 1.
21 Martineau, *Cinnamon and Pearls*, 70.
22 Deborah Logan, *Harriet Martineau, Victorian Imperialism, and the Civilizing Mission* (Farnham, UK: Ashgate, 2010), 13.
23 Ibid., 15–16.
24 Martineau, "England's Foreign Policy," *Westminster Review* 61 (1854): 190–232 (191 and 193). I have written elsewhere on Martineau's disillusionment with imperialism as expressed through this article. See *Translation, Authorship and the Victorian Professional Woman* (Farnham, UK: Ashgate, 2011), 119–21.
25 Smith, *Wealth of Nations*, 131.
26 Martineau, *Cinnamon and Pearls*, 1.
27 Logan, *Harriet Martineau*, 6–7.
28 Martineau, *Cinnamon and Pearls*, 3.
29 Ibid., 6–7.
30 Ibid., 7.
31 Ibid.
32 Smith, *Theory of Moral Sentiments*, 290.
33 Regenia Gagnier, "On the Insatiability of Human Wants: Economic and Aesthetic Man," *Victorian Studies* 36:2 (1993): 125–53 (128).
34 E. P. Thompson, "The Moral Economy of the English Crowd in the Eighteenth Century," *Past and Present* 50 (1971): 76–136 (90).
35 Smith, *Theory of Moral Sentiments*, 290.
36 Martineau, *Cinnamon and Pearls*, 22–23, emphasis added.
37 Sen, *Poverty and Famines*, 1–2.
38 Ibid., 3.
39 Gagnier, *The Insatiability of Human Wants: Economics and Aesthetics in Market Society* (Chicago, IL: University of Chicago Press, 2000), 1.
40 Sen, *Poverty and Famines*, 1.
41 Sara Millman and Robert W. Kates, "Toward Understanding Hunger," in *Hunger in History: Food Shortage, Poverty, and Deprivation*, ed. Lucile F. Newman (Oxford: Blackwell, 1995), 3–24 (9).
42 David Ricardo, *On the Principles of Political Economy, and Taxation* (London: John Murray, 1821), 93–94.
43 Martineau, *Cinnamon and Pearls*, 20.

44 Ibid., 20.
45 Ibid., 20–21.
46 Ibid., 21.
47 Yuki Masami, "Meals in the Age of Toxic Environments," in *The Routledge Companion to the Environmental Humanities*, eds. Ursula K. Heise et al. (New York: Routledge, 2017), 56–63 (57–58).
48 Martineau, *Cinnamon and Pearls*, 72.
49 Ibid., 75.
50 Ibid., 48.
51 Ibid., 53.
52 See ibid., 49.
53 This reference to the Kandy Nayak Dynasty, who were the rulers of Ceylon, with Kandy as their capital, 1739–1815, helps position the historical timeframe of Martineau's tale.
54 Martineau, *Cinnamon and Pearls*, 45. Emphasis added.
55 Ibid.
56 Masami, "Meals," 61–62.
57 Sen, *Poverty and Famines*, 12.
58 "Base-level health" is a problematic term in itself because statistics are used to determine what is average and acceptable, narrative concepts that are easily shifted for the convenience of the privileged. However, in Martineau's text, it is evident that there is not meant to be a question regarding whether or not the Cingalese are healthy or diseased; the question is more around who (or what) is responsible for their disease and starvation.
59 Martineau, *Cinnamon and Pearls*, 45.
60 Ibid.
61 Ibid., 46.
62 Ibid., 42–43.
63 Ibid., 63.
64 James Vernon, *Hunger: A Modern History* (Cambridge: Harvard University Press, 2007), 1.
65 Martineau, *Cinnamon and Pearls*, 85–86.
66 Ibid., 110–11.
67 Ibid., 111.
68 Akhil Gupta, "Farming as a Speculative Activity: The Ecological Basis of Farmers' Suicides in India," in *The Routledge Companion to the Environmental Humanities*, eds. Ursula K. Heise, et al. (New York: Routledge, 2017), 185–93, (186).
69 Martineau, *Cinnamon and Pearls*, 119.
70 Ibid., 120.
71 Ibid., 122.
72 Thomas R. Malthus, *Principles of Political Economy*, ed. John Pullen (Cambridge: Cambridge University Press, 1989), 448.

4 "I Have Tried to Write Truthfully"

Fictions of Science in Women's Writing of Nineteenth-Century Political Economy

Sarah Dredge

Looking back from 1871 to her setting of 1820, George Eliot in *Middlemarch* describes hopeful housing-reformer Dorothea Brooke's frustration at the use of political economy as "that never-explained science which was thrust as an extinguisher over all her lights."[1] Eliot's novel here registers a response to political economy in women's writing in the nineteenth century that commonly recurs. Very similar in tone to Mr. Brooke's use of political economy to silence Dorothea ("'Young ladies don't understand political economy, you know,' said Mr. Brooke, smiling towards Mr. Casaubon"[2]) is the reception given to writer and reformer Bessie Parke's 1854 *Remarks on the Education of Girls*: "Bless the women! let them study Political Economy if they please – but let it be to tell their children, and to fit themselves to help their husbands and brothers to think soberly and well."[3] Elizabeth Gaskell in her 1848 Preface to *Mary Barton* explains directly her refusal to address the "system" of political economy in writing her social realist novel about striking workers, saying: "I know nothing of Political Economy, or the theories of trade. I have tried to write truthfully; and if my accounts agree or clash with any system, the agreement or disagreement is unintentional."[4] As these examples show, to take part in social debate, from the very local context like Dorothea's, to the much more broadly political like Parkes' and Gaskell's, the language of political economy had become a central condition and testing ground with great popular reach, but one that seemed framed to exclude women as agents.

At the same time, it is noticeable how difficult, yet almost unavoidable, it was for mid-nineteenth-century women arguing for the right to work, earn and be recognized as full and individual subjects in society to deal with political economy: either to challenge its assumptions and resist its authority, or to employ its terms in their own cause. In spite of repeated attacks which evoked political economy to reject its call for professional and paid work for women, or dismissed women writers' own usage, former editor of the proto-feminist *English Woman's Journal* Emily Davies nevertheless complained at contributors' articles "setting Political Economy at defiance."[5]

One response of the *EWJ* to an attack that used the terms of political economy to argue against female professional work was to look back to earlier writing and point out the existence of important female forerunners from *within* mainstream political economy:

> Our contemporary triumphs over our assumed ignorance of Political Economy: women, he thinks, can know nothing of such things. We should have thought that the name of Mrs. Marcet, who by her writings so ably instructed young people in the principles of that science...might have occurred to our censor: we should have thought that he might have remembered how Miss Martineau laboured to impress upon the people the duties of self-reliance and prudence in marriages, at a time when the great truths of political economy were scorned and derided by all classes of English statesmen, and were thought too "low" and revolutionary to be even mentioned in a journal so respectable as the "Saturday Review."[6]

Marcet and Martineau are presented as practitioners within the field of political economy as well as professional writers; in both these senses, via their writings, they are agents within the social body as constructed by the domain of the economy: they "instructed" and "laboured."

However, it is notable that the *EWJ* article makes no mention of the distinctive feature beyond their gender that is shared by Marcet and Martineau, that both used forms of fiction as their mode of explication.[7] The *EWJ* descriptions seem on the contrary to use only terms that suggest the firmest of truth claims: "principles," "science," "great truths." The elision of their shared use of fictional genres perhaps suggests a fear that this could weaken the *EWJ*'s case regarding women and political economy, as if this could evoke instead connections to more familiar tropes of female writing: emotion over reason, imagination over fact, story over science, the personal over the abstract. Furthermore, a key process in the development of political economy as a discrete field of knowledge had been its differentiation from the aesthetic field increasingly associated with the feminine.[8] Calling attention to female economic writers as producers of imaginative literature could seem to undermine the use to which the *EWJ* wanted to put them, as founding practitioners of the science of political economy.

And yet, precisely *because* it did not seem to be competing on the ground of authoritative political discourse—the treatise, government report, the "Inquiry" (as per Adam Smith), the "Essay" on "Principles" (Malthus, Ricardo and others use "Principles" in their titles)—fiction could enable women writers more easily to enter into public conversation on social and political issues, increasingly conducted in the language of political economy.[9] Fictional forms also offer another kind of service in acting as media for the testing of political economy, which is what, by situating its truths in representations of various "real-world" contexts, Marcet and Martineau's texts both do implicitly. By placing their explication of the theories within fictional narratives (though with very different degrees of development), I will argue that the scenarios that Marcet and Martineau depict both refuse in their literariness to be reduced to the certainties of "laws," and evoke parallels with the fictionalizing process of the models of political economy. They can therefore can suggest alternative ways of reading economic "systems" that could complicate those claims to authoritative truth that are evident in its terminology of "science," "law," and "principle."

I do not want to claim, however, that Marcet and Martineau passively use a form—the literary—that undercuts their conscious efforts to teach political economy. I want instead to give them more credit than they gave themselves, as critical practitioners rather than mere explicators of political economy. An examination of Marcet and Martineau's political-literary practice makes visible the mutually revealing connections between the practice of fiction and economic theory, which over the preceding decades had been increasingly defined in opposition to each other. Under such scrutiny, the models and agents of the discourse of political economy, though presenting themselves as truths and facts, come into clearer focus as hypothetical models which have more in common with the suppositional status of fiction than they might wish to admit.

"Queen Bees or Working Bees?": Domestic or Political Economy

There is a telling print spat between periodicals the *Saturday Review*[10] and the *EWJ* in the late 1850s over the latter's right to argue for professional female employment. Though not its explicit subject (which is the campaign for women's right for paid work), the dispute hangs on which journal is correctly using the terms of political economy. The *SR* article exposes clearly that political economy, as the journal understood it, relied on dominant contemporary social constructs presented as facts: foundational terms such as "worker" and "labour," for example, which can now be seen as gendered constructs rather than abstract categories. In "Queen Bees or Working Bees?" the journal argues that:

> Men do not like, and would not seek, to mate with an independent factor, who at any time could quit – or who at all times would be tempted to neglect – the tedious duties of training and bringing up children, and keeping the tradesmen's bills, and mending the linen, for the more lucrative returns of desk or counter.[11]

By referring to a working woman as a "factor," this comment rhetorically tries to imagine a woman as simply a gender-neutral worker, but at the same time signals the impossibility of doing so by posing the issue in the context of her desirability as a man's "mate." A female worker is always primarily a hopeful wife-to-be, and therefore a prospective dependent, and so *cannot* function as the self-interested individual assumed by the labour market: her place within the normative social model of the heterosexual reproductive order precludes her from the basic starting point of the agent of political economy. The impossibility for the journal of applying the term "independent factor" to a woman is further underlined as the writer cannot imagine her work outside of the domestic environment. The unremunerative labours of childcare and housekeeping are her work, marking out that her duties are to others: their motivation and reward is love, not money, and cannot be calculated. This is presented as so self-evident, that to imagine otherwise is worthy only of mockery. The revenge exacted on the female worker puts her securely back in her subordinate gendered position: she does not "seek" or "like": she must wait to be sought and liked. Without the gloss of domestic ideology to ennoble its duties (via the "Queen" of the title), when "women's work" is de-coupled from the idea of the wife and bestowed upon these "factors," it becomes unproductive tedium.[12] What is ruthlessly revealed here is the dependence of the discourse of political economy, as inherited by popular usage in the mid-nineteenth century, on the orthodox sexual economy—and hence the problems experienced by those attempting to write women into political economy as economic agents.[13]

Though the female worker's economic agency cannot be recognized within this use of the terms of political economy, her failure to achieve her place in society can be:

> Married life is woman's profession; and to this her life training—that of dependence—is modelled. Of course, by not getting a husband, or losing him, she may find she is without resources. All that can be said of her is, she has failed in business and no social reform can prevent such failures.[14]

Here the illusion of a separate affective economy of the home, protected from the commercial logic of the market, is discarded, and women's place as inevitably dependent within an all-encompassing economy is revealed. In presenting this as natural and unescapable, the *SR* can use the language of political economy—"factor," "resources," "business," "lucrative," "returns"—to take a social *ideal* of gender relations (the dependent domestic woman) and harden it into scientific base. It is thus made impervious to reform because a logical inevitability: "All that can be said." And this is a society in which, according to *British Parliamentary Papers* of 1834, 52% of factory workers (including children) were female, and the 1851 census—even given all the problems of using this to record female paid work—produced figures showing that 30.2% of working age females were occupied in paid employment.[15] Clearly, some heavy ideological lifting was needed to maintain the idea of the leisured wife, and the version of the "natural" family that this image upheld, and it is striking that the terminology of political economy is mobilized to that end.

Although the female life at home is a "profession" and a "business," it is clear that such usages imply that the standard subject of political economy is inevitably a man. Political economy, therefore, functions to mask the fact that the laws of the market rested on some *a priori* assumptions—over who worked, what counts as work, which labours contribute to wealth or are "unproductive"—rather than a full reflection of social realities. The *SR*, in this example, thus perpetuated the gender truths of patriarchal society, reproduced from within the foundational categories of political economy: male duties lie in the market economy, female in the domestic. In Lorraine Daston's "On Scientific Observation," discussed in the Introduction to this volume, she pithily states that "it is habit that makes perception of the world possible": observation is produced by experience; it is trained, and so the observing eye helps create the object or knowledge it perceives. She adds that "at the same time… we lose the ability to see something that contradicts the form."[16] As the argument and language of the *SR* show, the worker, the agent of political economy, was constructed as a male by the habitual perception of the patriarchal society, an "observational" habit which *SR* reflects and perpetuates

But the response to the *SR* in the *EWJ* showed a refusal to give up the ground of political economy; it not that its principles or terms could be challenged, but that the exclusion of women from the purview of political economy was itself flawed:

> If it be well to maintain wages by keeping women out of employment, it must be advisable to incapacitate some other portion of our fellow-citizens for the same purpose. Why not declare all men of more than fifty too old for work? Why not banish from the market all dark, or all fair men; all Whigs or all Tories; all Peelite or all Radical gentlemen? In fact why not adopt any arbitrary principle of exclusion…?[17]

In rejecting women's invisibility within the practice and discourse of political economy, this passage attempts to correct the *SR*'s reading of the term "man" in political economic language. The *EWJ*'s female persona challenges the assumption that the subject of political economy is male by refocusing difference upon men. She points out that great variations are encompassed within the term "man" as the abstract human, but the only one that appears to invalidate participation even within the terms of the discourse is gender. To attempt to assert its right to use political economy to argue *for* middle-class women's right to earn, the article seeks to place women as agents within the discourse of political economy itself. It does not accept the failure of the *SR* to see women as possible workers and earners, but by staging its argument within the linguistic field of political economy, the *EWJ* does not challenge the overall validity of that discourse. Following Daston, the *SR* simply cannot see a woman and recognize her as an autonomous economic agent.

By insisting that the "man" of political economic theory is the gender-neutral "human," the *EWJ* article follows Priscilla Wakefield, who in her 1798 *Reflections on the Present Condition of the Female Sex; with Suggestions for Its Improvement* had argued of Adam Smith that his use of the male pronoun encompassed both sexes;[18] in practice however, this reading was difficult to uphold, and the *SR*'s assumption reflected the norm. As Kathryn Sutherland has argued,

> Smith's account of those joined psychological and technical considerations, which together define progress as the generation of wealth, entailed at the level of language and ideology an influential redescription of the sexual division of labour. This served to suppress the female contribution and to categorise work as a male preserve.[19]

Smith's political economy depended upon the assumption that subjects would all act in their own best interests. Smith writes:

> man has almost constant occasion for the help of his brethren, and it is in vain for him to expect it from their benevolence only. He will be more likely to prevail if he can interest their self-love in his favour, and show them that it is for their own advantage to do for him what he requires of them.... It is not from the benevolence of the butcher, the brewer, or the baker, that we expect our dinner, but from their regard to their own interest. We address ourselves, not to their humanity but to their self-love, and never talk to them of our own necessities but of their advantages.[20]

The presupposition of self-interest as the prime motive of the labour market is presented as a human universal—he claims that it is "human nature" "to truck, to barter, to exchange."[21] But the conception of femininity we are exploring in this chapter demonstrates that founding human nature on self-interest made it very difficult, by the early nineteenth century, to apply this model to women. By this moment, therefore, the apparently gender-neutral term "human nature" refers very strongly to biological man.[22]

Including women in the ranks of the self-interested individual ran contrary to the cherished notion deriving from domestic ideology of the self-denying woman: in *The Women of England* (1839), Sarah Ellis states that the "selfish woman may not improperly be regarded as a monster."[23] If the marketplace was conceived as a place of self-interested competition (as per Smith), in order to maintain the idea of a moral society in counterbalance to this, the home was imagined as the site of altruistic love and self-denial and associated with the self-sacrificing woman. Here was the place of the "benevolence" rejected by Smith in the *Wealth of Nations* as a motivator of the "human" propensity to exchange. Domestic ideology offers a site for the sympathetic aspect of human nature articulated in Smith's *A Theory of Moral Sentiments* which begins:

> How selfish soever man may be supposed, there are evidently some principles in his nature, which interest him in the fortunes of others, and render their happiness necessary to him, though he derives nothing from it, except the pleasure of seeing it.... That we often derive sorrow from the sorrows of others, is a matter of fact too obvious to require any instances to prove it.[24]

Smith's later description of the exchanges of the market finds little room for such sympathy,[25] but it is this selfless care for the good of others that governs domestic ideology, placing it in the home and in the domestic woman. Thus, an ostensibly gender-neutral political economic discourse comes to be understood in a way which reinforces the gender divisions of nineteenth-century social thought, presenting a problem for women who sought recognition for their work.

At the same time, ideas derived from political economy informed the articulation of social roles, evident in Ellis's description of the wife's social function:

> How often has man returned to his home with a mind confused by the many voices, which in the mart, the exchange, or the public assembly, have addressed themselves to his inborn selfishness, or his worldly pride; and while his integrity was shaken, and his resolution gave way beneath the pressure of apparent necessity, or the insidious pretenses [*sic*] of expediency, he has stood corrected before the clear eye of woman, as it looked directly to the naked truth, and detected the lurking evil of the specious act he was about to commit. Nay, so potent may have become this secret influence, that he may have borne it about with him like a kind of second conscience, for mental reference, and spiritual counsel, in moments of trial; and when the snares of the world were around him, and temptations from within and without have bribed over the witness in his own bosom, he has thought of the humble monitress who sat alone, guarding the fireside comforts of his distant home; and the remembrance of her character, clothed in moral beauty, has scattered the clouds before his mental vision, and sent him back to that beloved home, a wiser and a better man.[26]

The gendered differences set out here make clear that a woman must explicitly reject for herself the version of "human" nature on which the exchanges of the market rely. Ellis had previously in the same chapter suggested that this must be a willed act, opening up an acknowledgement that these gender differences are social ideals and not essential:

> it is necessary for her to lay aside all her natural caprice, her love of self-indulgence, her vanity, her indolence—in short, her very *self*—and assuming a new nature...to spend her mental and moral capabilities in devising means for promoting the happiness of others, while her own derives a remote and secondary existence from theirs.[27]

Woman's only agency is renunciation, and the assumption of a moral "view" precluded from the "confused" spaces of "mart" or "exchange."

These quotations come from a chapter called "Influence" which makes clear that women's proper moral action, in this wealth-seeking society, is to relinquish the idea of acting directly in favour of hoping to *influence* her husband (fathers and brothers are also mentioned, though this section addresses wives). This is evident in the passage just quoted as all *action* is removed from the wife: all the verbs are associated with the husband, and her influence works without any word or act of hers. Her power is located in her eye that can see clearly, through the "specious acts" urged by competitive exchange, but only in the home, as if we were entering here a completely other visual domain which produces ontologically different objects of perception (what is naturalized profit seeking in the market becomes a "specious act" in the home). But this vision only works to inspire better acts in others, not to enable the woman to perform them herself or compel them in others. It is in no way clear how this monitoring and influence works upon the husband. The influence must be "secret" because it cannot be acknowledged; it operates only within the private space away from public view, and silently, so that the husband's predominance cannot be thrown in doubt. She is "potent" but only insofar as the man recognizes recalls and acts upon his idea of her image, and only while she stays "guarding the fireside comforts of his distant home." As a "clothed" "character," she barely has physical presence at all. Woman's influence, acquired via her "clear eye," is made central to a moral society, but only insofar as she herself avoids pursuing her own interests in the public assembly or in public notice (or else her moral authority would disappear). This intangible power then magically turns drudgery into moral mission, and balances out the moral failings of the market to uphold the idea of a moral society.[28]

These qualifications suggest, like the brutal market logic directed by the *SR* at women attempting to transgress categories of meaning, that the construction of the domestic realm as separate and not governed by the (lack of) ethics of the market was a consoling illusion. In the next chapter on education, Ellis baldly states "Never yet, however, was woman great, because she had great acquirements; nor can she ever be great in herself—personally, and without instrumentality—as an object, not an agent."[29] There is a double act of imagination here, first—as Poovey argues in *The Making of the Social Body*—to disaggregate a set of economic concerns from all else that could be seen to be connected to it and to make a specialized domain, with its own rules (such as of gender) and institutions,[30] and second in managing to redefine work so as not to *see* women as working—either in paid labour out of the home, or in performing non-paid domestic work (or drudgery as the *SR* and Ellis see it). Concepts of "business" or "the mart" derived from political economy, as deployed in these usages by the *SR* and Ellis, therefore depended upon an understanding that agents work for their own best interest, leaving domestic ideology in the private home, represented by the domestic woman, to uphold the values of altruistic benevolence and self-sacrifice that Adam Smith had largely excluded (at least in the motivation of individuals) from the human instinct to trade.[31] The production of a domain of the economy that could dispense with moral motivations in favour of self-interest demands that this morality is protected elsewhere, in order to maintain the ethical claims of a society that saw itself as Christian. Domestic ideology and political economy are thus mutually dependent in shoring up the idea of a moral society; each relies on ideas of gender difference, carefully policed as we see in the examples of the *SR* and Ellis, which are ensured by a gendered reading of space and function.

It is important to note that while Ellis criticizes the lack of morals of the market (in strong terms: "the mammon of unrighteousness—the moloch of this world"[32]), she nevertheless, as much as Adam Smith, assumes that the dominant mode of her society is "the propensity to barter, truck, and exchange one thing for another."[33] The arguments over usage of political economy in the *SR* and *EWJ*, and, from a different angle, Ellis's attempt to create an antidote in the moral withdrawal of women to the home, each show that the assumptions of human nature and the exigencies of the market set out by theories of political economy had become widely accepted by the mid-nineteenth century. Bringing together politics, trade, and finance, theories of political economy established the key terms and models for understanding the workings of public society and the relations of individuals within it. Women who sought to reflect on, participate in, and even change, their society, could not ignore the language or precepts of political economy, even while, as a discourse understood to be predicated on masculine subjects, it seemed to resist them. Domestic ideology and political economy thus colluded in removing from view self-governing female social agents.

The *EWJ*'s invocation, therefore, of Marcet and Martineau in the mid-nineteenth century was important not only in showing women's ability to understand political economy and in suggesting its application to women, but also in identifying female writers within the discipline of political economy itself. The extract quoted above boasts of these female writers as instrumental, not external, to the process of disseminating and explicating political economy throughout society (not merely to a gendered readership), and so enabling its centrality within wide areas of public debate, and this "at a time when the great truths of political economy were scorned and derided by all classes of English statesmen."[34] In failing to acknowledge their fictional mode of intervention however, and by writing within the terms of political economy, I argue that the *EWJ* in this article in fact acquiesces to the categories of a discourse that could not recognize their arguments. Marcet and Martineau's *literary* engagement with the theories of political economy, by contrast, offers the possibility of a genuinely different conceptual framework, one that could enable new perspectives on economic gender relations to emerge.

Fiction and Political Economy

Jane Marcet and Harriet Martineau, however, do not straightforwardly call for a reinterpretation of the economic domain that would acknowledge female inclusion. Marcet and Martineau consistently write of the "truths" of political economy that readers simply need to be taught so as to understand their experiences and duties in society. This appears to accept the *a priori* assumptions political economy states as fact.[35] Effectively then, Marcet and Martineau presented their works as explications of received truth. This suggests that they were not interested in *challenging* the version of society that these theories of political economy held up as natural, but rather in teaching their female readers to better understand their place within it. Both have often been seen by modern critics as mere mouthpieces of what Michèle Pujol in *Feminism and Anti-Feminism in Early Economic Thought* has called the "malestream" of classic political economy.[36] Martineau's article, "On the Duty of Studying Political Economy" (1832), asserted that people "must become practically acquainted with the principles of political economy, before they can expect to have their interests properly taken care of by the government."[37] Marcet's Mrs. B. states:

> There is scarcely any history or account of voyages or travels that does not abound with facts and opinions, the bearings of which cannot be understood without some previous acquaintance with the principles of political economy: besides, should the author himself be deficient in this knowledge, you will be continually liable to adopt his errors.[38]

Both then concurred with the view that a proper understanding of society was only to be obtained via political economy. Even more explicitly than the *EWJ* article discussed above, they assert that the study of political economy is a positive duty on each individual, the dereliction of which seems to incur deserved ignorance and—for Martineau—exclusion from government protection. There is no sense in this that the "truths" of political economy itself could be questioned.

But both employed fictional methods that went counter to the increasingly spare discourse of the political economic texts they claimed merely to teach, represented best by Ricardo, of whom Claudia Klaver writes that his method "enable[d] him to strip his human representation of all features except those directly related to his economic point."[39] Partially reversing this methodology was in effect a claim to correct the development of the discourse itself. Illustrating and conversing upon economic truths is configured as adding something necessary. And one way in which Marcet and Martineau make use of such illustration, and differ from both political economy itself and the writing of the *SR*, is in refusing to gender the agents of political economy.

Hence at the heart of the project of *disseminating* knowledge of political economy is also the act of *reshaping* it, to assert the participation of women as active agents in the social body, including in its economic activities. The quotation from Martineau above speaks of those needing to inform themselves on political economy as "people," and Marcet chooses not just a female explicator but a young woman as the auditor needing to learn the centrality of political economy in understanding her social environment. In so doing, their texts make clear that they are not ignoring gender; they are simply assuming that women must be seen as (and see themselves as) part of the economic *dramatis personae*, not solely domestic supporters excluded from active participation in the male economic world.[40] Admittedly, Marcet's Mrs. B. does present adult women primarily as mothers, who act as teachers in the transmission of political economy to their children, but she is as good as her word in presenting the science in a "familiar" context, in the literal sense that the theory is located and exchanged within the family:[41] it is grounded in a world of women and children. Shifting their explanation of economic laws into this different context through their fictions, Marcet and Martineau rebalance political economy towards the human and the individual.

Problematizing Truth Claims: Three Prefaces

To explore these issues in more detail, I want now to look at three prefaces that highlight and seek to manage the relationship between the "science" of political economic theory, the process of exemplification, and fiction. These are the prefaces of Jane Marcet to her *Conversations on Political Economy* (1816), of Harriet Martineau to *Illustrations of Political Economy* (1832) and Elizabeth Gaskell's 1848 preface to her industrial novel *Mary Barton*, from which my title quotation derives.

It is noticeable that each writer feels that her work's combination of content and form is new and needs justification through some form of introductory remarks.

Gaskell's preface to her first novel offers a perspective on the earlier attempts of Marcet and Martineau to create a hybrid genre that could use fiction to represent and thus reflect upon society. Gaskell's novel is a form of fiction classed as a "social problem novel," a genre that claims close relation to observed and observable social realities, but seeks to do more than explicitly "teach," and which critics have claimed owes much to the example offered by Martineau,[42] herself influenced by Marcet. Gaskell's preface also seems to owe much to Martineau in the issues it addresses and the solution it proposes: fiction that can reflect society in order to educate readers on how better to *see* social dynamics, not (as with Sarah Ellis's disembodied fireside "monitress") by withdrawal from the taint of the market, but by insisting that readers witness its effects and sympathize with its sufferers. In emotive language, Gaskell redeploys in her preface the affective responses of the familial realm (which Rachel Ablow has allied closely to the novel form[43]) to industrial relations between workers and capitalists, in reaction against faceless systems—"theories of trade"—that exert inhumane control. Claiming to represent the lives of those she saw around her "truthfully" in an implicit distinction from "theories of trade," Gaskell mobilizes the affective powers of the novel, and of the family, as a new means of insisting on and consolidating human relations in capitalism, which are otherwise rendered in abstract terms, or ignored, in political economic discourse.

Gaskell's preface to her first novel defends her fictional treatment of social conditions, under the guise of an apology. After a description of why and how she came to write this novel, and what she had observed of the poverty and anger of working—and nonworking—people in Manchester, she writes (as I quoted above):

> I know nothing of Political Economy, or the theories of trade. I have tried to write truthfully; and if my accounts agree or clash with any system, the agreement or disagreement is unintentional.

At first sight, her tone is self-effacing. The preface is full of modifiers denoting opinion over fact: "they seem to me"; "it is not for me to judge"; "If it be an error." But though her language seems to defer the ground of political response to political economists, Gaskell sets an implicit challenge: despite the apparent acknowledgement of feminine ignorance of political economy with "I know nothing," she talks about her writing as "truthful" while "Political Economy" (its capitalization bestowing importance but also emphasizing its separation from the life her novel describes) is presented contrastingly as "theories" of trade. She asserts a right to this truth claim by virtue of having engaged with and experienced the social conditions of the labouring poor in a *material*, not *abstract*, context, which her novel then represents: "I saw," and gave "attention to the expression of feelings"; "I reflected," she states, and so claims a right, again in emotive language, to "give some utterance to the agony which, from time to time, convulses this dumb people."[44] In this context, her language of feeling rather than system is not apology but a reorientation of social discourse back to the human and the humane; the words "sympathy" and "anxious" recur and she speaks of "merciful deeds" and "helpless love" towards "widow's mites." Her chosen medium of sympathetic engagement, Gaskell suggests, enables her to represent the social relations around her "truthfully," and if this disagrees with any "system," her deceptively self-effacing words suggest the system is at fault.[45] The system has mistranslated social relations and so silenced the people. She ends by reaffirming her right to authority on the basis of observable evidence:

> To myself the idea which I have formed of the state of feeling among too many of the factory-people in Manchester, and which I endeavoured to represent in this tale (completed above a year ago), has received some confirmation from the events which have so recently occurred among a similar class on the Continent.[46]

It is by *not* learning to see the people around her only through political economy's systems as "labour" (refusing to become the experienced scientific observer that Daston discusses) that she had correctly diagnosed and predicted the eventual uprising of the poor against those the system benefitted, those better able to enjoy the fruits of their pursuit of self-interest.

Asserting her observations against others' theories, Gaskell enters a debate that Marcet and Martineau's prefaces also address, on the relative value of abstract "systems" or "theories," on the one hand, and narrative illustrations on the other, as modes of describing and thus reflecting—and reflecting on—society. While each method claims to produce authentic representations of observable reality, the strategy rests either on ever greater *abstraction* to produce a clearer model that can be applied to all levels of society (though perhaps only recognizable to an expert view), or on (variously) detailed represented *examples* of events or relations whose value comes from being familiar, and in which the operation of broader processes can be observed. Mary Poovey has written in *Genres of the Credit Economy* of the movement within the development of political economy to present itself more like a science than an embodied description of society, relying on abstract models, avoiding complicating factors, excising exceptions and obscuring qualifications deriving from a complex social picture, to create the impression of a factual basis for the new science.[47] This moves away from a representation that any member of society ought to be able to recognize, into arcane language and models that can only be fully understood by being schooled within the discipline itself. As such, it takes the ability to comment on the organization of social relations and the distribution of shared resources away from the affective realm now associated with women—familiar communities, personal ties, charitable and philanthropic relations—and resolutely into the masculine sphere of professionalized relations, reified knowledge, dehumanized processes.

Despite writing explicitly to disseminate political economy rather than criticize its inhumanity, and without calling (as Gaskell did) upon a countering discourse of sympathy, the prefaces of Marcet and Martineau both argue that abstractions can fail to convey meaning to ordinary readers, who nevertheless need to know how to apply them to their lived experience. Martineau states: "The reason why we choose the form of narrative is, that we really think it the best in which Political Economy can be taught, as we should say of nearly every kind of moral science. Once more we must apply the old proverb, 'Example is better than precept.'"[48] Marcet's Mrs. B. says of the use of fables in educating children on morals that "a principle abstractly laid down is beyond their comprehension."[49] Although her example associates this method with teaching children specifically, it is this same form that the *Conversations* employs, both in its own practice, and within that, in the frequent use Mrs. B. makes of illustrative examples and scenarios throughout. Although with apparently opposite intent, Martineau's preface uses many of the same strategies as Gaskell's: systems are compared to observations; she too uses emotive (not necessarily sympathetic) language to talk about the effects of social inequality; misunderstanding between rich and poor is noted, and the fictions that follow are presented as a mode of communication. In this literary practice, Marcet and Martineau each found a space for dialogue, both as professional female writers and theorists of political economy in their own right.

Though early theorists used brief narrative examples either based on claimed observation, such as Adam Smith's "fire-engine" boy who devised a quicker way of opening the boiler valve,[50] or abstract exemplifying figures like his "armourer" or sauntering "country weaver,"[51] they are mere thumbnails sketches of typical workers, rather than individual characters with a range of responses to various stimuli. The tendency is always to work to greater levels of abstraction to clarify the law or system, at the expense of evidential detail.[52] By Book 4 of the *Wealth of Nations*, Smith is speaking admiringly of the "system" of the French Physiocrats (though he disagrees with their insistence on agriculture as the sole source of a country's revenue and wealth), and uses objective language of abstraction to discuss the domain of political economy: "system," "truth," "principles," "science." He writes:

> This system, however, with all its imperfections is, perhaps, the nearest approximation to the truth that has yet been published

> upon the subject of political economy, and is upon that account well worth the consideration of every man who wishes to examine with attention the principles of that very important science.[53]

And it is noteworthy that to "examine" the "principles" of the "science," it is to a "system" that readers are referred, not a comparison with observation of the society it claims to describe. David Ricardo's 1817 treatise *On the Principles of Political Economy and Taxation* went further in eliminating personalizing details, and his references to workers are more like factors in an equation: "If a day's labour of a working jeweller be more valuable than a day's labour of a common labourer, it has long ago been adjusted, and placed in its proper position in the scale of value."[54]

Martineau's preface acknowledges that treatises on political economy are self-referential rather than addressing themselves directly to the outward conditions they claim to describe, which thus makes them inaccessible, and their claims to truth doubtful, to the uninitiated: "The works already written on Political Economy almost all bear a reference to books which have preceded, or consist in part of discussions of disputed points."[55] But for Martineau, this is merely the stage that the science has reached rather than, as Gaskell implies, a problem inherent within its principles:

> It is perfectly natural that when certainty began to be obtained and regularity to come out of the confusion, formality should be the order of the day; that truths should be offered in a cold and dry form, and should be left bare of illustration, and made as abstract and unattractive as possible.[56]

Martineau endorses the impulse of the new science to present itself *as* a science, but it is here that she asserts her own intervention. The final stage in the development of the new science is the communication of the "truths" so that they can be understood and applied. She argues that this is best done not through what is alienated from recognizable reality and therefore strange, but through the "familiar," and this is best achieved with a "picture"[57] and a "story": "The story of a merchant in Turkey, in contrast with one of a merchant in England, will convey as much truth as any set of propositions on the subject, and will impress the memory and engage the interest in a much greater degree."[58]

Martineau therefore wants to put *back* the detail that the abstract models of political economy had to transcend in order to construct their principles, but in such a way as to still make visible what she sees as the structural underpinning to chaotic reality; literary strategies provide the means for her to do so. The same "truth" is on offer via story as by bare proposition for Martineau, but the value is the greater as memory and interest will make it better absorbed and accepted. Rather than arguing, like Gaskell, from within a (gendered) discourse of sympathy for individuals (like the "widow's mites") that makes its point through *difference from* political economy, Martineau claims authority over both the "abstract" models and "familiar" description, presenting this as the latest development of the science of political economy.

Jane Marcet's preface is much more deferential to the theorists she claims merely to elucidate, but she too offers *her* representation of their principles as fulfilling a key role in communicating a science that had become too "abstruse" and "difficult"[59] for the population it so deeply concerned. Marcet is also more limited in her use of fictive strategies. She refers to her mode as "conversations" or "dialogues" and is suspicious that the claims of fiction could overwhelm the demands of the theory: she insists that adherence to "strict consistency of character... might have often impeded the elucidation of the subject."[60] Nevertheless, the creation of characters placed in a fictional (though limited) scenario, whose conversations "gave her an opportunity of raising objections, and placing in various points of view, questions and answers, as they had actually occurred to her own mind," enable her to "illustrate the subject" better than a "more didactic composition."[61] This suggests that some openness to what we would see as the multilayeredness of fiction, in opposition to simple didacticism, best suits her purpose. She does imply that every objection is thereby met, which would close down openness to different readings, but the paragraph prior to this had admitted that "a few of the most abstruse questions and controversies in Political Economy have been entirely omitted, and that others have been stated and discussed without any positive conclusion being deduced."[62] Though she puts this down to "the author's limited knowledge" and the "real difficulty of the science," she then declares that "when the soundness of the doctrine has appeared well established" it has been "stated conscientiously," which reserves her right to retain her own judgement on what is sound.[63]

The prefaces of Marcet and Martineau both then affirm but simultaneously complicate the abstract propositions of political economy, the hybrid mix of statement and fictive exploration seeming necessary to explicate a science that had attempted to present itself as simply truth. From their descriptions of their texts, Marcet and Martineau's arguments for using literary techniques suggest something missing in these abstractions; the "truths," if there, cannot be seen without help from a different representational mode, and one that departs from what had become the norms of the domain of the economic (to employ again Poovey's useful term), reattaching it to the affective realm against which it defined itself.[64] The "clear eye" needed here to complete the representation of society offered by economic theories was not that of the silent domestic women by her fireside imagined by Ellis, but one that offers a broader vision and could place abstract laws back in the context from which they ultimately derived, and claimed to explain.

Scientific Fictions: Illustrations and Conversations

Despite this, the truth claims for political economy in Marcet and Martineau's texts often seem predicated on a *contrast* with literary representation. Marcet's Mrs. B. and her pupil Caroline discuss this in relation to Oliver Goldsmith's "The Deserted Village":

MRS. B: Ignorance of the principles of political economy is to be discovered in some of the most elegant and sensible of our writers, especially amongst the poets. That beautiful composition of Goldsmith, the Deserted Village, is full of errors of this description, which, from its great popularity, are very liable to mislead the ill-informed.

CAROLINE: I should almost regret to learn any thing which would lower that beautiful poem in my estimation.

MRS. B: Its intrinsic merit as a poem is quite sufficient to Edition: current; Page: atone for any errors in *scientific principles.* Truth is not, you know, essential to poetic beauty; but *it is essential that we should be able to distinguish between truth and fiction.*[65]

This contrast between "scientific principles" and "poetic beauty" clearly places truth on the side of science, with literary writing presenting a deceptive representation of society. In this reading, poetry, or literature, does not offer a different form of truth claim, or an alternative perspective; the poem is just wrong. Mrs. B. had previously said "so many things are intimately connected with the science of political economy, that if you persevere in your resolution [to remain in ignorance], you might almost as well condemn yourself to perpetual silence."[66] To be ignorant of political economy takes away the right to comment on society; Mrs. B. allows no room for a dissenting perspective. For Mrs. B., literature is operating in a completely different realm with only aesthetic rather than direct relations to material society, and therefore—so long as readers are aware of this—its departures from what she sees as correct representation do not matter. *Contra* Romantic manifestos of the period, for Mrs. B., great literature has no access to deeper truth, but its "beauty" can be an end in itself if divorced from applicability to actual social relations. Goldsmith's poem, however, could "mislead" those minds not fortified by training in political economy; masquerading as "truth," the "beauty" of his poem—its literariness—could lead readers astray. In a later conversation Caroline learns that political economy offers "a safer road than that in which my imagination had first wandered" to the same end of "the happiness of our fellow creatures."[67] Mrs. B.'s comparison of literary and scientific truth claims shows the difficulty Marcet creates by trying to separate her own literary production from that which she sees as deriving from and appealing to the imagination; linking her own practice to the "truths" of political economy, she aims to thereby dispel "ignorance." Combining what her speaker nevertheless declares to be two different ways of seeing and writing, the literary and the economic, Marcet must then be careful to *dis*entangle their associations. But it is a distinction that cannot consistently be upheld when her own use of scenario and illustration through exemplary types invokes political economy's reliance on similar forms of indirect representation in modelling typical behaviours. In challenging the claim of fiction to speak truth in her own apparently truth-stating fictional composition, Marcet threatens also to expose cracks in political economy's claim to delineate pure "scientific principles."

So although Marcet and Martineau's use of fiction is a key aspect of their mode of intervention in this "familiar" context, both try to *control* its threat to undermine political economy's firm truths, and thereby highlight the risk that the medium could challenge its overt message. The precepts of political economy that Martineau and Marcet sought to teach, with their apparently firm laws and predictable events, demanded a kind of reading that was similarly unambiguous and, while made difficult due to the use of specialized terms, uncomplicated: a "denotative" not "connotative" reading as Mary Poovey puts it.[68] Readers were to absorb and accept the lesson offered, not engage imaginatively and emotively. This suggests that explanations or illustrations that provided *too much* material detail, and hence an overly complex social picture, or which excited the imagination beyond the needs of the explication, threatened to obscure the view of the operation of its laws, leading to (within the terms of the discourse) mistaken identification of the real causes of misery: possible misreadings. This concern may be reflected in the significant textual scaffolding that supports both texts: each has an explanatory Preface, Marcet also has an Introduction within the fictional narrative, and Martineau appends a list of principles at the end of each tale.

Marcet's *Conversations* tries to manage this threat by voicing objections—alternative readings—through the character of Caroline, which could then be refuted and corrected by Mrs. B. Each time, Caroline declares herself convinced by Mrs. B., thus modelling the desired response from the reader: "You have completely removed all my scruples"; "I think I now have a very clear idea"; "I find I must give up the point"; "There is no withstanding your attacks."[69] Martineau seeks to control interpretation with her "Summary of Principles" at the end of each tale, which states the laws that have been illustrated and so attempts, like Mrs. B. to insist on a right way of reading.

Slippages will occur, however, where the scenes related by Martineau, or the interactions between Mrs. B. and Caroline, do not quite attain the denotative reading required, and interpretation can undermine the idea of the stated "truth." Mrs. B.'s justification of the unequal ownership of land ends with the statement that "But whatever may have been the original causes of the division of land, and whether or not they were equally apportioned at first, it is impossible to prevent inequality from arising afterwards."[70] This acknowledgement of the irrational or unknown within the principle of property ownership derives from the fuller description of the laws and their history that the conversation form and creation of character has demanded. In a departure from Caroline's usual swift capitulation, in this case it takes several objections and long explanatory paragraphs from Mrs. B. before she demurs, and with more qualifications than usual (33–36). In spite of Marcet's stated prioritization of explication over characterization, this seems to be necessitated by the construction of a young woman as interlocutor, of whom society more often expects sympathy than rationalized acceptance of others' suffering: "Yet poverty frequently arises from sickness and misfortune, which render men unable to work; and, under such circumstances, it is hard to suffer the penalty incurred by idleness."[71] By imagining a text on political economy being read in the home, and by both genders, Marcet has had to do more than state logical conclusions to make their effects seem morally acceptable.

Martineau's *Illustrations* are more complex as narratives than Marcet's *Conversations*, both in order to represent more fully the different concepts of political economy in social contexts, and to appeal to those who read for pleasure. She, too, wanted to avoid the *merely* didactic tale, objecting in her Preface to "works that pretend to be stories, and turn out to be catechisms of some kind of knowledge which we had much rather become acquainted with in its undisguised form."[72] Her narratives aim therefore for exemplification not catechism, and go far beyond Marcet in breadth of the former and escape of the latter.[73] But this fuller embrace of fictional representation left her texts more open to two ways of reading, both the denotative that her "Summaries" demanded and the connotative that fiction encouraged. As these summaries underline, she is still aiming to convey "knowledge" to her readers, but in inviting a more complex response than the simple acceptance demanded by a "catechism," she opens up a space for apparent disagreement between meanings produced in readers by her tales, and the conclusions she then insists that they draw. The deaths of children due to malnourishment and subsequent disease in "Weal and Woe" (and even matricide, though distanced onto India and China[74]), and the sufferings of the workers and again children in "A Manchester Strike," are represented to show the effects of poor understanding of political economy on the ignorant poor, but they also reveal the frightening way in which the welfare of the poorest is dependent upon chance: the weather, crop failure, movements of fish stock, resulting price fluctuations. The profiting of capitalists from the poverty of their workers is also unavoidably represented, for example in "A Manchester Strike" when owners shown at the beginning of the tale to be arrogant and callous defeat their workers' strike by waiting for the latter to be starved back to work, and one of the worst profits from the lowered wages after the strike.[75] A pitiful little scene in "A Manchester Strike" where the good daughter of the focalizing family, made sickly by work, has to agree to sell her pet bird, her only joy, as they cannot afford to feed it, invokes every sentimental trope to elicit reader sympathy: "A halfpenny is as much to us now, child, as a guinea is to some people; besides we could get money by Billy. Ah! I knew that would make you cry to say so."[76] These sympathies are not easily satisfied by the reassurance in the "Summary" that the condition of workers may best be improved by (and the capitals are in the original): "ADJUSTING THE PROPORTION OF POPULATION TO CAPITAL."[77] Depicting want falling upon particular children, named individuals whose stories we have followed, rather than an abstract idea of "population," evokes a response that a precept may not easily contain.[78] A concluding statement that enacting principles of political economy can ameliorate the suffering of a greater number, though not all, may not make these representations of suffering seem happily resolved, or social inequality just. "These evils may be delayed by promoting the increase of capital, and superseded by restraining the increase of population," states the summary to "Weal and Woe in Garveloch."[79] This follows the narrative of the tale, however, in which the unrestrained population already in existence suffers for the prior failure successfully to promote the "increase of capital" (dependent anyway in this case on fish stock and changing environmental conditions). Emotive language subsequently slips even into the expression of the "Summary of Principles": "evils," "miseries," "horrors."[80] This chillingly resists the abstracting tendencies of other terminology employed, such as the "preventative check"—sexual restraint—that alone could reduce instances of "ultimate checks"—death.

This is not to say that all literary techniques work against the principles being represented. In relating the theories back to the lived reality from which they supposedly derived with at times such brutal honesty, these fuller narrative descriptions of Marcet and Martineau then needed extensive textual apparatus in order to establish the validity of the "truths" being taught, especially when, as above, they seemed to work against what might be felt to be morally just. A brief list of strategies employed could include voiced and countered dissent, "strawman" figures to illustrate poor economic practice,[81] rehearsal of political economic law presented as dialogue, commentary from a third person narrator, and principles stated outside of the fictional frame to govern its reading. Both Marcet and Martineau had to work hard to place the foundational figure of "economic man" in a representation of society without exposing him as a monster: this is particularly the case when his position is expressed—as always in Marcet and often in Martineau—via female characters. Representing these principles in this doubly feminized vehicle threw into relief its callous calculations. The reviews of Martineau's work in *Frasers* expressed outrage that population control was being discussed by a young unmarried female writer,[82] and the *Quarterly Review* criticizes the doctrines of the tales as "unfeminine."[83] Reactions to Martineau's gender cannot be disentangled from responses to the principles being illustrated in these reviews, and while this exposes the inevitability of gendered reading of women's work (even the positive reviews equate her work to her gender), in this case too it serves to emphasize the cold logic of the theories by contrast with associations of the feminine.

To make the texts work as effective fictions by providing the representative examples through which they seek to teach, Martineau and, though to a lesser extent, Marcet have to flesh out these human subjects of the discourse, and thus expose the inadequacy, and the implausibility, of the economic man constructed by the logic of the political economy they present as truth. In "Weal and Woe in Garveloch," for example, this figure seems to be split between the husband and wife Ella and Angus, or Ella and her friend Katie, who repeatedly have to remind each other of the proper economic action or inevitable social outcome, and keep each other's emotion in check. The correct rational choices of characters must be discussed, explained, and validated by other appropriately acting characters in order to humanize some chilling statements or decisions, such as that of Katie and Ronald, who love each other, not to marry so as not to add greater population strain to limited community resources. Katie and Ella (who is also Ronald's sister) discuss this:

> "Do not you think, Ella, that there are more parties to a marriage than is commonly supposed?"
>
> "There is a party," replied Ella, smiling, "that if it could be present, would often forbid the banns; and it is this party that Ronald has now consulted."
>
> "You mean society."
>
> "Yes. In savage life, marriage may be a contract between a man and woman only, for their mutual pleasure; but if they lay claim to Edition: current; Page: the protection and advantages of society, they are responsible to society. They have no right to provide for a diminution of its resources; and therefore, when they marry, they form a tacit contract with society to bring no members into it who shall not be provided for, by their own labour or that of their parents. No man is a good citizen who runs the risk of throwing the maintenance of his children on others."
>
> "Ah, Ella! did you consider this before your ten children were born?"
>
> "Indeed, Katie, there seemed no doubt to my husband and me that our children would be well provided for.... My husband and I shall be careful to teach those of our children who are spared to us how much easier it is to prevent want than to endure it."[84]

I have quoted at length here to show how the fictional scenario attempts the explanation, defence, and elaboration of an issue that runs counter to common feeling, or even conventional moral instruction (here to marry). The voice of "society" is embodied in a character so that it can state its interests, which run counter to the (proved irrational) desires of the individual. The claims of affection and "pleasure" must be balanced against rational assessment of available resources and need for population, in a calculation that is in stark contrast to the emotional primacy often associated with fiction, by being situated in the context of a detailed depiction of a small community no longer able to feed its inhabitants. The inhumanity of the laws of population must be explained by putting them back in a human context, but reinterpreted and presented via careful narrative methodology. The terms of this discussion of love and marriage are completely recast into the language of rights, responsibilities, calculations and contracts, but the occluded register of affective connection is continually evoked by its surprising absence. The female viewpoint and the form of domestic fiction create expectations that the working out of the laws of political economy, as Martineau presents them, prohibits, thus throwing into stark relief the affective considerations that the theory will not recognize.

Controlling multiple narrative possibilities so as to reveal the appropriate truth is a necessary part of both texts in their aim to function as instructive tools. But fiction's ability to direct the reader's view of reality and present it as "true" is also a powerful tool for both Marcet's and Martineau's pedagogic aims. This too can create revealing parallels with the methods of political economy required to create abstract laws out of the actions of innumerable individuals, which also will depend on the framing of the viewpoint and of the choices of the viewer. Martineau's narrator actually draws attention to this careful selection of the appropriate "reality" in this passage from "Weal and Woe," which explains its choice of location:

> In large cities, the mind of the observer is perplexed by the movements around him. The comings and goings, the births, deaths, and accidents, defy his calculations, and there are always persons at hand who help to delude him by talking in a strain which would have suited the olden time, but is very inappropriate to the present state of things...and while their advice is in the ears, and their example is before the eyes, and there is no lack of inaccurate explanations why our workhouses are overflowing, our hospitals thronged and our funeral bells forever tolling, it is difficult to ascertain the real state of the case. But when observation is exercised in a narrow range, the truth becomes immediately apparent.[85]

The narrator warns the reader that in looking at bustling cities and trying to establish principles for social organization, we often fail to see the action of the laws of political economy. He or she does not do this to suggest the inadequacy of the laws that cannot accommodate complexity: the error is with the view. The narrator thus chooses a small fishing village to represent, and within that focuses on a few characters, in order to illustrate the laws of population control, supply and demand. The narrative does this via the central (female) character ("Many would be of Ella's opinion, if they could, like her, see the operation of the principle of increase within narrow bounds") in order to maintain the realism of the tale, but nevertheless draws attention to the process of creating a representation that makes the law work.[86]

What is interesting is that this explanation signals its own method and figures its limitations. The language of this passage itself attempts to apply terms suggesting a scientific experiment—"observer," "calculations," "explanations," "ascertain"—while registering how this risks being overturned by the sheer excessiveness of the social scene: "perplexed," "defy," "delude," "inappropriate," "inaccurate." What is not explicitly acknowledged, and that Gaskell's Preface seems to imply, is that the multiplicity of social relations and needs may be more than a set of economic theories can sufficiently explain. The failure of the view of the city to fit the theory is presented by the language of this passage as a *deception* (like Goldsmith's poem) enacted by the city and its inhabitants upon the would-be economist. The "truth" asserted by the theory does not seem to be challenged by the inability of the observer to recognize it in this environment, and therefore it is not the theory that must change but the parameters of observation and representation. While the small town and island setting of Garveloch enables the clarity of the laws to be revealed (as the kind of labour and resource is limited), this is not a simple transparent application of law to situation; the situation is also manipulated to make the law work. There is little chance on the small island for diversification of labour by the creation of new industries, and so when the fish stock disappears, this fishing community must reduce, by death or emigration, until it shrinks back to a sustainable size.

In repeating and evoking the methods of the political economist by abstracting to a degree that makes the theory clearly visible, Martineau's narrator exposes the degree to which the truth claims of the system are reliant on a pre-decided set of criteria: which factors must be made visible or deemed extraneous in order to offer the appropriate set of proofs. Does this fictional representation of the "scientific" principle exemplify its truth, as the narrator states—"Many would be of Ella's opinion"—or does it draw attention to the constructedness of the *principle* as a hypothesis or fiction, that justifies a particular representation of social relations? Perhaps that association with the female observer, by stepping away from the figure of the self-interested masculine subject associated with the public world governed by political economy, helps in this process of drawing attention to the selective processes of representation. Though claiming only to "illustrate" rather than produce knowledge,

Martineau's identification of the rational perspective of the text with a female character is one of the ways in which her work actively intervenes in the discourse of political economy, and can question some of its founding assumptions.

Conclusion

"Economic man," the subject of late eighteenth- and nineteenth-century political economy, was the constructed aggregate of the actions and choices of those individuals deemed to be engaged in producing, distributing, and consuming the "wealth of nations" and represented the ideals of the dominant gender ideology which produced it and which it reinforced. Adam Smith acknowledged this to some extent by recognizing the effects of *custom* in producing the version of human nature upon which his theories rested.[87] But the effect of his presentation of economic theories as "laws," which only hardened in those that followed him, tended to reinforce these ideals as innate and fixed. As Kathryn Sutherland writes, "By rendering the disciplinary model more exclusive at a theoretic and analytic level, he refines the social model which he purports to describe."[88] And despite his occasional acknowledgement in *The Wealth of Nations* that poorer women sometimes worked for wages, Smith "uses sexual difference as the paradigmatic—read, unalterable—inequality."[89] Women are then excluded from the foundational terms of participation in the market; gender difference obscured their identity within the domain of political economy.

The laws of political economy must start from somewhere; terms like "worker" must be fixed in order for the processes of the laws to act "universally." They thus take as their *a priori* the conventions of their society, and fix them further by building upon them systems and laws that assume these terms as universal, and therefore not visible to scrutiny. Marcet reveals the force of convention in constructing "truth" when Mrs. B. warns her pupil that "It is dangerous to trust your judgement when it leads you to conclusions so different from the established course of nature,"[90] though in citing "nature," and then referring it to "Dispensations of Providence," she masks its basis in custom. The interests of those not represented by this common view of human nature could not then be recognized; like Caroline's "judgement" such interests did not match the "established course" and so could not be recognized as valid.

Hence, to return to where I began, the *Saturday Review* could dismiss the idea of the female professional and earner, as, according to the view of what is natural that the journal recognized, women should be "Queens" and not "workers." The "disinterested" laws of the market were only disinterested to the extent that they reflected the interests and prejudices of whoever set the terms of the status quo. And this is why the theories of political economy particularly needed "illustrating" or "conversing" upon for the broad readerships of Martineau and Marcet's texts: its truths could not be assumed to be self-evident to those not themselves fitting the model the theories assumed. Though Marcet and Martineau sought to exemplify, they could not help but also *test* the ability of political economy to describe society, and it is revealing that Gaskell, closely following Martineau's fictional ground, uses similar strategies to *criticize* its truths as her precursor had to reinforce them.

The truth-testing is not all in one direction, however. While fiction's re-integration of broader human experience could challenge the abstractions that political economy had come to rely upon, the claims of realist fiction to represent society are also questioned by the comparison with the systematizing gaze of political economy. The illusion of reality that Martineau's fictions strive to create within the tales (between the summary of principles with which they begin and end) depends also on selection and reduction in order to present a "true" view of society, as do the social realist novels by Gaskell and Eliot to which my introduction referred. Gaskell's focus on sympathetic identification with romanticized "widow's mites," or the widely used marriage plot, can mystify socioeconomic ties and responsibilities as deceptively as the one-dimensional modelling of economic man in Ricardo. By the interplay—and often tension—between the two aspects of their hybrid genre, that want both to insist upon denotative and invite connotative readings, Marcet and Martineau can make visible the absolute mutual embeddedness of the economic and the social.

Claims made for political economy as a *science* that produced truth, as opposed to literature that produced beauty, masked the close parallels between the modelling of political economic systems and the strategies of fictional representation, but the turn to fiction to explain its truths to a readership that included those who did not necessarily fit the model of the economic agent (women, poor working men, children) inevitably exposed their similarities. Theorists and their explicators sought to present the laws of political economy as natural, editing out anomalies and differences under normalizing aggregates, and excluding the contribution of such anomalous subjects from its models (refusing to recognize most female labour as "productive," for example). But the use of fictional forms, in the process of exemplifying, also exposed fault lines in the theories and models of political economy as modes of representing the complexities and multiplicities of social relations and exchanges. Key amongst these is the often unstated (though reified in property, franchise, and marriage laws) fiction of economic *man*, the self-interested individual, whose construction ran so counter to the contemporary gender ideals applied to women.

Notes

1 George Eliot, *Middlemarch*, ed. W. J. Harvey (London: Penguin, 1965), 40. Eliot's narrative exerts a revenge that Dorothea cannot: the wielder of the quashing term in this case was her uncle Mr. Brooke; a worse example of masculine logic or practitioner of political economy could not be found.

2 Ibid., 39.
3 Bessie Rayner Parkes archive, Girton College, Cambridge. BRP 11:1/4. (No pages).
4 Elizabeth Gaskell, *Mary Barton*, ed. Stephen Gill (London: Penguin, 1970), 38.
5 Emily Davies to Barbara Bodichon, 14 January 1863, Bodichon II, Girton College Archive, B313. Bodichon was the co-founder of the *English Women's Journal* (hereafter *EWJ*), while Parkes was also an editor and contributor (and possibly one of those Davies was complaining of: her article "Apropos Political Economy" criticised the failure of political economy to recognise moral considerations).
6 Anon., "The '*Saturday Review*' and the '*English Woman's Journal*': The Reviewer Reviewed," *EWJ* 1 (1858): 201–4 (202).
7 I'm aware that the "Conversation" format is not always seen as fiction. Although Marcet's "Conversations" do not attempt, like Martineau's *Illustrations,* to present themselves as stories or to collectively constitute a novel, they are employing fictive scenarios and character to convey ideas and instruction. Michèle Cohen discusses conversation as part of a genre of "familiar format" texts as popular modes of instruction, and Marcet's use of this form, in "The Pedagogy of Conversation in the Home: 'Familiar Conversation' as a Pedagogic Tool in Eighteenth- and Nineteenth-Century England," *Oxford Review of Education* 41 (2015): 447–63 (447).
8 See Mary Poovey, "Aesthetics and Political Economy in the Eighteenth-Century: The Place of Gender in the Social Constitution of Knowledge," in *Aesthetics and Ideology*, ed. George Levine (New Brunswick, NJ: Rutgers University Press, 1994): 79–105.
9 This is not to claim, of course, that women could not and had not written political treatises without such fictional coverings, but it is noticeable how often when they do, their words are read as personal, imaginative, emotive anyway (the reception of Wollstonecraft's *A Vindication of the Rights of Woman* is an obvious example). The *EWJ* also struggled with accusations of bias because women writing about women could never be seen to attain the lofty disinterest, the ability to see all points of view, assumed by male writers writing about "man" in theories of society and the economy.
10 Hereafter *SR*.
11 Anon., "Queen Bees or Working Bees?" *SR* 8 (1859): 575–6 (576).
12 This is acknowledged in Sarah Ellis's *The Women of England*, a prime articulation of domestic ideology, which I discuss below. While stating that women's domain is properly the home and her duties domestic, she repeats the term "drudgery" to refer to domestic work. What lifts it to a high mission is the domestic woman's motivation to sacrifice self to others, as in this example: "the most servile drudgery may be ennobled by the self-sacrifice, the patience, the cheerful submission to duty, with which it is performed" (Sarah Ellis, *The Women of England, Their Social Duties, and Domestic Habits* (London: Fisher, Son & Co., 1839), 43).
13 The antithetical positioning of the terms "worker" and "woman" is also shown in another article on the same issue by Dora Greenwell in the *North British Review* in 1862: "If she is a physician, a lawyer, an artist, a factory weaver, she will be *that*, and not much besides; and the world will be poorer for the loss of a woman" (Dora Greenwell, "Our Single Women", *North British Review* 36 (1862), 62–87 (74)).
14 Anon., "Queen Bees or Working Bees?" 576.
15 Census collectors in 1841 were instructed that "The professions &c. of wives, or of sons or daughters living with and assisting their parents but not apprenticed or receiving wages, need not be inserted," thus hiding married women's paid work. Results are also skewed in 1851 by the relabelling of

other work as "domestic service" and excluding some agricultural labour, which again shows social ideals cast as hard data (Joyce Burnett, "Women Workers in the British Industrial Revolution," *Economic History Net*, accessed 31 January 2017, http://eh.net/encyclopedia/women-workers-in-the-british-industrial-revolution-2/). Sara Horrell and Jane Humphries examine data revealing a great deal of fluctuation in levels of married women's participation in household earnings in the period 1787–1865, both temporal and geographic, and discuss the difficulty of producing reliable figures. Even in the period of the lowest participation rate (1846–1865: the period in which this *SR* article is published), they produce a figure of 45.3% of married women in paid employment within their sample (Sara Horrell and Jane Humphries, "Women's Labour Force Participation and the Transition to the Male-Breadwinner Family, 1790–1865," *Economic History Review* 48 (February 1995): 89–117 (Table 1, 98)).

16 Lorraine Daston, "On Scientific Observation," *Isis* 99:1 (2008): 97–110 (99).

17 Anon., "The Reviewer Reviewed," 202.

18 'He does not absolutely specify, that both sexes, in order to render themselves beneficial members of society, are equally required to comply with these terms ["that every individual is a burthen upon the society to which he belongs, who does not contribute his share of productive labour"]; but since the female sex is included in the idea of the species,...their sex cannot free them from the claim of the public for their proportion of usefulness' (Priscilla Wakefield, *Reflections on the Present Condition of the Female Sex: With Suggestions for Its Improvement* (Cambridge: Cambridge University Press, 2015), 1–2).

19 Kathryn Sutherland, "Adam Smith's Master Narrative: Women and the *Wealth of Nations*," in *Adam Smith's Wealth of Nations: New Interdisciplinary Essays*, eds. Stephen Copley and Kathryn Sutherland (Manchester, UK: Manchester University Press, 1995), 97–121 (97).

20 Adam Smith, *Wealth of Nations: A Selected Edition*, ed. Kathryn Sutherland (Oxford: Oxford World Classics, 1998), 22. Discussing the difference in human nature assumed between Smith's earlier work, notably the *Theory of Moral Sentiment* and the *Wealth of Nations*, William Grampp identifies the "overwhelming force of his self-interest" (William D. Grampp, "Adam Smith and the Economic Man," *Journal of Political Economy* 56:4 (194): 315–36 (328)).

21 Smith, *Wealth of Nations*, 21.

22 John Stuart Mill differed from other key theorists of political economy by attempting to include women as agents in his version of the economy, though he too struggled to find a way to value female domestic labour as productive, and imagined that on marriage a woman would always take marriage and motherhood as her profession. See Michele Green, "Conflicting Principles or Completing Counterparts? J. S. Mill on Political Economy and the Equality of Women," *Utilitas* 6:2 (1994): 267–85 and Nancy Hirschmann, "Mill, Political Economy, and Women's Work," *The American Political Science Review* 102:2 (2008), 199–213.

23 Ellis, *The Women of England*, 73.

24 Adam Smith, *The Theory of Moral Sentiments*, eds. D. D. Raphael and A. L. Macfie (Oxford: Clarendon Press, 1976), 9.

25 This is the issue of "the Adam Smith Problem," though see the qualifications of this discussed in the Introduction to this volume, which I will also refer to below.

26 Ellis, *The Women of England*, 53.

27 Ibid., 45.

28 "English homes have been much boasted of by English people, both at home and abroad. What would a foreigner think of those neat, and sometimes elegant residences, which form a circle of comparative gentility around our

cities and our trading towns? What would he think, when told that the fathers of those families have not time to see their children, except on the Sabbath-day?" (Ibid., 57).

29 Ibid., 64.

30 Mary Poovey, *The Making of the Social Body: British Cultural Formation 1830–1864* (Chicago, IL: University of Chicago Press, 1995), 8–9. Poovey describes how the "domain" of the "economy" was formed in the eighteenth century, by disaggregating financial transactions from the contexts in which the term "economy" had been understood: household management "with all the financial, ethical and domestic responsibilities that an early modern household entailed" (ibid.).

31 The theory of the "invisible hand" argues that though individuals would always act in their own self-interest, the aggregate of individuals so doing, perhaps with some providential help, produced greater productivity and hence greater social good: "by directing that industry in such a manner as its produce may be of the greatest value, he intends only his own gain, and he is in this, as in many other cases, led by an invisible hand to promote an end which was no part of his intention" (Smith, *Wealth of Nations*, 292–1).

32 Ellis, *The Women of England*, 52.

33 Ellis's whole discussion in this section of her book makes clear that contemporary society had become so exclusively concerned with wealth creation, that the different moral values of women were particularly necessary. It is notable that she sees this as inevitable, even necessary for Britain to maintain its global position (as do theorists of political economy and Marcet and Martineau), but requiring the especial moral influence of women, fostered in private and enacted primarily in the domestic realm, in order uphold an equal moral force (ibid., 56–57).

34 Anon., "The Reviewer Reviewed," 202.

35 Marcet, writing in 1816, drew largely on Malthus, Jean-Baptiste Say and Smith, though David Ricardo's ideas were familiar to her before the publication of his *Principles* from discussions in her home and some critics note her specific engagement with him in the *Conversations* (see Hilda Hollis "The Rhetoric of Jane Marcet's Popularizing Political Economy," *Nineteenth-Century Contexts* 24:4 (2002): 379–96 (380) and Evelyn L. Forget "Jane Marcet as Knowledge Broker," *History of Economics Review* 65:1 (2016): 15–26 (16, 21–2). Martineau, writing 16 years later and much more extensively, has more influences to draw upon, though she followed the framework of James Mill's *Elements of Political Economy* and always saw herself as Malthusian. See Deborah Anna Logan, Introduction to *Illustrations of Political Economy: Selected Tales*, by Harriet Martineau, ed. Deborah Anna Logan (Peterborough, ON: Broadview, 2004, 22, 17)

36 Michèle Pujol, *Feminism and Anti-Feminism in Early Economic Thought* (Aldershot, UK: Edward Elgar, 1992), 200.

See, for example, Deirdre David, *Intellectual Women and Victorian Patriarchy* (London: Macmillan, 1987) and Ann Hobart, "Harriet Martineau's Political Economy of Everyday Life," *Victorian Studies* 37 (1994), 223–51. Joanna Rostek notes the "contradictions inherent in Martineau's argumentation" with regard to essentialist notions of gender" ("Female Authority and Political Economy," in *Proceedings of the Conference of the German Association of University Teachers of English* 35, eds. Silvia Mergenthal and Reingard M. Nischik (Trier, Germany: Wissenshaftlicher Verlag Trier, 2013), 21–33 (27)). Ella Dzelzainis discusses this tendency at greater length in "Feminism, Speculation and Agency in Harriet Martineau's *Illustrations of Political Economy*," in *Harriet Martineau: Authorship, Society and*

Empire, eds. Ella Dzelzainis and Cora Kaplan (Manchester, UK: Manchester University Press, 2010), 118–37 (119).

37 Harriet Martineau, "On the Duty of Studying Political Economy," *Monthly Repository* 6 (1832): 24–34 (26).

38 Jane Marcet, *Conversations on Political Economy* (London: Spottiswoode, 1816), 8.

39 Claudia Klaver, *A/Moral Economics: Classical Political Economy and Cultural Authority in Nineteenth-Century England* (Columbus: Ohio State Press, 2003), 19–20.

40 For more detail on Martineau's presentation of "women's active economic role," see Lana Dalley's excellent discussion in "Domesticating Political Economy: Language, Gender and Economics in the *Illustrations of Political Economy*" in *Harriet Martineau: Authorship, Society and Empire*, 103–117, especially 113.

41 Marcet, *Conversations on Political Economy*, iii.

42 See especially Catherine Gallagher, *The Industrial Reformation of English Fiction: Social Discourse and Narrative Form, 1832–1867* (Chicago, IL: University of Chicago Press, 185), 61, which discusses the "social problem novel" and Martineau's influence, and Josephine Guy, *The Social Problem Novel: The Market, the Individual and Communal Life* (London: Macmillan, 1996).

43 Rachel Ablow, *The Marriage of Minds: Reading Sympathy in the Victorian Marriage Plot* (Stanford, CA: Stanford University Press, 2007), 4–7.

44 Gaskell, *Mary Barton*, 38.

45 Her emphasis on sympathy being opposed to systems recalls the vexed issue of the relationship between moral categories and political economy inherent from the construction of political economy as a science and exemplified in the "Adam Smith problem," as discussed in the Introduction to this volume.

46 Gaskell, *Mary Barton*, 38. She meant by this the revolutions of 1848, popular uprisings which began in France in February of that year, and spread to much of Europe.

47 Mary Poovey, *Genres of the Credit Economy: Mediating Value in Eighteenth- and Nineteenth-Century Britain* (Chicago, IL: University of Chicago Press, 2008), 223–5. This is observable even in a comparison between the writing of David Ricardo in *Principles of Political Economy and Taxation* and Smith's *Wealth of Nations* (which, as his own Preface states, Ricardo sets out respectfully to correct and refine; see *Principles of Political Economy and Taxation*, Library of Economics and Liberty, accessed 1 May 2017, www.econlib.org/library/Ricardo/ricP.html).

48 Martineau, *Illustrations of Political Economy*, xiii. Ella Dzelzainis very usefully discusses Martineau's 1833 article "The Achievements of the Genius of Scott" in which Martineau makes an argument for fiction that "took 'moral science, politics, political economy, social rights and duties' and 'the birth of political principle' as its subject" (see "Feminism, Speculation and Agency," 120).

49 Marcet, *Conversations on Political Economy*, 11.

50 Smith, *Wealth of Nations*, 17.

51 Ibid., 23 and 16.

52 Though see the Introduction to this volume for a discussion on the way Smith added qualifications to some of his statements in later editions, to "render many of his key phrases more subjunctive".

53 Smith, Wealth of Nations, 389.

54 Ricardo, *Principles of Political Economy and Taxation.*

55 Martineau, Illustrations of Political Economy, xi.

56 Gaskell, *Mary Barton*, xii.

57 Martineau, Illustrations of Political Economy, xi.
58 Ibid., xii.
59 Marcet, *Conversations on Political Economy*, v.
60 Ibid., v.
61 Ibid., v–vi.
62 Ibid., iv–v.
63 Ibid., v.
64 Poovey, *The Making of the Social Body*, 6–7.
65 Marcet, *Conversations on Political Economy*, 8–9; my emphasis.
66 Ibid., 7.
67 Ibid., 36.
68 Poovey, *Genres of the Credit Economy*, 300.
69 Marcet, *Conversations on Political Economy*, 38, 41, 52 and 54.
70 Ibid., 33.
71 Ibid., 34.
72 Martineau, *Illustrations of Political Economy*, xiii.
73 There are 25 tales, set in different countries depending on the context, and featuring mainly different characters, though some tales return to a set of characters to apply slightly different situations and principles.
74 Ibid., 101.
75 Ibid., 211.
76 Harriet Martineau, *Illustrations of Political Economy: Selected Tales*, ed. Deborah Anna Logan (Peterborough, ON: Broadview, 2004), 206 (hereafter *Selected Tales*).
77 Ibid., 216.
78 Joanna Rostek also notes that the "complexities and afflictions of poverty" represented in the *Illustrations* at times "bursts the purposes of her taxonomy;" see "Managing the Unmanageable: Paradoxes of Poverty in Harriet Martineau's *Illustrations of Political Economy*" in *Narrating Poverty and Precarity in Britain*, eds. Barbara Korte and Frederic Regard (Berlin: De Gruyter, 2014), 35–55 (53). Claudia Klaver comments that "Martineau's narrative form at times exposes logical flaws within the economic theory she intends to promote;" see *A/Moral Economics*, 59.
79 Martineau, *Selected Tales*, 136.
80 Ibid., 140.
81 Both Marcet and Martineau required the construction of a "savage" or "Irish" straw-man to contrast against the civilised "economic man" ("Weal and Woe in Garveloch" employs both). The implausible excesses committed by these figures also make the representation of their "civilized" counterpart upon which it rests seem less reliable.
82 William Maginn, "On National Economy: Review of Miss Martineau's 'Cousin Marshall,'" *Fraser's Magazine for Town and Country* 6 (1832), 403–13 (403).
83 Quoted in Martineau, *Selected Tales*, 423.
84 Ibid., 112.
85 Ibid., 115.
86 Ibid., 115. In Martineau's practice here, the explicit identification of this with a female subject's perspective itself counters some central assumptions of the theory.
87 See Grampp, "Adam Smith and the Economic Man," 331.
88 Sutherland, "Adam Smith's Master Narrative," 113.
89 Poovey, "Aesthetics and Political Economy in the Eighteenth-Century," 90.
90 Marcet, *Conversations on Political Economy*, 35.

Part II

Political Economy and Its Others

Section 3

Vision, Surveillance, and the Corporation

5 Malthus's Vision

Ekphrasis and Corporate Sovereignty

John O'Brien

We remain in the thrall of a vision of society that was first formulated by Thomas Robert Malthus in his 1798 *Essay on the Principle of Population*. This is, famously, a fairly bleak vision of the future, one where the pressures of population growth are continually checked by the finitude of natural resources. It has nonetheless proven to be a persuasive vision. Even now, the doctrine known as "neo-Malthusianism" colours, with some justice, contemporary concerns about population growth, resource depletion, and climate change.[1] This is a *vision* in the metaphorical sense, a conceptualization of the present and future of humanity that calls upon the reader to join him in a shared imagined prospect of a political economic scene. But it has its roots in Malthus's consistent use of *visual tropes* in his writing. This is a formal feature of Malthus's writing that economists and economic historians do not discuss, but is hard to ignore once you begin to notice it. Malthus's recourse to the visual rhetoric starts at the beginning of the 1798 version of the *Essay*. The book opens with well-known description of its occasion in Malthus's conversations with a "friend"—his father—about William Godwin's essay on avarice in his periodical *The Enquirer* in 1797.[2] There Malthus describes the *Essay* that follows as simply an attempt to get his ideas out in writing "in a clearer manner" than he had been able to do in dialogue.[3] As he did so, he goes on, "the subject opened upon him" causing him to think that "the least light" that he could shed on the topic would be received "with candour" by a readership that would need only "the most cursory view" of society to be convinced of the correctness of his thesis.[4] A few more examples: Malthus is "shedding light" on a subject that others like Godwin and Condorcet have "shut their eyes to."[5] The entire book is a "sketch of the state of society," one that accumulates multiple "observations" on the subject.[6] And, when Malthus notes in beginning the 1803 edition of the *Essay*, that there are indeed positive checks to population in the form of people delaying marriage, it seems quite natural for him to describe this as the work of "foresight."[7] As he anticipates the reception of his argument in 1798,

Malthus (speaking in the third person) describes his object of study as though it were a painting:

> The view which he has given of human life has a melancholy hue, but he feels conscious that he has drawn these dark tints from a conviction that they are really in the picture, and not from a jaundiced eye or an inherent spleen of disposition.[8]

The language could be drawn from the discourse of the picturesque, or from the gothic novels of Malthus's contemporary Ann Radcliffe, works that at first glance seem very distant from the topics to which Malthus would go on to address in the *Essay*. But political economy, aesthetic theory, and fiction must share a common language, one that belongs to none of them more than to the other; metaphors are available for all to use. For Malthus, metaphors of vision are very frequently the vehicle through which he apprehends the objects to which political economy as a discipline directs its attention. Sight is the *master metaphor* of the *Essay*, the figure of speech that organizes its rhetorical stance towards its object of study. Society is a picture that Malthus's prose describes. In so doing, Malthus can be imagined as a rhetorician working in the mode of the classical form of *ekphrasis*, the "speaking forth" of an object or image that cannot speak for itself. By referring to the sister art of painting as he writes in the still-new discipline of political economy, Malthus hopes to give his argument objectivity; as a picture, a thing in the shared world, his controversial thesis cannot be ascribed the "jaundiced eye" of his subjective beliefs.[9] The ekphrastic turn of Malthus's work is one of the secrets of its enormous success.[10]

Writing about the history and philosophy of science, Lorraine Daston observes that the concept and practice of "observation" is both "everywhere and nowhere," universally understood to be essential, but also "invisible because it is generally conceived to be so basic as to merit no particular historical or philosophical attention."[11] Malthus's ekphrastic rhetoric has similarly escaped notice. In this essay, I read Malthus's use of visual tropes as a means of creating a position from which knowledge of an economy can be conceived as a thing to be observed, an object of scientific inquiry of the same order as natural phenomenon. In deploying a rhetoric of ekphrasis so freely but so modestly as not to call attention to it, Malthus discovers a set of what Caroline Levine has recently called "affordances": "the potential uses or actions latent in materials or designs."[12] Malthus and the political economists who have followed his lead find in the register of the visual a set of affordances that gave their arguments persuasive power. It created a sovereign vantage point from which to make authoritative claims. Such a vantage point admits, as we shall see, a comprehensive perspective that raised the question of population from a local, to a national, to a global issue. But it also reaches a kind of limit when Malthus finds himself arguing for the interests of a new kind of sovereign, the modern corporation, which challenges the transparency of the prospect that his prose aims to construct.

Ekphrasis

In its strictest sense, ekphrasis is a mode internal to imaginative literature. It is most prominently a species of poetry in which a poet gives voice to an object that originated in the plastic arts such as a painting or a sculpture. For the literary critic Murray Krieger, the ekphrastic mode is "introduced in order to use a plastic object as a symbol of the frozen, stilled world of plastic relationships which must be superimposed upon literature's turning world in order to 'still' it."[13] The best-known example in the English-language tradition (one that is, as it happens, contemporary with Malthus) is John Keats's "Ode on a Grecian Urn" (1820), in which the poet contemplates the human activity—singers, lovers, priests—depicted on an ancient funerary urn, calling upon its "silent form" to "tease us out of thought/as doth Eternity."[14] The mode, as its Greek name would suggest, has its roots in antiquity, and its *locus classicus* there (as a long critical tradition has established) is Homer's description of Achilles' shield in book 18 of the *Iliad*. I do not have room to quote Homer's long and beautiful set piece (which deserves to be read in its entirety) at any length here, but it is worth noting that the shield that Vulcan forges for Achilles, though framed by images of the cosmos, is decorated with images of the entire society; it depicts cities with wedding feasts, courts, and battles, as well as agricultural workers toiling in fields, vineyards, and pastures. It is an image of political economy, one that Homer's description takes as a prompt to pause and articulate what Krieger thinks of as the "plastic relationships," the intricate web constituting the society whose trajectory would be altered by the outcome of the war to which Achilles is about to return. Although the reading of poetry is a temporal act, one that requires the reader to take in words sequentially, ekphrastic poetry aspires to suspend time, to use the metaphor of the image apprehended in the mind's eye as a way of holding at bay the constant flux and temporal change of a culture. Krieger here implies, without quite explicitly saying, that ekphrasis is a metaphor for literature itself, that all of imaginative writing enacts just this kind of halting of the movement of the world to focus a reader's attention on an object that is temporarily stilled for the sake of contemplation.

Political economy shares the same language as literature, and, for Malthus, the same problem of attempting to render a complex, dynamic object. Malthus's recourse to what I will call a version of economic ekphrasis is his way of meeting the challenge of representing the temporal process whereby, as the *Essay* famously argues, human population grows at a pace that outstrips the production of the resources it needs.

The "melancholy hues" of the "picture" he paints with words derived from the fact that the image that the *Essay* constructs, above all else, is that of a mathematical relationship, one between the increase in the food supply (which, Malthus argues, proceeds arithmetically), and the increase in population (which he believes proceeds geometrically). This ratio between the ratios of population increase and the increase in subsistence forms, Malthus writes, the "general outline" of his argument. The ratio itself is the still object, the picture that will get filled in by the details that follow in the course of the *Essay*.

Were Malthus writing today, it is a certainty that his description of these relationships would come accompanied by a set of graphs and charts that would provide numerical support, but would at the same time constitute something closer to a literal picture of the situation that the narrative is describing. The practice of what Edward Tufte has called the "visual display of quantitative information" was being developed by, among others, the French physiocrat François Quesnay, who constructed his famous *Tableau Économique* 1758 in order to depict the relationship between the categories of what Quesnay terms *dépenses productives* (investment in agriculture), *dépenses stériles* (investments in industry), and *depenses du revenue*, the annual revenue from both.[15] The "economic picture" that Quesnay draws is in effect a chart of the relationship between investment and return. Quesnay himself noted that such a picture helped do what language could not, writing to Mirabeau that his *tableau* "brings before your eyes certain closely interwoven ideas which the intellect alone would have a great deal of difficult in grasping, unravelling and reconciling by the method of discourse."[16] But Quesnay's practice did not yet create a template that others were able to follow, and it is not surprising that Malthus did not include graphical information in this book (although he does reprint the tabulation of births, marriages, and deaths in Prussia, Lithuania, and Pomerania that Richard Price had imported from Johann Susmilch's pioneering empirical research from the 1750s and 1760s); it was not yet an expectation that a treatise in political economy feature that kind of picture. Language, rhetoric, was still the first-order tool that the political economist had at his disposal. The proliferation of metaphors of visuality and sight—in short, the construction of a whole ekphrastic register—is born of Malthus's felt need to make language do work that a later generation of economists would very likely let graphs perform. Malthus strikes a modern reader as a clear, even eloquent writer. But that is at least in part by comparison with the work of modern economists, who no longer feel the need to persuade exclusively—and perhaps even primarily—through language. We shall see that when it is called for by the situation, Malthus can be quite evasive as well.

It is not as though the recourse to the visual was inherent, however, in the topic of human population. Such visuality is *not* typically found in the previous writers on the question of population. For example, David Hume's essay "Of the Populousness of Ancient Nations" (1752), which Malthus identifies as one of his influences, is almost relentlessly non-visual, or even rigorously anti-visual. It is almost impossible while reading this text to gain a visual idea of the things that Hume is describing as he uses Roman historians to argue that there were more people in the ancient world than in eighteenth-century Europe. Another text that Malthus cites, Benjamin Franklin's *Observations Concerning the Increase of Mankind* of 1755 includes the word *Observations* in the title, but the essay that follows is not given to a lot of figurative language of any kind.

Similarly, the most proximate writers on population, the clergymen who had conducted an extensive debate on the topic of population through the course of the 1780s and 1790s, were not in general a rhetorical model for him, though it seems very clear that Malthus's interest in population derives in no small part from the fact that he was professionally a member of that group. Malthus was a clergyman, taking holy orders in 1789, and we know that he was very concerned with the struggles of poor people in his own parish, in particular with the struggle for subsistence faced by many during the years of hardship in the mid-1790s. To the extent that we can reconstruct it, his 1796 essay *The Crisis* (which was never printed; the manuscript was lost sometime after the 1830s) seems to have been, in the first instance, a critique of the Pitt government for failing to meet the needs of the labouring poor. Malthus was surely speaking from his position as the church's representative in a parish that was hit particularly hard. But the question of the population had always been a concern for pastors, who needed to count their flock. Starting in 1538, this became a legal responsibility, as clergymen were from this point on required to keep records of births and deaths.[17] Such records were not studied, or even gathered systematically, however, which meant that no one really knew whether the population in the British Isles was increasing or decreasing, and that led to a spirited debate conducted among members of the clergy in the 1780s. A key text and prompt in this debate was Richard Price's *Essay on the Population of England and Wales* (1780), which argued (incorrectly) that the British population was declining. Other clergymen, such as John Howlett and William Wales, responded to counter Price's argument.[18] There is no need to get into the thick of their arguments back and forth, which were inconclusive, because until the first census of Britain in 1801—a census undertaken in part in response to Malthus's *Essay*—no one had enough data to decide the question either way. Of these writers, however, only Price uses a visual register of language with any frequency, a tendency hinted at in the title of his most important book, *Observations on Reversionary Payments* (1772), and followed through to a certain extent there and in his writings on population per se. Price's *Essay on the Population of England*, for example, uses the term "observations" again and again to describe the data that he and other others have gathered about the population. It is no surprise, then, that Price is another source that Malthus names as an influence, though it would be hard to make the case that Price has anything like the level of ekphrastic rhetoric that Malthus would deploy.

A more significant source for Malthus's rhetorical stance is the writers of a generation earlier, the 1750s. Robert Wallace's 1753 book *A Dissertation on the Numbers of Mankind* (another book cited by Malthus as a precedent) is a very important source. Wallace, whose book was initially undertaken as a refutation of David Hume's "Of the Populousness of Ancient Nations" anticipates a fair amount of what Malthus would go on to say almost a half century later; he argues, for example, that the natural rate of increase of the population would see the human population double every 33⅓ years were it not for what he terms "the distressed circumstances of mankind."[19] More to the point here, Wallace anticipates the intensely *visual* shape of Malthus's *Essay*. Again, I can only as it were sketch the general picture: Wallace wants, he says, to "set things in a clearer light" than Hume, to offer "a distinct and compleat view of the various migrations of mankind."[20] Of the numerous writers cited by Malthus as his sources, Wallace offers both much of the substance of the argument and, just as crucially, a rhetorical stance that Malthus will adopt.

Or, perhaps it is better not to understand the relationship between Wallace and (to a lesser extent) Price's deployment of a visual register and the more thoroughgoing ways in which Malthus uses it as a case of influence in the sense of one author consciously echoing another's prose style. Rather, we can imagine that Malthus, Price, Quesnay, and Wallace are all straining against the limits of language to construct a way in which to conceptualize the complicated interrelationship of multiple factors in the entity that would only later come to be reified as "the economy." We can take that rhetorical move as a sign of a felt crisis in the ability of language to represent an economic system that was understood now to be less about the movement of money and things (let us call this, for lack of a better word, mercantilism) but of the interrelationship between things and a dynamic human population that now greatly complicated the ability of the writer to describe it. The political was now put into political economy, raising the discourse from in many cases literally a parochial matter to a national concern.

For Quesnay and the authors of mid-century, the viewer of the economic picture would have been the sovereign for whose eyes such an image would be available to aid wise decision making. In France, it was easy to personalize this conception in the figure of the monarch. In the British context, the observer is less easily identified as a specific person with a name and a place. Robert Wallace, for instance, produced his *Dissertation on the Numbers of Mankind* in the first instance for the Philosophical Society of Edinburgh, a group that included Hume and

Adam Smith, and who constituted the initial *audience* for his argument in the literal sense, as he read it aloud to them in one of the Society's regular meetings. The "we" of his book, the readers who assess the tables of population growth he constructs in order to gain a better "prospect" of the movements of humankind over the ages, are educated men who contribute to public debate. They are the heirs to the position of the landed gentleman, the early eighteenth-century ideal that, as John Barrell has articulated, were able to have a "comprehensive view" of their society by virtue of their lack of having any particularized interest, as in a specific trade or profession.[21]

Adam Smith's *The Wealth of Nations* (1776) demonstrates how the confidence by which this perspective might be embodied in a single person is becoming strained to the point of fracture. Again and again in his treatise—a crucial text for Malthus as both a theorist and an educator—Smith posits, not the body of a sovereign monarch or that of a disinterested gentleman or public-spirited citizen, but what he calls "the whole body of the people" or "the great body of the people" as the entity that is interested in the topic of political economy.[22] Given the specific framing of Smith's study, which addresses the wealth, not of individuals or monarchs, but of nation-states, that corporate body is imagined as the population of each of the various nations of the world, with their competing interests that are nonetheless related systematically. Smith constructs what has become famous as an "invisible" system, one guided by a "hand" that no body, individual or collective, can see. *The Wealth of Nations* and the knowledge system of political economy that it and Malthus's *Essay on the Principle of Population* helped found is predicated on the belief that such invisible relationships can be made manifest to the reader. This is an instance of what W. J. T. Mitchell has called "ekphrastic hope," the belief that by outlining a still picture of the object to be studied, the writer might transcend the limits of the medium of prose and lead the reader to a new vision: "when we discover a 'sense' in which language can do what so many writers have wanted it to do: 'to make us see.'"[23] Much has been written about Smith's description of the pin factory, where, he says, "I have seen a small manufactory of this kind" produce "upwards of forty-eight thousand pins in a day," a striking testimony to the power of the division of labour.[24] What is less remarked is that Smith offers this example, which he calls "trifling," largely to illustrate a limit case that does not actually reflect the way that "the general business of society" is organized:[25]

> In those great manufactures, on the contrary, which are destined to supply the great wants of the great body of the people, every different branch of the work employs so great a number of workmen, that it is impossible to collect them all into the same workhouse. We can seldom see more, at one time, than those employed in one single branch.[26]

The ekphrastic hope here is that the discourse of political economy can enable "the great body of the people" to see what can no longer been seen by a single, sovereign spectator.

But, as Mitchell argues, the hope that ekphrasis carries is typically accompanied by what he calls "ekphrastic fear," the anxiety that the object might actually come to life "when we sense that the difference between the verbal and visual representation might collapse, and the figurative, imaginary desire of ekphrasis might be realized literally and actually."[27] When Malthus turns his attention in the 1810s to the question of educating young men to administer the population of India, that fear becomes activated. In works written to defend the East India College, the sovereign position of the reader becomes far less stable than it is in the *Essay*, the prospect less perspicuous. In part, this is probably due to the politically charged nature of these texts, the fact that they were designed as interventions into a complicated and contentious argument about the nature and the future of the College. But it also, I will suggest, has something to do with the way that the College itself bore witness to, and was the servant of, a new kind of sovereign, the corporation, which had a vision of its own. Neither Malthus nor Smith has a way of accommodating the "coming to life" of this aspect of the economic picture, and the problem continues to colour the discipline that their writings help found.

The Corporation

Malthus became the first professor of Political Economy at a college or university when he was given an appointment at the East India College in July 1805. He spent most of his adult life as member of its faculty.[28] In hiring Malthus to be one of the first faculty members at the College, the Company's Directors were capitalizing on the fame that Malthus had gained from the *Essay*.[29] But the Directors were also making a tacit statement about the importance of Malthus's attention to population and demography as the centrepiece of political economic thinking to the question of how best to prepare civil servants to administer an enormous area of territory that contained, as Malthus put it, "60 millions of Asiaticks," which was more than five times the number of people in the British Isles.[30] Though it was authorized by Parliament, the East India College was not founded under the auspices of the church or the state, but under those of the British East India Company, whose interests it was designed to serve. Its students were boys between the ages of 15 and 18, who were expected to complete at least 2 years of study—in European history and also Indian history, in math, in political economy, in drawing, in composition, in the Sanskrit, Hindustani, and other languages that they would use in the subcontinent, and also in fencing and, for a while, dancing. Students did not receive a degree. But they did take, and have to pass, a series of examinations in order to be certified for the

Company's service. The very existence of a College in Hertfordshire was the product of a debate over the nature of the institution that could best accomplish the Company's goals; its location, the terms under which students would be admitted, the curriculum, and the kinds of competence that students would need to demonstrate to go on to work for the Company. What Malthus called the College's "enlarged and enlightened views," on educating young men for the role of colonial administrators, had to do with the universality of its curriculum and the way that it extended the logic of quantification, not just to the population that the Company administered, but to the administrators themselves. Such a stance represents a surprising but perhaps inevitable affordance that emerged when Malthus yoked a rhetoric of visuality to the project of supporting an institution that was poised to claim a very different kind of sovereignty than the political bodies imagined by Smith.

The most important documentary record of Malthus's long career at the East India College are two essays that he published to defend the Company in Parliament, one in 1813 and one in 1817. The pamphlets have the characteristically long and uninformative names for political essays of the time: the first is called *A Letter to the Right honorable Lord Grenville Occasioned by Some Observations of His Lordship on the East India Company's Establishment for the Education of Their Civil Servants*, and the second is *Statements Respecting the East-India College with an Appeal to Facts in Refutation of the Charges Lately Brought Against It in the Court of Proprietors*. These are peculiar pamphlets in many ways, as they tend to skirt issues rather than address them explicitly. Unlike most of Malthus's other writings, their tone is tendentious rather genial, their argumentation convoluted rather than, as in the *Essay on the Principle of Population*, bracingly straightforward. We can take these as symptoms of the complications in the College's mission, which occluded the interests it served.

The East India College in Hertfordshire was established by act of Parliament in 1804, with the stated intention of providing a training for young men who would go on to serve as administrators for the East India Company. But there was an unstated intention as well. This was to create an institution that would outflank the College at Fort William, Calcutta, that had been created by Richard Wellesley, the Duke of Wellington's older brother, who was Governor-General of the Company and resident in Calcutta. Wellesley's extraordinary *Notes with Respect to the Foundation of a College at Fort William* (1800), a public essay addressed to the East India Company's board in London, announced, as Eddy Kent as recently pointed out, "a *fait accompli*... an audacious act of insubordination" as Wellesley described the institution that he had already established in Calcutta to train young British men who had entered the Company's service.[31] Kent argues persuasively that Wellesley's *Notes* has to be considered a key text in the history, not only of the

East India College and the Company that it served, but in the ideology of British imperialism itself, as "the first imperial text to suggest the need for a systematic production of a corporate identity," one in which being an employee of the Company was the equivalent of being a servant to a national project.[32] Pursuing the interest of the nation would now take the place of the pursuit of private gain that characterized the careers of the first cohorts of Company employees in the eighteenth century, and that had ultimately led to corruption so thoroughgoing as to result in public scandals, most spectacularly the impeachment trial of Warren Hastings (1788–1795). Wellesley's College in Calcutta, however, asserted a level of control over the training of the Company's employees that exceeded what many members of the Board of Directors in Britain were willing to grant, and the East India College in Hertfordshire was established to serve as a counterweight that would render Wellesley's College pointless. The two colleges were rivals but they were extensions of the same corporate entity and were ultimately accountable to the same national parliament.

This is why in his essays Malthus does nothing but praise Wellesley and the College that he founded in Calcutta. He does so in terms that will by now be resonant. Observing that the growth of the British empire in the Indian subcontinent required a system of education capable of producing more administrators than had ever been deployed before, Malthus testifies that "the penetrating eye of the marquis Wellesley saw this deficiency in so strong a light, that he thought himself imperiously called upon, as governor-general, to provide a remedy for it."[33] Malthus's praise for Wellesley's "penetrating eye" is completely empty and intentionally misleading, however, since Wellesley's College at Fort William was designed to do precisely the kinds of things that the College at Hertfordshire was created to fend off. The College at Fort William largely taught languages; it offered extremely practical knowledge for the young men who would then be dispatched around the Company's territory. It seems to have done this job quite well. More than that, the College at Fort William became the home base for the first generation of British scholarship on Indian cultures. A number of faculty members there collected books and manuscripts, translated texts from south Asian languages into English and vice versa. The College at Fort William took seriously the project of immersing itself and its students in the culture that it hoped to govern.

The Company's Directors in London were not particularly interested in promoting a deep knowledge of south Asian culture. Quite the opposite was the case. One of their fears was that their employees would come to sympathize too much with the cultures of the subcontinent, losing their primary loyalty to the Company. It was easy to cast this assimilation to the local in racist and orientalist terms. Malthus does this, for example, when he describes how Calcutta offers "all the temptations to indolence and sensual indulgences peculiar to a warm and luxurious climate."[34] Malthus speculated, on the evidence "of the most undoubted authorities," that students who arrived in Calcutta without appropriate preparation in England itself would be drawn into enormous debts by Indian moneylenders eager to ensnare them in financial situations that could place the company itself at risk:

> Interest accumulates upon interest, the increasing salary is unable to discharge the increasing debt; and, not only all prospect of a return to Europe, with a competency, is for ever closed, but the honor and integrity of the persons thus embarrassed are endangered, and the service suffers in the tenderest point.[35]

Malthus's scenario fits the stereotype of Indians as both devious and sensuous, laying traps for innocent Europeans that must be guarded against through the intellectual inoculation of abstract philosophical education. The creation of the East India College at Hertfordshire was intended, among other things, to cancel out the influence of Wellesley's college in Calcutta, indoctrinating students at home in what Malthus calls "British feelings."[36]

The Hertfordshire College was embattled from the outset, frequently attacked in the London press, and often called upon to defend itself in Parliament. The most frequent pretense offered in Parliament and the print media for closing the college is that the boys there acted much like you would expect 15- to 18-year-old boys to act who were being supervised by a bunch of men who, like Malthus, were knowledgeable in their fields but had absolutely no experience in pedagogy or in running a school. Students constantly got themselves into trouble: brawling with local residents, shooting off pistols, rioting against the faculty, in a couple of cases essentially mutinying against any discipline at all and forcing classes to be shut down for several days at a time before truces were declared. These disruptions often ended up in the newspapers; they were an enormous embarrassment to the College and to the Company. But the newspaper and Parliamentary campaigns were driven more by Hertfordshire College's resistance to the traditional patronage system than to the indiscretions of the students that constituted much of the public case for closing it. Malthus hints at this in the *Letter* when he observes that the patronage system had made it impossible for the College's faculty to enforce discipline by having "the power of expulsion" available as a sanction.[37] Students very frequently had powerful allies who could appeal any decision made by the faculty members at the College to the directors of the company, who would almost always rule in their favour.

What the East India College in Hertfordshire did that cut against the grain of the patronage system was subject students to a regime of quantification. Exams were graded, and students were ranked, to use Malthus's language, "each individual in the numerical order of his relative merit."[38] Such a ranking system was not in itself particularly novel in the world, but it was novel in the history of the East India Company, in which junior employees had never faced such a ranking system. The students in Hertfordshire become numerical evidence themselves. Malthus offers a breakdown of what we might now call something like time to degree, and includes the evidence of several years to demonstrate that the students who go through the programme there are able to assume their full position as writers more quickly than those who had gone immediately to Calcutta upon their appointments, and had to learn while in India. The Hertfordshire College was thus in Malthus's terms a quantifiably more *efficient* operation than had been in place before. Students were positioned within a regime of numbers, which Malthus wields to argue for the College's success and its right to have priority in the training of the Company's future administrators.

Such a program absorbed the students themselves—not only their training, but the assessment of them as human resources for the Company's service—into much the same system of abstraction that characterized the Hertfordshire College's curriculum. Where the College at Fort William emphasized South Asian languages and history, the curriculum that Malthus taught in stressed subjects like British common law and European political economy. These were believed to express universal forms of knowledge that could be projected globally, and knowledge of them would create students with the kind of enlightened "views" that would enable them to govern, not the distinctive peoples of the Indian subcontinent, but its people in the aggregate, considered now in terms of a *population.* Although surprisingly little has survived that would help us know exactly how Malthus taught, what we have makes it clear that his goal was to make his students into exegetes of Adam Smith's *The Wealth of Nations.*

It is at first blush no surprise to see Malthus bringing in *The Wealth of Nations* for support as he defends the Hertfordshire College in 1817. But to do so is inherently tricky because Smith famously hated corporations, which, he argued, come to constitute an interest of their own, one that has no necessary overlap with the interests of individual shareholders or the nation that authorized it. "Such exclusive companies [as the East India Company]," he writes, "are nuisances in every respect; always more or less inconvenient to the countries in which they are established, and destructive to those which have the misfortune to fall under their government."[39] Indeed, the interest of the "merchants and manufacturers" who incorporate themselves as monopolies runs counter, Smith argues, to the interest of "the great body of the people" of a nation, who will always seek the most advantageous deal for the state.[40] For Smith, the quintessential corporation is indeed "the mercantile company which oppresses and domineers in the East Indies."[41] Writing as an employee of the very same Company that had served as Smith's exhibit A for the perniciousness of the commercial corporation, Malthus has to radically misread Smith's argument in *The Wealth of Nations*. This is a peculiar moment in Malthus's 1817 *Statements*, his last public work in support of the Hertfordshire College, one that is that is difficult to parse grammatically. Here is Malthus:

> One of the great objections urged by Adam Smith against the government of an exclusive company is, that their interests, as a sovereign, are generally considered as subordinate to their interests as individuals, or as a body of merchants. In the establishment of the East-India college, the feelings of the sovereign conspicuously predominated; and the public did justice to the disinterested motives and the enlarged and enlightened views which prompted the decision.[42]

This starts out by more or less accurately describing Smith. But Malthus then turns Smith's argument upside-down to support precisely the opposite of what *The Wealth of Nations* argues. The question comes down to the relationship between the words "interest" and "sovereign." Smith had seen their confluence as the heart of the problem with the corporation as an entity. For Smith, it is precisely by gaining a kind of sovereignty that corporations come to form an interest of their own, one that threatens the interests of nation-states that, as the title of his book suggests, Smith imagines as the central agents in the global economic system. The problem for Smith is not, as Malthus says, that the "interests, as a sovereign" of the company subordinate the interest of the individuals who make it up, but quite the opposite, that the interests of individuals become combined and therefore newly empowered by being brought together within an incorporated institution. By selectively paraphrasing (rather than citing) Smith and interpreting his words in ways that severely distort his argument, Malthus hopes to forestall the argument that "the sovereign," the Company itself, might be considered as an entity that has the power to overcome the self-interest of its own shareholders and install a system that stymied the patronage networks of old. The awkwardness of Malthus's prose is what a poker player might call a tell for the awkwardness of his situation. As a faculty member of the College, he is called upon to defend it against its opponents; as a writer addressing a Parliament whose members enjoyed the power of using their influence to help people gain places in the Company, he cannot attack the patronage system directly; as the nation's most famous political economist, he must support his argument with the authority of the discipline in the person of his most important predecessor.

Malthus's paragraph ends, of course, with precisely the kind of formulation that would horrify Smith but that is entirely consistent with the rhetorical stance that he adopted throughout his writing career. It was the "enlarged and enlightened views" of the sovereign East India Company that is responsible for the establishment of a Company that modernized the education of colonial administrators. Here it is the *Company,* not the author or the reader that has an expansive view, "seeing" the overall situation abstracted from the particulars of individuals and their desires and claims, and acting for the benefit of a comprehensive and transcendent interest. We have moved past the rhetorical form of ekphrasis, where the author speaks on behalf of the silent object, to that of corporate personification, where the company becomes rhetorically a person. The Company has attained the sovereignty that was once reserved for persons, specifically in Malthus's earlier works, the reader. At the same time, the young persons who are being trained in England to work for the East India Company in the Indian subcontinent were now being subjected to a new regime of quantification to render them fit for the Company's purposes. The debate over the College is a small moment in the history of the East India Company, and also of the corporation's relationship to human beings. As he vindicates the ways of the East India Company, Malthus marks a moment in the advance of the corporation's expansion of quantification into new realms of personhood as well as terrain.

When it is deployed to imagine how the Company exercises its sovereignty over its people—both its workers and the 60 million inhabitants of its domain in India—the ekphrastic mode discovers a new affordance in Malthus's hands. It enables Malthus to silently confer a kind of agency on the Company that we are now quite familiar with, but that had little precedent in political economic discourse, the agency of personhood. Malthus's essays are bound in their moment and situation, but they offer a clue to results that would be far-reaching. As Timothy Mitchell has pointed out,

> The oldest and largest of the British colonizing corporations, the East India Company, had played an important role in producing the modern science of economics. Three leading nineteenth-century political economists, James Mill, Robert Malthus, and John Stuart Mill, spent their working lives as employees of the company; and after its nationalization and renaming as the India Office, as we know, it gave the most famous economist of the twentieth century [John Maynard Keynes] his first employment.[43]

In the hands of Malthus, the rhetorical stance of ekphrasis played a constitutive role in the formation of the discipline of economics, as it formulated the object of study for which the discipline must give voice. Does the fact that the relationship between the person and the corporation continues to be a fraught one owe something to the way that so many of its earliest thinkers and writers were embedded within the foremost

Company of the day? Such a question is unanswerable in those terms, of course. But the continuing power of the corporation suggests that it might be time for us to move beyond the vision that Malthus first put in place, and that has to some extent held us captive ever since.

Notes

1 Even those who argue against Malthus's claims, such as Geoffrey Clark, construct their arguments in his terms. When, in his book *A Farewell to Alms*, Clark attempts to understand why it was that the Industrial Revolution occurred first in Britain, his answer is framed as an argument about how humanity first broke free from what Clark calls the "Malthusian trap" whereby "short-term gains in income through technological advances were inevitably lost through population growth" (Clark, *A Farewell to Alms: A Brief Economic History of the World* (Princeton: Princeton University Press, 2007), 1).
2 Thomas Robert Malthus, *An Essay on the Principle of Population*, ed. Philip Appleman (New York: Norton, 2004), 15.
3 Ibid.
4 Ibid.
5 Ibid., 18.
6 Ibid., 34, 51.
7 Thomas Robert Malthus, *An Essay on the Principle of Population* (London, T. Bensley, 1803), 72.
8 Malthus, *Essay* (2004), 15–16.
9 Ibid., 16.
10 Malthus's recourse to visual tropes pre-dates the composition of the first edition of the *Essay* in 1798. Malthus's first known piece of political writing was entitled *The Crisis, A View of the Present Interesting State of Great Britain, by a Friend to the Constitution*. Written in 1796, this pamphlet-length piece seems to have been intended for publication but was never, for reasons unknown, printed. On *The Crisis*, see Patricia James, *Population Malthus: His Life and Times* (London: Routledge and Keegan Paul, 1979), 50–54. A few parts of *The Crisis* were printed in William Otter's *Memoir of Robert Malthus*, printed as appendix to the second edition of Malthus's *Principles of Political Economy* in 1836.
11 Lorraine Daston, "On Scientific Observation," *Isis* 99 (2008): 97–110 (97).
12 Caroline Levine, *Forms: Whole, Rhythm, Hierarchy, Network* (Princeton, NJ: Princeton University Press, 2015), 6.
13 Murray Krieger, *Ekphrasis: The Illusion of the Natural Sign* (Baltimore, MD: Johns Hopkins University Press, 1992), 265.
14 John Keats, "Ode on a Grecian Urn," in *Keats's Poetry and Prose*, ed. Jeffrey N. Cox (London: Norton, 2009), 460–62 (ll. 44–45).
15 Edward Tufte, *The Visual Display of Quantitative Information* (Cheshire, CT: Graphics Press, 1983), title page.
16 Quoted in Susan Buck-Morss, "Envisioning Capital," *Critical Inquiry* 21 (1995): 440.
17 David V. Glass, *Numbering the People: The Eighteenth-Century Population Controversy and the Development of Census and Vital Statistics in Britain* (London: Gordon and Cremosi, 1978), 15.
18 See Richard Price, *Essay on the Population in England, From the Revolution to the Present Time* (London: T. Cadell, 1780), John Howlett, *An Examination of Dr. Price's Essay on the Population of England and Wales*

(Maidstone: J. Blake, 1781) and William Wales, *An Inquiry into the Present State of Population in England and Wales* (London: C. Nourse, 1781).

19 Robert Wallace, *A Dissertation on the Numbers of Mankind* (Edinburgh: G. Hamilton and J. Balfour, 1753), 8.

20 Ibid., 2.

21 John Barrell, *English Literature in History: An Equal, Wide Survey* (New York: St. Martin's Press, 1983), 35.

22 Susan Buck-Morss drew my attention to this habit ("Envisioning Capital," 440.) For "great body," see, among many other places, Adam Smith, *An Inquiry into the Nature and Causes of the Wealth of Nations*, 2 vols. (London: Strahan and Cadell, 1776), 1:5; for "whole body," see, 1:86 and 2:371.

23 W. J. T. Mitchell, *Picture Theory* (Chicago, IL: University of Chicago Press, 1994), 152.

24 Smith, *Wealth of Nations*, 1:7.

25 Ibid., 1:5.

26 Ibid., 1:6.

27 Mitchell, *Picture Theory*, 154.

28 See Keith Tribe, "Professors Malthus and Jones: Political Economy at the East India College, 1806–1858," *The European Journal of the History of Economic Thought* 2:2 (1995): 327–54 (327).

29 Tribe notes that the Directors were also ensuring with this appointment as with the others they made that students' education would focus, not on subjects specific to India, but to the principles underlying abstract topics that, however much they were the product of European intellectual history, were believed to be universal: rhetoric, law, political economy ("Professors Malthus and Jones", 334).

30 Malthus, *A Letter to the Right Honorable Lord Grenville Occasioned by Some Observations of His Lordship on the East India Company's Establishment for the Education of Their Civil Servants*, (London: J. Johnson, 1813), 37.

31 Eddy Kent, *Corporate Character: Representing Imperial Power in British India, 1786–1901* (Toronto, ON: University of Toronto Press, 2014), 67.

32 Ibid., 68.

33 Malthus, *Letter*, 5.

34 Ibid., 24.

35 Ibid., 24–25.

36 Ibid., 20.

37 Ibid., 22.

38 Quoted in James, *Population Malthus*, 220.

39 Smith, *Wealth of Nations*, 1:91 and 1:641.

40 Ibid., 2:83.

41 Ibid., 1:89.

42 Malthus, *Statements Respecting the East-India College with an Appeal to Facts in Refutation of the Charges Lately Brought against It in the Court of Proprietors* (London: John Murray, 1817), 31.

43 Timothy Mitchell, *Rule of Experts: Egypt, Techno-Politics, Modernity* (Berkeley: University of California Press, 2002), 94.

6 Moral Surveillance after Malthus

Alex Deans

In his 1798 *An Essay on the Principle of Population*, Thomas Malthus formulates an indissoluble conflict between human needs and the manifest realities of nature, when he writes:

> Population, when unchecked increases in a geometrical ratio. Subsistence increases only in an arithmetical ratio.[1]

With its appearance of mathematical stringency, the principle of population authoritatively reframed not only problems inherited from earlier political economists concerning growth, the distinction of ranks, and the progress of civil society, but also questions arising from a sense of the cultural and social flux of the historical moment. The *Essay* coincided with the economic turmoil of the Napoleonic wars and a period of intense political attention to the problem of poverty, culminating in the Poor Law Amendment Act of 1834. The principle of population itself represented a critical challenge to the "natural justice" discourse that had shaped the conceptualization of the relationship between rich and poor by eighteenth-century political economists, replacing it with a conviction of the providential necessity of poverty.[2]

But if Malthus's *Essay* continues to be infamous for recommending the abolition of the poor laws and the privations of famine, disease, and war as necessary "checks" to "incipient population," equally striking is its account of subject formation as an effect of economic hardship.[3] In the first edition of the *Essay*, Malthus argues that the natural sanctions of economic scarcity find their providential significance in "the creation and formation of mind; a process necessary to awaken inert, chaotic matter, into spirit; to sublimate the dust of the earth into soul; to elicit an aethereal spark from the clod of clay."[4] In the second edition of 1803, Malthus omitted this necessitarian and theologically heterodox argument, and adopted a more voluntaristic model of *homo œconomicus*, which emphasized the individual's power of "moral restraint."[5] Sexual abstinence was now the preferred "preventive check" to excess population, relocating a key problematic of Malthus's political economy to the level of individual morality and reason. What Malthus described as "the object of securing the operation of the preventive check to population," thus necessitated a programme of pedagogic reform, directed at "the lower classes of society... to infuse into them a portion of that knowledge and foresight which so much facilitates the attainment of this object in the educated part of the community."[6]

This essay primarily considers the work of the Church of Scotland Minister Thomas Chalmers (1780–1847), perhaps the most committed and prolific adherent to Malthusian political economy. In doing so, it attempts to build on Mary Poovey's vital work on Malthus and Chalmers in *Making a Social Body* and *A History of the Modern Fact.*[7] Chalmers rose to national prominence as a preacher and social reformer in the manufacturing districts of Glasgow's east end in the 1810s, and was distinguished by the assiduity with which he attempted to convert Malthus's belief in the restraining power of individual morality into a technique of social reform.[8] Chalmers was convinced that the Presbyterian minister's power of scrutiny over his parishioners was the perfect tool with which to institute the "moral preventive check" that would preserve society from the worst effects of the principle of population, by instilling the lower classes with habits of forethought and sexual restraint.[9] In his social reform programmes and the sprawling treatise on *The Christian and Civic Economy of Large Towns* that followed, Chalmers thus elaborated an apparatus of socio-moral regulation that paid close attention to the role of surveillance in underwriting processes of subject formation among the ranks of the urban poor. Chalmers's "civic economy" was in every sense a disciplinary project, in which the order of the social whole would be maintained by a constant and visible surveillance of the lower classes, in turn furnishing the observer with an empirical knowledge of human character and its variations under different material circumstances. Such an approach promised to recalibrate political economy as a science capable of relating social phenomena on the level of populations, to the interaction of moral and material causes on the level of the individual. In this sense, what follows explores the way in which the concept of the population—an aggregate body given a central place in political economy by physiocratic uses of natural history, as Elizabeth Wallmann discusses in the present volume—was broken down to the level of individual subjects in early nineteenth-century Britain, in service of the new perspective on population offered by Malthus. This method of individuation perhaps reflected a post-French Revolution anxiety that populations were too big to be governed: mass embodiments of material needs and desires whose lack of reasoning or moral faculties were a threat to the social order.

Chalmers's use of surveillance as a technique of both knowledge production and social policy finds an illuminating parallel in Alexander Bailey Richmond's 1824 *Narrative of the Condition of the Manufacturing Population.* A former weaver, Richmond considers the key preoccupations of Chalmers's contemporary writings and projects: namely the moral and material plight of the lower classes in Scotland's industrial towns and cities (primarily Glasgow), and the articulation of moral and economic responses to Malthus's principle.[10] However, Richmond's *Narrative* also recounts its author's recruitment as a government spy, tasked with determining whether labouring-class radicals were plotting against the state during a period of ferment in 1816. Mirroring Chalmers's contemporary use of parochial surveillance, Richmond offers a striking defence of his spying activities, in which he argues that espionage is a valid instrument of social intervention in cases where the moral and material condition of the poor has deteriorated beyond the reach of conventional reform. The *Narrative* thus establishes a strange dynamic between Richmond's perspicacity as a labouring-class student of political economy, able to attribute popular discontent to a lucidly analysed matrix of economic determinants, and his role as a misguided spy, who claims to have believed that he could correct the behaviour of the radicals whose conspiracy he infiltrated.[11] The imbrication of Richmond's own analysis with the punitive mechanisms of state anticipates the extent to which the problem of poverty and the management of excess or aberrant populations would increasingly fall under the remit of institutions—prisons, hospitals, and schools—rather than the purview of political economists.

In their respective contributions to a burgeoning genre of popular political economy, both Chalmers and Richmond grapple with a problem that is simultaneously a practical one of how to maintain social order, and one of knowledge formation, or of the extent to which complex social and psychological factors could be admitted into political-economic analysis. That Chalmers and Richmond even entertained the latter question, already distinguished them from the parallel and ultimately more influential reformulation of classical political economy as a primarily mathematical discipline, concerned with the general "laws" that governed rates of value in labour and exchange.[12] Through subsequent developments, this approach would result in a knowledge practice that dealt neither in human subjects *per se*, nor in the aggregate subject of the population, but in abstract types such as the margin-calculating and utility-maximizing individuals of neoclassical and later forms of political economy.[13] Such models presume a generalizable individuality, characterized by a capacity for economic decision making, but can hardly be said to be concerned with interiority, or the social and material formation of human subjects. If this distinction might be seen to reflect a necessary refinement of political economy's disciplinary scope, it is also the case, as I argue below, that Chalmers and Richmond were responding to an emergent problematic of political economy that was presaged by Adam Smith in the *Wealth of Nations*: the moulding of disparate human characters by the division of labour and an industrial class system.

Thomas Chalmers: Political Economy and "Moral Habit"

Chalmers's written and practical interventions reflected an ongoing debate in the early nineteenth century—particularly between Malthus and David Ricardo—about the epistemological status of political economy, which Malthus famously held to bear "a nearer resemblance to the science of morals and politics than to that of mathematics."[14] Introducing the 1821 volume of *The Christian and Civic Economy of Large Towns*, Chalmers writes:

> [t]ill within these last fifteen years, the great topic of inquiry among our abstract politicians, was the theory of commerce; and the moral habit of the labouring classes, as founded on their religion, did not enter, as an element, or as a component part, into that theory.[15]

The injection of moral and religious concerns into political economy is couched here in a rhetoric of objectivity, authorized largely by Malthus and the putative status of the principle of population as a natural law. The goal of introducing a specialized knowledge of the human, and particularly labouring-class subject as a key variable of political-economic enquiry, had its roots in Malthus's *Essay* as both a critique and outgrowth of Smithian political economy. "The true and genuine situation of man on earth," as seen through Malthus's principle of population, rendered the task of rethinking the relationship between poverty and the progress of wealth and society a methodological as well as moral imperative.[16] As Mary Poovey writes, Malthus proposed in his *Essay* that by gathering empirical data on the poor as a social body, political economists might test to what extent their own claims proceeded from a knowledge of the generalizable desires and habits of the human subject.[17]

In this sense, Malthus was suggesting a revision or extension to the Scottish enlightenment's central knowledge project: what David Hume, writing in *A Treatise of Human Nature* had called "the science of Man."[18] In subjecting the moral and intellectual qualities of human beings to the rigor of "experimental philosophy," Hume and his successors proposed a unitary field of enquiry in which the principles of political economy—no less than those of moral philosophy—were traced back to the study of the passions and affections, even if Hume conceded the "impossibility of explaining ultimate principles."[19] As Albert O. Hirschman argues, this way of thinking was crucial to the eighteenth-century identification of the "acquisitive drive" as an innate characteristic of human beings that legitimized the pursuit of wealth on an individual level, and regularized behaviour at a macro-scale, allowing philosophers to link the principles of political economy to a common understanding of human nature.[20] Hirschman argues that for writers from Shaftesbury to Smith, self-interest appeared as one of the inborn characteristics of the human subject, but one that when moderated by reason, produced benign effects on both a private and a public level, distinguishing it from the destructive passion of short-sighted avarice.[21] For Hirschman, this distinction between wild and mediated passions is crucial to Smith's description, in the *Wealth of Nations*, of "the desire of bettering our condition, a desire which, though generally calm and dispassionate, comes with us from the womb, and never leaves us till we go into the grave."[22]

Indeed, this section of the *Wealth of Nations* as a whole is revealing of the way in which Smith's argument circumvents the need for either the empirical model of "moral habit" sought by Chalmers and Malthus, or the abstract representation of the economic individual deployed by later economists. While the "effort of every man to better his condition" appears "uniform, constant, and interrupted" from the detached perspective of the philosopher, the preceding passages acknowledge that this is merely the aggregate outcome of various passions and behaviours, in which the general trend towards mediated self-interest is "sufficient to compensate" for aberrant agents and factors. Rather than logical abstraction, Smith's modelling of human characteristics and behaviours in the aggregate is licensed by the rhetorical ability of his prose to move freely between different scales of description. It is this modulation of perspective, rather than an identifiable causal behaviour, that translates between individual and general—or aggregate—human tendencies. This moment in *The Wealth of Nations* then, might be taken as a precursor to the ekphrastic turn that John O'Brien attributes to Malthus elsewhere in this book: a use of visualization to overcome the difficulties of describing the complex social, productive, and exchange relationships that we have learned to call "the economy."

If this technique avoids the need for either an abstract model or particularized knowledge of the human subject at the historical moment in which Smith is writing, it does not foreclose the possibility of a future state of society, in which the balance of passions at an individual and aggregate level ceases to "maintain the natural progress of all things towards improvement."[23] Of particular relevance to Malthus and Chalmers's desire to infuse political economy with a knowledge of the poor is Smith's account in *The Wealth of Nations*, of the effects of the advanced division of labour upon the lower classes. There, Smith famously reflects that a labourer whose work requires the repetitive execution of simple mechanical tasks will effectively lose some measure of their humanity and become "not only incapable of relishing or bearing a part in any rational conversation, but of conceiving any generous, noble, or tender sentiment, and consequently of forming any just judgement concerning many even of the ordinary duties of private life."[24] In what Philip Connell calls a "latent paradox" of Scottish enlightenment thought, Smith's degraded labourer appears to lose the moderating influences of sympathy and reason, which render self-interest a quality of the civilized economic subject, rather than an ungovernable passion.[25] For Smith, this is a political-economic problem in which the characteristics of moral subjects resonate at the level of the population, for: "in every improved and civilized society this is the state into which the labouring poor, that is, the great body of the people, must necessarily fall, unless government takes some pains to prevent it."[26]

Smith's remarks make the case for state-organized public education and point to an instructive variation of the human subject in the figure of the mentally debased labourer, thus underlining the genealogical relationship between this passage in *The Wealth of Nations*, and the intellectual and social projects of Malthus and Chalmers's political economy. When applied to Malthus's notion that sexual restraint could operate as a preventive check against overpopulation, Smith's admonishment concerning the effects of manufacturing on the lower classes would have acquired an added urgency. Although reframed by the principle of population, Malthus shares a simultaneously ethical and methodological concern with Smith, when he writes in the *Essay* of the utility of recording "the observable differences in the state of the lower classes of society, with respect to ease and happiness."[27] While such observations would be expected to reveal the true effects of poverty in relation to broader fluctuations in wages and subsistence, they would also provide an inductive basis from which to investigate the susceptibility of human character to different social and material conditions. Thus Poovey writes that "Malthus's interest in the poor deconstructed the universal subject of eighteenth-century philosophy in the name of a cultural relativism written onto (what we would call) class."[28] But Poovey also argues that in this desire to retrench economic thinking in an empirical knowledge of the poor, Malthus was not proposing a strictly statistical project in the modern sense, so much as a way of understanding how the moral qualities of an "aggregate" subject, evident in the general "happiness" of the whole, were both produced by and involved in producing a nexus of socio-economic causality.[29]

For Malthus, the condition of what Smith had called "the great body of the people" appeared to be a problem of interiority as much as demography, maintaining political economy's epistemological roots in the moral philosophy of the eighteenth century. Developing both the Scottish enlightenment's science of man, and the more pessimistic strands of Smith's political economy, the moral modelling proposed by Malthus reflected the sense in which the principle of population married a large-scale economic problem to individual morality, through the figure of an aggregate human subject. This aggregate subject was distinguished from the physiocratic notion of the population that Elizabeth Wallmann discusses elsewhere in the present volume, by virtue of its ineluctably moral nature. Malthus's reconceptualization of political economy as an empirical as well as moral discipline, paved the way for Chalmers's dual application of surveillance as a mode of knowledge production that observed the habits and condition of the poor, and a corrective technique which sought to amend those habits by exposing them to the clerical gaze. By combining the methodological and practical rigors of political economy and the Christian social mission—a manoeuvre that he presents as a smooth dovetailing of isometric fields rather than a contentious disciplinary expansion—Chalmers retained many of the socio-political concerns of *The Wealth of Nations*, while locating his own avocation in the study and inculcation of economic morality.

The Principle of Population and the Paradox of Character

Echoing Malthus's invocation of the poor as a specific object of empirical knowledge, Chalmers's claim to have located a socio-political determinant in "the moral habit" of the lower classes, frames problems of government around the figure of a contingent and particularized human nature—tentatively theorized by Smith—on which are imprinted the material conditions of manufacturing and urbanization. But in *The Christian and Civic Economy*, Chalmers also gives the assumed interaction of human subjects with socio-economic forces a specific expression in the notion of character. In reference to Malthus's principle of population and its effects, Chalmers writes:

> the disciples of political science, however wisely they may speculate upon this question, are, if without the element of character among the general population, in a state of impotency as to the practical effect of their speculation... they want one of the data, indispensable to the right solution of a problem, which, however clear in theory, will, upon trial, mock the vain endeavours of those who overlook the moral principles of man.[30]

Chalmers's argument is striking for the way in which it presents the centrality of aggregate character to economic understanding as simultaneously an article of revealed truth, and the result of empirical findings yet to be made. This rhetorical play of the self-evident and the obscure is precisely what lends "the moral principles of man" their value in this formulation, as the sign which promises to disclose the meaning of the socio-economic text, and yet which always refers back to another layer of complexity.

Returning again to Wallmann's essay in the present collection, the above emphasis on character as "one of the data," appears to upturn the physiocratic understanding of populations as necessarily bodily, rather than moral in their composition. But we might also view Chalmers's recourse to character, like the figure of the population in the earlier, French political economy considered by Wallmann, as an instance of abstraction, in that it permits Chalmers to fix in concept, a series of relations otherwise dissolved in the temporality of the socio-economic medium. But if those who refused to account for the "element of character" were condemned to produce a partial view of social systems, Chalmers's attempt to reify the discourse of moral habit and character as a technique of reform or intrinsic function within a broader political-economic theory did not necessarily discover a new source of legibility within the body politic. Beyond the level of abstraction, Chalmers's notion of character seemed to describe something that was both obscure and variable, a reflection of complex class divisions and the particular conditions associated with them. In other words, character was both the solution and the root of the problem. For Chalmers and his contemporaries, the social specificity of character raised the possibility that individual human subjects—and thus the population at large—were governed more by arbitrary circumstance than a moral nature. Far from providing an anchor point for social reform, such a model of character would exert a reciprocal and disordering influence on its moral and socio-economic environment, continually reflecting and reproducing the discontents of the emerging industrial society.

This dilemma encapsulates what Jerrold Seigel calls "a perhaps paradoxical but… defining feature of nineteenth-century thinking, namely the heightened emphasis it gave at once to the prospect of human freedom and to the determining power of material circumstances."[31] For Seigel, an important expression of "the polarity of determinism and freedom as an element in the problematic of character and the sharper form it took in the nineteenth century" was represented by Robert Owen's assertion that "character is universally formed for and not by the individual."[32] Owen famously argued that defects in society as it currently existed derived from its adherence to the contrary and false supposition that "it is in the power of every individual to form his own character."[33] Notions of legal and religious guilt were an upshot of this flawed formula, and punished a criminality that was produced by external social factors beyond the control of the individual. Through his *New View of Society: or, Essays on the Principle of the Formation of the Human Character*, the famous socialist manufacturing community that he organized at New Lanark, and the "Institution Established for the Formation of Character" that the latter incorporated, Owen elaborated a model for the shaping of virtuous and happy individuals, through the transformation of the external forces which he believed were wholly determinate of human nature. The totalizing nature of Owen's project, relying on the precise use of moral and instrumental education, workplace supervision and the regulation of social life within the specially constructed and insular milieu of an industrial village, underlines the susceptibility of character—the putative object of reform—to myriad and otherwise uncontrollable influences.

For Chalmers as for Owen, the paradox of character was not merely epistemological. If the notion of character itself rested on shaky foundations, or simply named a reciprocal determinism that existed between individuals and their environments, the task of instituting a "moral preventive check" based on the plural exercise of individual rational restraint would be almost impossible. This problem was intensified by the nature of the principle of population itself, imagined to always be in operation in varying degrees of severity, through the effects of hunger and privation on the lower classes. Until the point of actual starvation, this entailed an ever-worsening state of need that worked to extinguish any spark of morality by normalizing the material and intellectual destitution of extreme poverty. Chalmers warns that society might thus be condemned to a self-perpetuating cycle of degradation. For:

> [s]o long as there is generally a low and grovelling taste among the people, instead of an aspiring tendency towards something more in the way of comfort, and cleanliness, and elegance, than is to be with in the sordid habitations of a rude and demi-barbarous country, will they rush, with precipitation, into matrimony, and care not how unable they are to meet its expenses, and forfeit the whole ease and accommodation of the future, to the present ascendency of a blind and uncalculating impulse.[34]

Here, the 'uncalculating' tendency of the lower classes becomes a symptom of their inadequate character. By the same logic, the capacity for economic self-interest, in the sense of understanding how the principle of population determines one's own prospects of happiness, becomes the product rather than prerequisite of moral restraint. Chalmers therefore posits that "[t]he tendency to excessive population, can only find its thorough and decisive counteraction, among the amended habits, and the moralized characters, and the exalted principles, of the people themselves."[35]

However this argument is qualified by an acute sense, acknowledged above by Chalmers, of the role played by material circumstances in a negative process of character (de)formation, in which the moral qualities of the individual are both determined by and determinate of the economic world which that individual inhabits. As we have seen, Robert Owen's solution to this paradox was to abstract the process of character formation itself from the distortive external pressures of economic life, within the carefully managed environs of New Lanark. For Chalmers, such an approach would have appeared counterproductive, because the mediation of those pressures—as expressions of the ratio between population and subsistence—was precisely what the reformed character of the lower classes was supposed to accomplish. It therefore fell to the intervention of the Christian philanthropist and a modified social apparatus to imprint character on an otherwise torpid population. In this sense, Chalmers's notion of character was ultimately, in Michel Foucault's terms, a "technology of power over the body."[36] We are perhaps a long way here from the opening gambit of *The Christian and Civic Economy of Large Towns*, where Chalmers, parsing Malthus's *Essay*, appears to posit that moral character is something latent in populations, and thus a necessary object of empirical enquiry for the political economist. But partly due to the complexities involved in determining character's relationship to these wider material dynamics, Chalmers's goal of reattaching an epistemological ligature between subjective interiority and large-scale economic phenomena gives way over the course of his argument, to a realization of the need to actively instill and manage the moral character of the poor from the top down.

Richmond's *Narrative*: Espionage and Industrial Society

Before finally turning to the practical element of Chalmers's project as described in *The Christian and Civic Economy*, I want to foreground my discussion by considering the intertwining of espionage, analysis, and correction in Alexander Richmond's *Narrative of the Condition of the Manufacturing Population*. Richmond's account illuminates the punitive uses of surveillance in lower-class populations during the early nineteenth century, underlining the disciplinary context of Chalmers's deployment of similar techniques. However, in terms of knowledge formation, Richmond's *Narrative* also provides a further perspective on the way in which a problem of political economy was gradually commuted into one of social organization and discipline, through a particular modelling of the moral and psychological factors seen to be at play in industrial society.

Richmond largely endorses Malthus's criticism of Adam Smith in the first edition of the *Essay*, that the growth of manufacturing and its revenue as a section of the total economy, tends not to proportionately improve the comfort and happiness of the lower classes, and that "the increasing wealth of the nation has had little or no tendency to better the condition of the laboring poor."[37] He therefore finds little fault with Malthus's pessimistic reassessment of the relationship between economic progress and "the happiness and comfort of the lower orders of society."[38] But in common with Chalmers, Richmond perceived that the effects of poverty were hostile, rather than conducive to the formation of rational or moral human subjects. Going further, he refutes outright the notion that poverty itself could operate as a preventive check against overpopulation, describing it as "a downright insult to men of understanding, when applied to a class who are once degraded."[39] Instead, desperate conditions would actively militate against the Malthusian check of "moral restraint." For:

> improvident breeding follows, as the necessary consequence of a blind indulgence of the strongest propensity of animal nature, which, at the lowest point, continues to operate with undiminished force. Excessive labour, scanty, unwholesome food and unhealthy occupation, will shorten the duration of life, and will produce a quicker succession of beings, but it will not lessen the absolute number; on the contrary, the increase will continue, until they are forced to prey upon the lowest garbage. Thus, the physical and mental process of degeneracy is confirmed and perpetuated, until brutality and ignorance render amendment or escape almost hopeless.[40]

Richmond's almost cannibalistic vision denudes and amplifies the infamous analogy included in the second edition of Malthus's *Essay*, reimagining the scene from outside the dining room, as guests are ejected from "nature's mighty feast."[41] For Richmond as for Chalmers, the problem of poverty is boiled down here to the reflexive mechanism by which the moral character of the poor both determines and is determined by immediate economic circumstances, which become more adverse as the ratio of population to subsistence increases. Moreover, Richmond's hypothesis holds Malthus's principle to be untrue under certain conditions, as populations might still increase on even the barest sustenance, rendering human life nasty, brutish, and short, but not necessarily diminished in terms of the absolute number of bodies. Richmond's interpretation renders the physiocratic model of population discussed by Wallmann in bleakly animalistic terms. In this account, Richmond also emphasizes the materiality of the human intellect itself, with moral inadequacy painted partly as the result of a poisonous diet, and any notion of character subordinated to the sexual urge.

For Richmond however, the corollary of this belief was not that the effects of the economic status quo were primarily natural forces that had to be accommodated, as Chalmers and Malthus argued, by a careful habituation of the lower classes. Rather, the structure of deprivation that Richmond observed appeared to him as the result of various mutable interests and contingencies that were best addressed through the revision of political-economic doctrine. Richmond's initial appeal then, was not to his fellow labourers' capacity for rational restraint, but to that of their masters. Richmond writes that by 1811 he had gained "a considerable degree of popularity" among his fellow weavers due to his involvement in a committee whose purpose was to litigate in favour of fixing minimum prices for woven goods. The organization: "consisted, with one or two exceptions, of practical men, acquainted only with the technicalities of their trade, and had no knowledge of the general theory upon which the arguments of our opponents were chiefly founded."[42] Richmond implies that his own knowledge of political economy, conversant in "all the arguments of Smith, Malthus, and the economists of the French school," meant that in disputes with masters and politicians: "the weight of the discussion, on the abstract points, fell on [him]."[43] But when Richmond refused the requests of local authorities to use his influence over weavers in the west of Scotland to disband a strike (illegal under the combination acts of 1799 and 1800), he was indicted and imprisoned in Paisley Jail. The case attracted the attention of several prominent Whig lawyers, including Francis Jeffrey and Henry Cockburn, the latter of whom records in his posthumously published *Memorials of his Time*, that Richmond's "organization and management" of the 1812 workmen's combination, "was better evidence of his talent than many men of high political station could have produced."[44]

Through Richmond's account of his role in organized labour, we can see how the "general system of '*surveillance*'" (Richmond's emphasis) that had insured the smooth running of the worker's combination in 1812, presented itself as a suitable model for the marshalling of a less ordered labouring-class population a few years later.[45] Richmond's experience of labouring-class self-organization appeared to refute the Malthusian notion that checks to population "ought to be effected by privation, vice and misery." Rather, he argued, the moral imperative when dealing with "beings possessing the power of ratiocination," was to secure the ascendancy of the intellect over the bodily passions, both on the level of the individual and the population.[46] In Richmond's words, "[t]he question... resolves itself into this; whether man should be placed under the government of his moral and intellectual faculties, or left the slave of his mere animal appetites and physical propensities."[47] Under the "deplorable" conditions in which he found the labouring classes in 1816, Richmond's materialist model of the human mind rendered the spontaneous manifestation of judgement and reason unlikely.[48] Yet through the judicious and covert agency of the spy, the effects of reason could still be set to work, even if rationality itself was largely absent from the population in question. Pressing his case, Richmond writes:

> until society is differently constituted, and governments have recourse to the primary principle of ameliorating the condition of the people, and resting the means of prevention in a superior education, and the diffusion of a better system of practical morality, I see no other remedy.[49]

Richmond's decision to intervene in lieu of the "primary principle" of a more broadly diffused capacity for reason is supported by the clarity of perspective and privileged knowledge of the whole afforded by the spy's ability to alternate between the milieus of both the suspect and the suspecting. This kind of infiltration is necessary Richmond argues, because:

> [n]one but minute and accurate observers are aware of the peculiarity of character and opinions, produced by insulated association among the different ranks of men, and their absolute ignorance respecting the true character and feelings of each other, as society is at present constituted.[50]

Richmond powerfully articulates the sense in which the "insulated association" brought about by class difference has become an obstacle to the theoretical or empirical comprehension of the body politic from the systematic perspective of the economist. The predictable abstractions of generalizable human tendencies and populations drawn upon by Smith—and as Wallmann discusses in this volume—the French physiocrats, give way here to highly differentiated class characteristics and aggregate expressions of irrational behaviour. The complexity of industrial society has rendered the perspective of the spy the only one capable of knowing the governed, or ascertaining certain principles of political economy in operation.

Richmond's account of a society impenetrably stratified by the disparate subjectivities produced by material conditions, returns us to Smith's vision in *The Wealth of Nations*, of "the great body of the people" deprived of their moral and intellectual faculties by the division of labour. Looking later into the nineteenth century, we might also see how this line of argument anticipates Marx's assertion that: "[i]t is not the consciousness of men that determines their existence, but on the contrary, their social existence determines their consciousness."[51] If for Marx and Engels this way of thinking about interiority as an element of political economy—or the critique of political economy—pointed to the inevitability of revolution, this possibility lay beyond the horizon of Richmond's analysis. Indeed, the revolutionary affirmation of class consciousness imagined by Marx seems unfeasible in Richmond's account, where such an event would be forestalled by the triumph of "animal appetites and physical propensities" among the lower classes. But the sense that consciousness is materially determined by socio-economic circumstance finds potent expression in Richmond's *Narrative*, just as it does in Chalmers's conflicted account of character and (as Seigel notes) the work of Robert Owen.[52] Richmond's critique of early nineteenth-century political economy rests on the way in which the labouring classes are continually pushed to the margins of subsistence, primarily by the speculation of manufacturers and markets, rather than by the principle of population itself. Thus in a reversal of the Malthusian appeal to the reformative facility of "moral restraint," Richmond envisages a "differently constituted" society as the solution to the problem of class-specific character determination. As we've seen, Chalmers too was alert to the susceptibility of intellect and morality to extrinsic material factors, calling for a more rigorous form of social intervention than that envisaged in Malthus's *Essay*. In this sense, I would argue, Chalmers's use of surveillance to instill morals in a lower-class population, can be seen in the same light as Richmond's substitution of aggregate rationality with the clandestine influence of the spy. In both accounts, the accretion of a social apparatus that is restraining as well as pedagogic, is revealed as the fallout of an inability—on a practical and social level as well as an intellectual one—to reconcile the principles of political economy with a coherent moral understanding of human nature. As I suggest below, what Richmond and Chalmers experience as an impasse of both policy and knowledge formation, would arguably crystallize under the regime of later nineteenth-century thinking as the so-called "Adam Smith problem."

Moral Surveillance and the Parish: The "Principle of Locality"

Like Richmond, Chalmers perceived the need for new ways to read and intervene in the complex moral systems of an antagonistic and fractured social field. In *The Christian and Civic Economy of Large Towns*, Chalmers was ostensibly putting into writing a system of philanthropic reform which he had tested in practice in the impoverished east end of Glasgow, only a few years after the same population had provoked the fears of rebellion and conspiracy that led to Richmond's deployment as a spy. As the Minister of St John's Kirk from 1819 to 1823, Chalmers assumed responsibility for poor-relief and pastoral provision in a district of around 30,000 people, with the material aim of eliminating pauperism and thus enacting—with some contextual qualifications—Malthus's "Plan of the Gradual Abolition of the Poor Laws."[53]

Chalmers objected to poor relief not only on the grounds that it removed a preventive check against overpopulation, but because in his view, it replaced the voluntary "kindness and the watchfulness of private charity" with obligation.[54] Chalmers's naming of "watchfulness" as one of the virtues he hoped to foster through the abolition of poor relief invokes the always latent interplay between voluntary visibility and surveillance as the means through which one's own moral character and those of others—both individually and in the aggregate—are normalized and maintained. In both his execution of the St John's experiment and his inscription of its methods in *The Christian and Civic Economy*, Chalmers emphasized a "principle of locality" that sought to reduce the effective distance between the minister and his individual parishioners, by interspersing the urban space between them with a subordinate lay clergy. The aim was to simulate the moral oversight which rural ministers were ostensibly able to exercise over their less populous parishes, where "the minister alone, or with a very few coadjutors of a small session, may bring the personal influence of his kind and Christian attentions to bear upon all the families."[55] Chalmers reasons that

> by dividing his parish into small manageable districts—and assigning one or more of his friends, in some capacity or other, to each of them—and vesting them with such a right either of superintendence or of inquiry, as will always be found to be gratefully met by the population—and so, raising, as it were, a ready intermedium of communication between himself and the inhabitants of his parish, [the minister] may at length attain an assimilation in point of result to a country parish, though not in the means by which he arrived at it.[56]

The passage suggests the level on which the economy of moral surveillance Chalmers established in his parish materialized a "paradox of disciplinary individualism" in which, for Poovey, "the individuality of every man is affirmed by his voluntary submission to the greater whole."[57] On this level, the St John's project might be interpreted in the same light as Malthus's parallel conceptualization of the sovereign gaze of the corporation, as discussed by O'Brien in his contribution to this volume. The agents involved in the apparatus of surveillance are bisected by their liberty to roam and their duty to report to the minister, by whom they are also endowed with the authority to question and observe. The system is decidedly hierarchical—even managerial—its effect simultaneously that of organizing the social relations of the parish and carrying the right of scrutiny embodied by the clergyman beyond the confines of his individuality, to superintend the formation of moralized characters in the parishioners. The project's dependency on the spatial manipulation of the community and its members reveals the extent to which Chalmers, like Owen, saw his ability to influence processes of interiority as dependent on extrinsic, environmental techniques. With reference to Richmond's almost contemporaneous use of surveillance, we can also see the way in which Chalmers's careful subdivision of his urban parish is proffered as an antidote to the "insulated association" endemic to industrial society. The process of opening up the social "intermedium" by breaking a population into individuals and households is tied to the governmental necessity of dismantling conspiracies and labourer's combinations.

Yet if one tendency of Chalmers's moral surveillance was to dissolve the threatening insularity of unregulated association, another was to install layers of inscrutability that mirrored Richmond's concealment of his own motives as a government spy. On this level, Chalmers seems to have pursued a similar end of substituting the moral agency of the philanthropist for that of the philanthropic subject. Animating Chalmers's constant enforcement of what he describes as a "moral regimen," through the segmentation of space and dispersal of the minister's gaze among the multitude, is an apparent desire to naturalize the dictates of Malthusian economics by repeatedly obscuring their rationale.[58] While it might be "a doctrine which stands on a firm basis of arithmetic," Chalmers acknowledges that labouring-class households would scorn the intrusion of a political economist intent upon demonstrating the implications of Malthus's *Essay* for their long-term welfare.[59] On the other hand, Chalmers argues that the Christian evangelist "might step into almost every dwelling-place—and engage the inmates in conversations of piety—and leave, at least, the sensations of cordiality and gratitude behind him." As their imperatives of moral restraint are aligned, the divine can accomplish the purpose of the economist with perfect efficacy, and without revealing the covert process of interpellation whereby the moral agency of the subject simply articulates Malthus's principles of political economy.

Contrary to its stated aim, Chalmers's *Christian and Civic Economy* seems to uphold an "unfortunate distance" between theological and political-economic thinking, asserting that the two fields are transparent in the eyes of providence and the minister, but refusing to close the gap between Christian morality and economic self-interest in the mind of the lower-class subject.[60] Chalmers's image of a labouring-class domesticity, whose inhabitants are left with only the "sensations" of paternalistic attention, performs an interiority which remains inaccessible to the observer, despite its rhetorical centrality to the mode of moral and economic argument. Just as Richmond circumvents his fellow labourers' powers of reasoning and agency through a covert attempt to direct their actions, the purpose of "conversation" in the St John's scheme is not rational exchange, persuasion, or the imparting of knowledge, but merely the production of tranquil "sensations," simulating the polite moderation of feeling that the labouring-class subject seems incapable of performing voluntarily. Here we might briefly reconsider a variation on "The Adam Smith Problem," as raised by the editors in their introduction to this book. If *The Wealth of Nations* imagined that a certain equilibrium of human characteristics and other factors would "maintain the natural progress of all things towards improvement" at the aggregate level, Smith's earlier but frequently revised *Theory of Moral Sentiments*, attributed this mediatory function at the level of the individual to the desire for sympathy and an ability to modulate the "pitch" of one's feelings, so that they might be shared with an "impartial spectator."[61] Richmond's spying activities and the surveillance of Chalmers's lay clergymen, might be seen as attempts to externalize a version of this normative function within lower-class populations, through organizational and disciplinary imposition. It is perhaps significant that in their attempts to reconcile political economy and morality through the diffusion of rational restraint,

Richmond and Chalmers are forced in practice to return to the "impartial spectator" of *The Theory of Moral Sentiments*, rather than the "invisible hand" of *The Wealth of Nations*, reconstituting the former in their unorthodox apparatuses of social reform.[62] That Chalmers's style of philanthropy becomes the servant of a *laissez-faire* policy justified by Malthus's principle of population, ironically makes it easier to imagine the very shift that *The Christian and Civic Economy* purports to forestall: a conceptual and practical divorce of the economic from the political and the moral. That the "The Adam Smith Problem" continues to warrant attention—despite numerous responses and reformulations—perhaps marks it as something alive in the diffuse socio-political tissue of capitalism, as much as in intellectual history.[63]

Notes

1 Thomas R. Malthus, *An Essay on the Principle of Population, as it Affects the Future Improvement of Society, With Remarks on the Speculations of Mr. Godwin, M. Condorcet, and Other Writers* (London: J. Johnson, 1798), 14.
2 On the role of natural justice in enlightenment political economy see Donald Winch, *Riches and Poverty: An Intellectual History of Political Economy in Britain, 1750–1834* (Cambridge: Cambridge University Press, 1996).
3 Malthus, *Essay* (1798), 99–100. On the moral and theological dimensions of the *Essay* see Boyd Hilton, *The Influence of Evangelicalism on Social and Economic Thought, 1785–1865*, (Oxford: Clarendon, 1988; repr. 1997) and Phillip Connell, *Romanticism, Economics and the Question of "Culture,"* (Oxford: Oxford University Press, 2001), 46.
4 Ibid., 353.
5 Thomas R. Malthus, *An Essay on the Principle of Population, Or A View of Its Past and Present Effects on Human Happiness; With an Inquiry into Our Prospects Respecting the Future Removal or Mitigation of the Evils Which it Occasions*, ed. Donald Winch (Cambridge: Cambridge University Press, 1992), 23.
6 Ibid., 274.
7 See Mary Poovey, *Making a Social Body: British Cultural Formation, 1830–1864* (Chicago, IL; London: University of Chicago Press, 1995), and *A History of the Modern Fact, Problems of Knowledge in the Sciences of Wealth and Society* (Chicago, IL; London: University of Chicago Press, 1998); see also Poovey's *Genres of the Credit Economy: Mediating Value in Eighteenth- and Nineteenth-Century Britain* (Chicago, IL: University of Chicago Press, 2008).
8 For a fuller account of Chalmers's career, see Stewart J. Brown, *Thomas Chalmers and the Godly Commonwealth in Scotland* (Oxford: Oxford University Press, 1982).
9 Thomas Chalmers, *The Christian and Civic Economy of Large Towns*, 3 vols. (Glasgow, 1821–1826), 1:16.
10 Alexander B. Richmond, *Narrative of the Condition of the Manufacturing Population and the Proceedings of Government Which Led to the State Trials in Scotland* (London: 1824; repr. New York: Augustus M. Kelley, 1971).
11 On the reception of Richmond's *Narrative* see W.M. Roach, "Alexander Richmond and the Radical Reform Movements in Glasgow in 1816–17," *The Scottish Historical Review* 51:151 (1972): 1–19. On espionage and

radicalism in Scotland during this period see Gordon Pentland, "'Betrayed by Infamous Spies?' The Commemoration of Scotland's 'Radical War' of 1820," *Past and Present* 201:1 (2008): 141–73.

12 See, for example, the preface to David Ricardo, *On the Principles of Political Economy and Taxation* (London: 1817).

13 See Dani Rodrik, *Economics Rules, Why Economics Works, When It Fails, and How to Tell The Difference* (Oxford: Oxford University Press, 2015), 100 and Donald Winch, "Marginalism and the Boundaries of Economic Science," *History of Political Economy* 4:2 (1972): 325–43.

14 Thomas R. Malthus, *Principles of Political Economy* (London: 1820), 1.

15 Chalmers, *Christian and Civic Economy,* 1:4.

16 Malthus, *Essay* (1798), 175.

17 See Poovey, *Modern Fact*, 285–88.

18 David Hume, *A Treatise of Human Nature: Being An Attempt to Introduce the Experimental Method of Reasoning into Moral Subjects*, 3 vols. (London: 1739–1740), 1:6.

19 Ibid.

20 Ibid., 9.

21 See Albert O. Hirschman, *The Passions and the Interests: Political Arguments for Capitalism before Its Triumph* (Princeton; Oxford: Princeton University Press, 1977; repr. 2013), 62–66.

22 Ibid., 66. Adam Smith, *An Inquiry into the Nature and Causes of The Wealth of Nations*, 2 vols. (London: 1776), 1:415.

23 Smith, *Wealth,* 1:416–17.

24 Ibid., 2:366–67.

25 Connell, 69.

26 Smith, *Wealth*, 2:367.

27 Malthus, *Essay* (1798), 33.

28 Poovey, *Modern Fact*, 286.

29 Ibid., 287.

30 Chalmers, *Christian and Civic Economy,* 10.

31 Jerrold Seigel, "Necessity, Freedom, and Character Formation from the Eighteenth Century to the Nineteenth," in *Character, Self, and Sociability in the Scottish Enlightenment*, ed. Susan Manning and Thomas Ahnert (New York; Houndsmills, UK: Palgrave Macmillan, 2011), 249–66 (255).

32 Ibid, 259; Robert Owen, *New View of Society: Or, Essays on the Principle of the Formation of the Human Character* (London: Printed for Longman, Hurst, et al., 1817), 33.

33 Ibid., 32.

34 Chalmers, *Christian and Civic Economy,* 8.

35 Ibid.

36 Michel Foucault, *Discipline and Punish: The Birth of the Prison*, trans. Alan Sheridan (London: Penguin Books, 1991), 189.

37 Malthus, *Essay* (1798), 312–13. See Richmond, 1.

38 Malthus, *Essay* (1798), 305.

39 Richmond, *Narrative,* 194.

40 Ibid., 195.

41 See Thomas R. Malthus, *An Essay on the Principle of Population; or A view of its Past and Present Effects on Human Happiness* (London: 1803), 531–32.

42 Ibid., 18.

43 Ibid., 35, 18.

44 Henry Cockburn, *Memorials of His Time* (Edinburgh: Adam and Charles Black, 1856), 326.

45 Ibid., 14.
46 Richmond, *Narrative,* 194.
47 Ibid.
48 Ibid., 53.
49 Ibid., 67–68.
50 Ibid., 76.
51 Karl Marx, *A Contribution to the Critique of Political Economy*, trans. N.I. Stone (Chicago, IL: Charles H. Kerr, 1904), 7. In relation to Richmond's *Narrative*, one might also consider Friedrich Engels, *Condition of the Working Class in England* (London; New York: 1891).
52 Seigel, "Necessity," 258.
53 See Malthus, *Essay* (1803), 536–48.
54 See Thomas Chalmers, 'Minutes of the Evidence Taken Before the Committee Appointed by the House of Commons, to Inquire into the State of Mendicity and Vagrancy in the Metropolis and Its Neighbourhood', *Edinburgh Review* 28:55 (March 1817), 1–31, 8.
55 Chalmers, *Christian and Civic Economy,* 89.
56 Ibid.
57 Poovey, *Social Body*, 103.
58 Chalmers, *Christian and Civic Economy,* 1:25.
59 Ibid., 18.
60 Ibid., 3
61 Adam Smith, *The Theory of Moral Sentiments* (London; Edinburgh: 1759), 3, 79.
62 Smith, *Wealth*, 2:35.
63 On responses to "The Adam Smith Problem" see, for example, Richard Teichgraeber III, "Rethinking Das Adam Smith Problem," *Journal of British Studies* 20:2 (1981), 106–23, and more recently, Keith Tribe, *The Economy of the World: Language, History, and Economics* (Oxford: Oxford University Press, 2015), 139–62.

Section 4

Political Economy and Affect

7 The "Adam Smith Problem" and the Retreat of Sentimental Virtue from the World

Mary Peace

It is now a "truth universally acknowledged" that the "Adam Smith problem" that exercised cultural theorists and historians from the nineteenth century onwards was the product of misreading. Richard Adelman and Catherine Packham define the "Adam Smith problem" in the introduction to this volume as "the apparent conundrum surrounding how...the moral philosopher who wrote *The Theory of Moral Sentiments* in 1759, could also write *The Wealth of Nations* (*WN*) in 1776".[1] How could the author of *The Theory of Moral Sentiments* (hereafter *TMS*), who "considers human nature as universally sympathetic, other-orientated, social and thus moral" have written the latter, which "treats human behavior as almost always self-interested and calculating"?[2] This essay will not seek to rekindle an "Adam Smith problem" but will argue that we can reach a better understanding of the origins of this misreading if we map Smith's works against the history of the evolution of sentimental ideas across literature and political economic discourse in the third quarter of the eighteenth century.

The period between the 1750s and the 1770s witnessed a gravitational shift in the dominant understanding of sentimental ideas.[3] During this period the polite, moral-sense discourse of sentimentality, which emerged in the writings of Francis Hutcheson, David Hume, and Adam Smith, was increasingly overwritten by primitivist, Rousseauvian ideas. The polite, refined moral sense, which had secured the ethical frameworks of literature, economics, and social policy in the 1740s and 1750s, was progressively usurped by a primitivist version of sensibility which was imagined to lack agency in the world and to be corrupted by it. This primitivist sensibility, I suggest, can be traced back through the philosophical elaborations of Jean-Jacques Rousseau to the literary sensibility of Richardson's later novels.

To provide a case study of this evolution, the essay will map Smith's two landmark texts, *TMS* and *WN*, respectively, against events in the career of that most sentimental of eighteenth-century figures—the Reverend William Dodd. Dodd was born in 1729, just six years after Adam Smith. He is significant in the context of this essay for the sentimental performances on which his career was founded but would ultimately founder; his Richardsonian novel of sensibility, *The Sisters* (1754); the affecting sermons which brought crowds flocking every Sunday to hear him preach at Chapel of the Magdalen House for Penitent Prostitutes (later the Magdalen Hospital); and the sentimental defence that he mounted in court in 1777 after being caught red-handed having forged the signature of his pupil the Earl of Chesterfield. The dates spanned by Smith's major publications roughly coincide with Dodd's own career in the public eye. Dodd makes his first appearance at the Magdalen House chapel as a polite, sentimental preacher in 1759 and is executed for forgery in 1777, after the failure of his sentimental pleas at the Old Bailey. Dodd's career, I will argue in this essay, offers us a graphic illustration of complex and changing nature of sentimental discourse and thus a context for better understanding the misreading which lead to the "Adam Smith Problem."

The Adam Smith Problem

TMS proposes that right moral judgement results from sympathetic identification with the feelings of an impartial spectator. For Smith,

> before we approve of the sentiments of any person as proper and suitable to that object, we must not only be affected in same manner as he is, but we must perceive this harmony and correspondence of sentiments between him and ourselves.[4]

It is this sympathetic identification which makes us overcome our selfish instincts—which renders us benevolent. And "proper benevolence," Smith states "is the most graceful and agreeable of all affections."[5] Indeed, the power of sympathy, Smith tells us in his 1790 edition of *TMS* is "a voice capable of astonishing the most presumptuous of our passions."[6] In *WN*, however, Smith seems to question the strength and indeed even the true virtue of our "benevolent" affections. Here Smith famously asserts that "[i]t is not from the benevolence of the butcher, the brewer, or the baker, that we expect our dinner, but from their regard to their own interest."[7] Benevolence, it seems, is here a weak virtue and indeed, in the light of a further statement in volume 2, may be understood as scarcely a virtue at all in relation to "the public good." Here, Smith states that:

> By pursuing his own interest...[the merchant] frequently promotes that of the society more effectually than when he really intends to promote it. I have never known much good done by those who affected to trade for the publick good.[8]

Smith's two texts struck nineteenth-century scholars as problematically at odds and it was out of this perceived discrepancy that "the Adam Smith problem" was born.[9]

More recently, however, Smith scholars have shown that a proper reading of these two works demonstrates a coherent system of thought across them both. The works, as Smith's distinguished editor D. D. Raphael argues, represent largely distinct areas of investigation. Raphael cites as evidence the account given by John Millar of the lecture series he attended on moral philosophy delivered by Adam Smith at Glasgow University. This was divided into four parts: the first "Natural Theology," the second "Ethics," the third "*justice*" and the last "political regulations…founded not upon the principle of *justice,* but that of *expediency.*"[10] Smith's publications, it is contended, were projected to follow this sequence of discrete topics. In the event Smith published a few essays on Natural Theology; moved on to a full explanation of "ethics" in *TMS;* made notes towards, but did not complete a work on *justice* and concluded his series by publishing *WN*—a work concerning "political regulations…founded… [upon] *expediency.*"[11] Moreover, even when issues of ethics and expediency do appear to overlap, as in Smith's declaration that we cannot look to benevolence to supply us with our necessary wants, Raphael argues that where *TMS* is concerned primarily with the formation of principles, *WN* treats of motives to action.[12] Perhaps the most compelling evidence offered by Raphael is that the sixth edition of Smith's *Theory of Moral Sentiments* was published in 1790, long after the publication of *The Wealth of Nations.* It was published with substantial additions by Smith, yet far from rethinking the conclusions of the original text, Smith's additions restated, expanded, and strengthened his original conclusion: that right moral judgement results from a sympathetic identification with the feelings of an impartial spectator.[13] There are substantial grounds, therefore, for understanding Smith's thought as a coherent whole.

Raphael's arguments are often convincing, but they do leave a problem for any scholar approaching *WN* from the perspective of the mid-eighteenth-century moral-sense philosophy in which Smith's *TMS* is considered to be a key player. Moral-sense philosophy forges its identity in dialogue with established classical-republican ideas. These ideas are centrally preoccupied with the moral implications of luxury—the relationship between economic development and individual and public morality. David Hume describes the formative role played by classical-republican theory for moral-sense theory in his *An Enquiry Concerning the Principle of Morals* (1751). In classical theory, he says:

> Luxury, or a Refinement on the Pleasures and Conveniences of Life, had long been supos'd the Source of every Corruption and Disorder in Government, and the immediate Cause of Faction, Sedition, civil

> Wars, and the total Loss of Liberty. It was, therefore, universally regarded as a Vice, and was an Object of Declamation to all Satyrists, and severe Moralists.[14]

By contrast, Hume argues, moral-sense theorists:

> prove, or attempt to prove, that such Refinements rather tend to the Encrease of Industry, Civility, and Arts, regulate anew our *moral* as well as *political* sentiments, and represent, as laudable and innocent, what had formerly been regarded as pernicious and blameable.[15]

In his essay "On Luxury," Hume argues that in a luxurious society "mens [sic] temper is soften'd as well as their knowledge improv'd," and then their "humanity appears still more conspicuous; and is the chief characteristic, which distinguishes a civiliz'd age from times of barbarity and ignorance."[16] In Hume's arguments, at their most sanguine, indulgence in luxury actually produces the refinement and self-regulation that prevents such luxury from corrupting the body politic. As he argues in his essay "Of Refinement in the Arts," "The more men refine upon pleasure, the less will they indulge in excesses of any kind."[17]

As Nigel Wood points out in a recent essay, Smith's "immediate preparation for the *Theory of Moral Sentiments*...combined a concern for rhetoric with ethics...[he] would not have been associated with economic theory in the year 1759."[18] Yet, we certainly find here a version of Hume's argument about the beneficial effect of commerce on the refinement of true virtue. Virtue is not achievable in solitude, Smith asserts, for it is in society:

> that [man] first views the propriety and impropriety of his own passions, the beauty or beauty or deformity of his own face. To a man who from his birth was a stranger to society, the objects of his passions, the external bodies which either pleased or hurt him, would occupy his whole attention...Bring him into society, and all his passions will immediately become the causes of new passions. He will observe that mankind approve of some of them and are disgusted by others.[19]

This is extremely reminiscent of Hume's statement in his essay "Of Refinement," that

> [t]he more these refin'd arts advance, the more sociable do men become; nor it is possible, that, when enrich'd with science, and possest of a fund of conversation, they shou'd be contented to remain in solitude, or live with their fellow citizens in that distant manner, which is peculiar to ignorant and barbarous nations. They flock into cities; love to receive and communicate knowledge; to show their

> wit or their breeding; their taste in conversation or living, in cloaths or furniture...So that beside the improvements they receive from knowledge and the liberal arts, 'tis impossible but they must feel an increase of humanity, from the very habit of conversing together, and contributing to each other's pleasure and entertainment.[20]

Smith's argument does link the refinement of the moral sense to social commerce, and though there is no explicit reference to the growth of luxury, there is a distinct echo of Hume's arguments in this idea. Smith is clearly still working within the parameters of a polite moral-sense discourse which, in the face of classical-republican ideas, is attempting "to prove, that...Refinements rather tend to the Encrease of Industry, Civility, and Arts, regulate anew our *moral* as well as *political* sentiments."[21]

WN, however, marks a distinct departure from this moral-sense discourse. This departure is paradoxically rendered most conspicuous by attempts to include the latter text in this earlier tradition. It is argued, for example, in Eleanor Courtemanche's recent work, *The Invisible Hand in British Fiction*, that *WN* can be understood in terms of the moral philosophy of the mid-century in terms of its concern to reconcile luxury and morality. "The idea that capitalism can be virtuous is taken for granted today," Courtemanche argues, is a direct result of the *WN*.[22] But this argument would have sounded at the very least jarring to the ears of the mid-century moral-sense theorists. *WN* has shaken entirely free of the classical-republican underpinnings of moral-sense theory. It no longer subscribes to the idea that luxury can refine the virtues of the individual; instead it takes ethics out of the proper sphere of individuals in order to transfer it to the "invisible hand" of the capitalist system itself. It removes the need for individual virtue to be part of the equation which results in "public good," and insists instead on what Courtemanche has described as the "ironic" virtue which results from the individual's unencumbered indulgence of their private appetites and desires.[23] If there is any validity in the argument that *TMS* and *WN* are both works of moral philosophy, it must lie, I think, in John Guillory's statement that *TMS* can be read as laying "the groundwork for the discipline's eclipse."[24] From the perspective of mid-eighteenth century polite moral-sense theory there is, I suggest, a clear "Adam Smith problem." By mapping Smith's two texts against the history of the gravitational shift in the emphasis of sentimental discourse more generally during the course of the eighteenth century, we can, I think, go some way to understanding this apparent discrepancy.

The Gravitational Shift

In *Sentiment and Sociability*, John Mullan argues that Samuel Richardson's novels bear witness to a shift in sentimental discourse, at least in literary terms. Whereas *Pamela* (1740) seems full of a moral-sense confidence in the power of sentiment to transform the world, by the time Richardson publishes *Clarissa* in 1748–1789 this confidence has receded and we find "habits of sociability" as "limited or exceptional, only just surviving in a world in which fellow-feeling was rare and malevolence prevailed."[25] The literary phenomenon is at this stage in stark contrast to the much more optimistic professions of contemporary moral-sense philosophy. It is striking, however, that these elegiac notes can be heard outside the literary context in France from 1750 in the writings of Rousseau—a writer who was a profound admirer of Richardson. In Rousseau's view, declared the *Monthly Review* in 1758, "there was never a romance equal to, or even so beautiful as Clarissa, in any language whatever."[26]

Rousseau's *First Discourse* (1750) was the winning entry of a competition set by the Academy of Dijon to answer the question of "Whether the re-establishment of *arts* and *sciences* has contributed to the refinement of manners?" Controversially, Rousseau won with a passionate indictment of the arts and sciences as inextricably bound up with luxury and thus the moral corruption of individuals and the body politic. The "sweetness of character, and that urbanity of manners" which results from the refinement of manners in a luxurious society, Rousseau argues, has "the appearance of virtue without possessing one."[27] The *First Discourse* "made such a noise in *France*" that William Bowyer saw fit to publish a translation in England in 1751. Bowyer's "Preface" to his translation is typical of the initial reception of Rousseau's ideas in England. Bowyer acknowledges it as both "one of the finest pieces of oratory" and extremely dangerous in its "persuasion."[28] Rousseau's version of moral sentiment is dangerous in that it offers no accommodation with a polite world.

Over the next decade Rousseau developed his ideas in philosophical and educational treatises and in his vastly influential novel, *Lettres de Deux Amans* (1760) (more commonly referred to as *Julie ou, la Nouvelle Héloïse*). Together these works represent an extended critique of the moral-sense philosophical commitment to economic progress. Rousseau proposes instead that human beings are born with a natural sensibility that is universally destroyed by contact with luxurious civilization. Truly "Innocent and virtuous men," he states, lived in "the simplicity of primitive times."[29] He describes these primitive times as a "beautiful coast deck'd by the hands of nature, towards which we still turn our eyes, whilst with regret, we find ourselves moving from it."[30]

In 1755, Rousseau published his *Discours Sur L'Économie Politique*, translated into English in 1767 as *A Dissertation upon Political Economy*. Rousseau's version of how a political state should be governed occupies much of the same ground as the writings of the moral-sense theorists. Like them, Rousseau's work is clearly in dialogue with classical-republican political theory: "nothing [he argues] can be substituted in the place of morals, for the support of government."[31] Cultivation of individual virtue is therefore paramount, but as you'd expect, he does not subscribe—at least officially—to the idea that such "humanity" can be engendered by living in a luxurious society. Like the classical-republican theorists, Rousseau considers that the refinements attendant upon luxury do not lead to true virtues and will always lead to moral corruption. Where Rousseau differs from the classical-republican theorists is in the value that he places on the "beautiful coast deck'd by the hands of nature" from which we are moving away. For Rousseau, nature is the originary source of virtue, and though modern man is always already in a fallen world, he must still be governed by its values. Rousseau has one foot in the tradition of moral-sense philosophy because he grounds individual virtue in our natural sensibilities—though, in this fallen world, he imagines sensibilities must be brought back to their true nature by education and protected from the corruptions of luxury.

We have therefore two versions of sentimental discourse circulating at this period, both grounded to some extent in the senses. One, at its most sanguine, sees sentimental virtue promoted and cemented by civilization; the other sees native sensibility as corrupted by civilization, only surviving in isolation or retreat from the world, in conditions which reproduce the prelapsarian state of nature as far as is possible.

The Reverend William Dodd's Double Sentiments

The relationship between the polite and primitivist sentimental discourses at the mid-century is vividly illustrated in a case study of Dr William Dodd. Dodd, as the author of a primitivist Rousseauvian novel in 1754 and a poster-boy for moral-sense charitable enterprise in the late 1750s and the early 1760s, very much inhabits both strands of sentimental discourse, and his career illustrates the gravitational shift in the culture of sentiment which took place in the third quarter of the eighteenth century.

When, in 1758, Jonas Hanway, the merchant-philanthropist founder of the Magdalen House, described the qualities that he desired to see in the Chaplain who would preside at the institution, he insisted that the ideal candidate should

> be a man of distinguished piety, with a very peculiar zeal in the great cause of Christianity; a man of good sense and politeness, with that kind of humanity which arises from a knowledge of the human heart.[32]

Hanway's description seems to have been perfectly tailored for William Dodd. In a review of *Reflections upon Death,* Dodd describes his own style as at once "elegant and nervous—neither careless nor yet affected."[33]

The terms "elegant" and "polite" and "sentimental" dominate descriptions both of his life and his preaching.

Dr Dodd, though once referred to as "Chaplain Extraordinary" in the Magdalen House literature, was in fact never the official chaplain at the Magdalen.[34] He was, however, by far the most famous and popular preacher to deliver sermons at the chapel and, in 1761, the governors were so pleased with him that they voted to pay him £100 per annum in order to preach in the chapel every Sunday.[35] "His eloquence," we are told in one of the accounts of Dodd's trial, famously

> melted the hearts of his hearers; they forgot there was such a passion as avarice, and they considered it even as a privilege granted them to support their afflicted fellow-creatures.[36]

Dodd was, moreover, famous for his elegant and luxurious dress and manner. As Samuel Foote's play, *The Cozeners* depicts him in 1778, Dodd

> doesn't pore, with his eyes close to the book, like a clerk that reads the first lesson, not he! But all extemporary, madam; with a cambric handkerchief in one hand, and a diamond ring on the other: And then he waves this way, and that way; and he curtsies, and he bows, and he bounces.[37]

Dodd was the embodiment of the refined and polished sentiments imagined by Hanway. His sermons attracted Royalty, the fashionable and the elite. Following the success of his performances at the Magdalen House chapel, in 1763 he was appointed as "chaplain in ordinary to the King," and subsequently promoted to the even higher post of "Chaplain to his Majesty." According to Gerald Howson's biography, after these promotions he began:

> to affect an ostentation of manner and dress. He bought a coach so that he would not cut too humble a figure when arriving at St. James's Palace.[38]

Dodd, would display himself and gossip at Hyde Park every day, and generally distinguish "himself by his gaiety of appearance at all public places."[39] Dodd frequented all the fashionable and, by novelistic convention, risqué new public spaces of the capital: Ranelagh Gardens, Chelsea, Vauxhall Gardens, Marylebone Gardens, and Bayswater.[40] Dodd's star reached its zenith in 1765 when he was invited to become tutor to the son and heir of Philip Dormer Stanhope, Earl of Chesterfield. Dodd toured Europe with Chesterfield and describes how he "enjoyed the felicity of seeing life under its most brilliant and varied aspects."[41] Dodd seemed to be dining out most splendidly on the moral-sense sentimental promise that luxury and virtue could be reconciled.

Indeed, we even find Dodd explicitly rehearsing the polite moral-sense philosophy of Hume in his *A Sermon on Job* at the Magdalen House Chapel in 1762. Here he cites Hume's *Remarks on Benevolence* in order to praise the altruistic behaviour of mercantile men and financiers. "Remarks on *Benevolence*" Dodd asserts, is a text which is "impossible to read without approbation."[42] "Benevolence," Dodd continues, is "the highest perfection, not only of men, but of angels" and it is "a pleasing reflection, that amidst the prevalence of selfishness and dissipation...in the present day...works of benevolence never abounded more."[43] The establishment of the Magdalen House, Dodd says, addressing the merchant financier founders of the institution, "abundantly testifies [to] the delicacy of your sentiments, and the strength of your judgements."[44] Dodd is confident not just in the virtue of benevolence and its ability to transform the world but also in its ability to be produced by the world. Dodd may not quite have established "benevolence" as a motive sufficient for the butcher, the brewer, and the baker to feed the population from the goodness of their hearts, but he was certainly confident that it could underwrite good works in the world.

In Dodd, the moral-sense founders of the Magdalen House seemed to have found the most perfect exponent of the possibility of marrying virtue and luxury. Dodd was indisputably "polite," but what is most instructive about Dodd as a sentimental case study is that he inhabited both a primitivist and polite moral-sense sentimental discourse from the start. Dodd is appointed as a "polite" sentimental preacher, but his own conception of the idea of politeness, as laid out in his novel *The Sisters* (1754), four years before the opening of the Magdalen House, has much more in common with Rousseauvian primitivism than with polite moral-sense philosophy. *The Sisters* is a sentimental novel in the style of Richardson's *Clarissa*. It tells the story of two sisters who travel to London to make their fortunes, only to become the victims of sexually predatory aristocrats. Dodd's novel clearly echoes Richardson's pessimism in *Clarissa* at the impossibility of reconciling virtue with the world.

Dodd's use of the word "polite" in *The Sisters* is one of the clearest indications of these literary sympathies. In the novel we are told that the male protagonist, Mr. Fortebrand,

> liv'd what the gay world calls a polite life: he had genteel apartments at the other end of town, occupied by as genteel a lady; he was constant at every public place, intimate with every person of quality and taste, and deep in the secrets of the town, insomuch that he was esteem'd one of the most knowing, as well as the most gallant men of the town.[45]

A polite life for Dodd in 1754 with his literary cap on is a life of luxurious sexuality. There is scarcely a single moment in Dodd's novel in which the luxury of modern society can be seen to refine the moral sense, or where politeness and elegance are not synonyms for corruption. The novel does sound the odd note of moral-sense sentimentality. The narrator, for example, certainly echoes the sentiments of some of Hume's *Essays* when he muses:

> how amiable is wisdom, when adorn'd and beautified with elegance and delicacy: in a female lovely and engaging, how doth sense shine, how doth goodness appear with lustre more than her own?[46]

But beyond this, the representation of the elegant and "polite" life as morally corrupt is the absolute rule. The novel sets itself up as a "retirement" narrative, in which the author claims authority to "erect a light-house for the benefit of future mariners" on the grounds of having retreated from the "busy world and escap'd from the tumultuous sea of pleasure and libertinism."[47] In modern education, we are told, the "nobler and more important things are wholly pass'd by; and the precepts of religion esteem'd unnecessary to be taught, and too *well known,* or at least too unpolite to be inculcated."[48] Indeed the evils that befell the sisters is attributed the "polite" education given to them by their mother.[49] When the sisters find themselves in the corrupt, luxurious world of high society, the dominant adjective used to describe the situations is "polite." The procuress, Mrs. Searchwell, is described as "a laughter-loving merry-hearted dame, whose engaging politeness soon won over unwary maidens."[50] And later, when Lucy has been seduced and has become herself a courtesan, she describes her party as "no less polite than the best."[51]

The Limits of Sentimental Virtue in *The Sisters*

The possession of a delicate moral sense is certainly a prerequisite for virtue in Dodd's *The Sisters.* The ideal imagined readers of the novel are addressed as those "whose hearts overflow with tenderness, and whose gentle bosoms are the seats of pity and compassion."[52] The good characters overflow with tears at the sight or description of misery. The extent to which tears gush from characters' eyes is the most reliable register of their virtue. The narrator and Caroline are constantly described as drowning in tears, and the production even of a single tear is the sign that all virtue is not lost. Yet passions are not, as in Hume's *Essays*, refined and cultivated into a "delicacy of taste"; rather this quality is represented as innate but invariably corroded by commerce with the world. As Dodd explains:

> FALLEN as we are among evil times and evil men, it requires no small caution to guide ourselves aright, and to pass thro' life, our

> virtue unshaken, and our principles uncorrupted. We cannot peep out, and receive no damage: we find so little to strengthen us in goodness, so much to establish us in evil that the best heart, the more it is conversant with the world, by degrees dissolves into luke-warmness, and at length totally relaxes the reins to the furious drive of passion and pleasure.[53]

The moral sense in *The Sisters* is offered as a touchstone of virtue, but it is simultaneously represented as an extremely fragile, elusive and in some cases an entirely illusory source of virtue: it cannot be relied upon to moderate and contain the excesses of the world. Dodd's sentimental characters are frequently overwhelmed by their sensibility. Their lack of self-control renders them entirely helpless. When Mr. Jaison receives bad news, his "heart was too full for utterance: he cou'd not speak, it throbb'd too quick, and the faculties of his soul were too much tied up with eager expectation."[54] Sentiment is a fragile and wayward quality here and is in no sense refined by its commerce with the world.

The heart of the novel beats for a Rousseauvian version of natural, unrefined sensibility, but as the novel makes clear, such virtue cannot survive in the world, and Dodd, like many of his proto-Evangelical contemporaries, looks ultimately to religion and propriety to police such sensibility in the world. It is Mrs. Hodson who embodies these supplementary virtues: she is described as very much in possession of sensibility: she is "a woman of the greatest tenderness, as well as goodness of heart."[55] However, she is also a beacon of propriety and religion. Her heart is subject to the dictates of propriety and the will of God. When Mrs Hodson discovers that her friend Caroline is secretly engaged to her nephew, propriety triumphs over the dictates of her heart. She writes to her brother, old Mr. Jaison, to inform him that his son is making a match with a penniless girl. The narrator assures us that Mrs Hodson

> was no enemy to *Caroline*, but on the contrary wish'd her well in every part of her life: nor can any such matter be inferr'd from her proceeding in the manner above related with regard to her nephew. She doubtless therein judged and acted very rightly: well knowing the impropriety there was in such a match without the consent of Mr *Jaison*'s father, well knowing the breach of duty, which must be made thereby, and the calamities, which wou'd be probable therefore to befall him.[56]

Propriety is shown here to be the rightful guide of morality, however much it may pain the heart.

In a similar vein, Mrs Hodson is shown to have no time for the unrestrained outpourings of the heart, as we learn when she reprimands Mr. Sanson for his excess of grief on discovering his daughter is "ruin'd": "Hold sir, let me entreat you: forbear these rash ventings of your passion;

and bear yourself with patience becoming a man and a Christian."[57] For Mrs Hodson, all promptings of the human heart should ultimately be subjugated to the will of God. It is not difficult to imagine that the sympathies of Dodd's ideal imagined readers are with Sanson, for, as we have been told, these are readers "whose hearts overflow with tenderness, and whose gentle bosoms are the seats of pity and compassion."[58] But the official moral of the novel is that such sentimental virtue is insufficient without the supplement of religion and propriety.

William Dodd, then, occupies two different and ostensibly conflicting sentimental discourses in the early years of his career. In his literary persona, he espouses primitivist sentimental ideas which link luxury with corruption, but in his civic persona and as "Chaplain Extraordinary" at the Magdalen House for Penitent Prostitutes, he explicitly voices the moral-sense ideas of Hume.

Politeness—Sentiment—Primitivism

Dodd's ability to inhabit both the polite and the primitivist sentimental discourses at the mid-century suggests that they were not necessarily perceived as conflicting by contemporaries. Indeed, as I have argued elsewhere, it is more helpful to think of sentimental discourse in the mid-century as a continuum between the sanguine politeness of Hume's writing and the elegiac pessimism of Rousseau's primitivism.[59] Historically this is supported by the considerable professions of mutual respect and love with which Hume and Rousseau began their famous friendship. In 1763, Hume positively gushes in his expression of regret at not being in London to host Rousseau after the latter has been forced into exile. In response to Madame de Boufflers, who is attempting to secure an invitation to London for Rousseau, Hume replies: "Good God! madam, how much I regret my being absent…on this occasion…there is no man in Europe of whom I have entertained a higher idea, and whom I would be prouder to serve."[60] And later in 1765 when the deal has finally been brokered, Rousseau declares to Hume: "your great views, your astonishing impartiality, your genius, would lift you far above the rest of mankind, if you were less attached to them by the goodness of your heart."[61]

The mutual respect for each other's work, which found root in their mutual distrust of reason, and their commitment to the idea of a universal moral sense, was cemented, at least initially, by their mutual indulgence of precisely this sense. Soon after Hume first met Rousseau he declared:

> He has an excellent warm heart; and, in conversation, kindles often to a degree of heat which looks like inspiration. I love him much, and hope that I shall have some share in his affections.[62]

Rousseau, it seems, reciprocated. As he stepped foot on the "land of liberty," we are told, "he leaped on his illustrious friend's neck, embraced him without uttering a word, and covered his face with kisses and tears."[63]

As key Enlightenment figures sharing a commitment to the value of the senses, Hume and Rousseau had much in common. But in life, as in philosophy, their ideas of nature and the heart were ultimately incompatible. Hume and Rousseau fell out notoriously badly and Rousseau fled to the "wilds" of Derbyshire. Hume's response was to question whether Rousseau had cultivated sufficient resources to enjoy solitude. The delicacy of Rousseau's passions had not, he suggests, been adequately transformed into a delicacy of taste. Rousseau, Hume asserts

> has reflected, properly speaking, and studied very little; and has not indeed much knowledge. He has only *felt,* during the whole course of his life; and in this respect, his sensibility rises to a pitch beyond what I have seen any example of: but it still gives him a more acute feeling of pain than of pleasure. He is like a man who were stript not only of his clothes, but of his skin, and turned out in that situation to combat with the rude and boisterous elements, such as perpetually disturb this lower world.[64]

The episode illustrates how much the two Enlightenment sentimental philosophers had in common, but also the ultimately incompatible nature of their views. It suggests, I think, both the extent of the common ground between the polite and the primitivist sentimental philosophers, but also disparities, which would become increasingly apparent as the primitivist version of sentiment gained ascendancy in the world of both literature and political discourse in the second half of the eighteenth century.

The Ascendency of Primitivist Sentimental Discourse

In the early 1750s, Rousseau's ideas had been greeted predominantly as "sophistical" and often, indeed, as highly dangerous, certainly outside the literary context. But in 1760 Rousseau's novel, *La Nouvelle Héloïse* was greeted as a "brilliant success" and heralded the rise of Rousseau's reputation more generally in England in the 1760s. So much so, that it was, as I have described, to England that he turned for refuge after the adverse reception of *Émile* (1762) in France forced him into exile. Once here, he was by all accounts the absolute centre of attention, to the point that his host, Hume, was once slightingly referred to as "the shower of the lion."[65] Rousseau was a star in London; *La Nouvelle Héloïse* was much lauded and his ideas as well as his ingenuity seem to have found an appreciative audience.[66]

Rousseauvian primitivist ideas were increasingly coming to dominate the understanding of sentimental ideas in the 1760s in the literary world. A novel such as Henry Mackenzie's *Man of Feeling* (1771) is typical in representing the native virtue of the protagonist as surviving only in retreat from the world. Perhaps most illustrative of this sea change is Henry Brooke's multi-volume *History of a Fool of Quality* (1765–1770). This novel has been read as a both an "extensive and radical defence of commerce against landed wealth" and as a novel "more deeply stamped with the seal of Rousseau—the Rousseau of the second *Discourse* and of *Émile* than is any other book of the period."[67] It is both: the first few volumes chart the contrasting education of two brothers—one reared a luxurious aristocrat, the other a virtuous merchant refined by his commerce with the world; the last few volumes chart the education of the next generation in which virtue is represented as spontaneous and in retreat from the world.[68] Brooke's novel, published between 1765 and 1770 enacts the ascendancy of primitivist sentimental ideas in this period.

It is perhaps not surprising then to find these ascendant cultural truths spilling over from literature into the world. Responses to the translation of Rousseau's *Discourse upon the Origin and Foundation of the Inequality* (1761), still register a degree of scepticism about the applicability of Rousseau's ideas in the modern world, but there is also a much greater sympathy.[69] A 1762 article in the *Critical Review* exemplifies this softening towards Rousseau. The article starts by rehearsing a critique of Rousseau's second *Discourse*, but then launches into a much more searing critique of moral-sense philosopher John Millar for his arguments against Rousseau in *A New Estimate of Manners and Principles: Or, a Comparison between Ancient and Modern Times*. The reviewer concludes that Millar is to Rousseau "as a dwarf climbing up the knees of a colossus."[70] In same year, the writer Oliver Goldsmith can be found agreeing with Rousseau that any

> attempt to introduce the sciences into a nation of wandering barbarians, is only to render them more miserable than even nature designed they should be. A state of simplicity is best fitted to a state of solitude.[71]

Goldsmith follows Rousseau's argument to the extent that he believes the refinement of the arts and sciences is only appropriate for nations which have already become populous and luxurious.[72] By 1762, Rousseau's second *Discourse,* it seems, was attracting as much attention as his novel had at the beginning of the decade, and much of it was supportive.

There are signs, also, that sensibility is increasingly being perceived as a problematic moral compass in the world of charity. Just four years after William Dodd's polite sentimental sermonizing at the Magdalen Chapel, we find a distinctly Rousseauvian sentimental note sounded in Newton

Ogle's *A Sermon Preached at the Anniversary Meeting of the Governors of the Magdalen Charity* (1766). This text argues, in a familiar sentimental vein, that "A greater Delicacy of Frame, a greater Sensibility" is characteristic of the female sex and that "this Constitution was intended by Providence to fit them for the Place they hold, and to be the Cause of that Happiness in the Creation, which another Kind of Constitution would not so well have produced."[73] Here, we are ostensibly again on a moral-sense territory which makes a virtue out of "Delicacy" and "Sensibility," and sees these attributes as a bulwark against corruption. But Ogle's views prove decidedly less sanguine. He goes on to argue that

> in this corrupt World Things are out of Order! That very Constitution, which the Author of Nature intended for good, too often exposes them to an unequal Contest, and instead of being for their Welfare "becomes unto them an Occasion of Falling."[74]

Ogle's views are decidedly Rousseauvian. Luxury and commerce, for Ogle, are not forces for refinement. Indeed, he says:

> as the Intercourse of Mankind increases, so do the Causes of Temptation. Luxury and Leisure multiply the Number of Seducers, Licentiousness introduces Opportunity, and vast Difference of Fortune often makes the Tempter too strong for the tempted.[75]

Ogle's sermon proceeds in unmistakably Rousseauvian manner. We are told that "It is in rich and polished States that Vice and Misery are found in their greatest Extremes."[76] Ogle does refer to the "Many Advantages [that] attend the Increase of Wealth and Power," but, states, "Great Wealth produces great Inequality, great Inequalities great Luxury; these open new Veins of Vice, and tend unavoidably to corrupt those whose Condition less allows of Corruption."[77] It is not possible, Ogle admits, to return to a "State of Simplicity," and instead he proposes the introduction of "Correctives and Palliatives" such as the Magdalen House, "as may prevent the Increase, though they do not wholly remove the Cause, of Evil."[78] Like Dodd in *The Sisters*, Ogle is proposing to supplement the virtue of sensibility, for he can find no accommodation between virtue and commerce.

In the 1750s it seems, William Dodd was able to inhabit both the polite and primitivist discourse without any apparent contradiction between the two. Indeed, Dodd's biographer, Howson, speculates that Dodd was invited to preach at the Magdalen House Chapel not

> *in spite* of his rubbishy novel but *because of* it; in other words, because some well-intentioned but uncritical alderman believed it showed Dodd to be one clergyman at least with a genuine concern for, and experience of, this subject [prostitution].[79]

But as in the culture more generally this understanding of "politeness" was straining at the seams, and evidence that Dodd's understanding and embrace of the role of "polite" preacher was not associated with much moral refinement, was beginning to emerge.

In 1766, Dodd lost vast sums of money on an investment in a private chapel for the rich and famous.[80] Then, in 1772, Dodd and his wife were discovered trying to bribe their way into the living of St. George, Hanover Square. As a result, Dodd was sacked from his post of Chaplain to the King.[81] After several years of scandal and rumours, Dodd was caught red-handed in February 1777 having attempted to forge the signature of the Earl of Chesterfield on a bond for £4,200, and was brought to trial. Six months later Dodd was hanged at Tyburn. His attempted fraud had been a desperate attempt to pay off the vast debts accrued by a life of considerable luxury. Dodd was styled a victim of the "extravagance of the times, which involves us all in the madness of living beyond our incomes."[82] It was clear that "a delicacy of sense" had failed to moderate his appetites.

Dodd inevitably fell back, however, in his defence, on the sentimental narratives which had underpinned his early career. Dodd styles himself above all as a "victim of circumstance," and it is in this vein, that Dodd makes his appeal to his former pupil, the Earl of Chesterfield. Dodd pleads that he had "no intention to defraud my lord Chesterfield."[83] He appeals to Lord Chesterfield's "tenderness for me, as my pupil," stating "I love him."[84] At this point, we are told, Dodd "wept bitterly."[85] When Dodd finally recovers his composure, he concludes: "I hope he will, according to that mercy that is in his heart, shew clemency to me."[86] But, we are told "his lordship paid not the least regard to his tears."[87] In sharp contrast to the description of Dodd at the height of his sentimental powers preaching at the Magdalen Chapel, his eloquence is no longer able to melt:

> the hearts of his hearers; [so that] they forgot there was such a passion as avarice, and they considered it even as a privilege granted them to support their afflicted fellow-creatures.[88]

The plea for the essential goodness of his heart to be recognized falls on deaf ears. By the time of Dodd's trial such sentimental virtues had become known almost exclusively for their weakness, corruptibility, and lack of agency in the world.

When, after judgement of death was pronounced, Dodd was asked if he had anything to say in mitigation of the judgement, his reply amounted to a complete renunciation of the sentimental ideas which had driven his public life and works:

> Being distinguished and elated by the confidence of mankind, I had too much confidence in myself…I did not consider the danger of vanity, nor suspect the deceitfulness of my own heart.[89]

Like many of his contemporaries in the world of religion and philanthropy, Dodd ultimately abandoned all belief in the idea that the heart offers a sufficient moral compass with which to navigate the world and embraces evangelical ideas. Indeed while in prison awaiting his sentence Dodd consciously renounced the polite Anglicanism which he had so heartily advocated throughout the middle of the century and threw himself into the arms of those very impolite Methodists who "in the days of his prosperity he had often cast a slur upon."[90] For the Methodists God, and not man, nor even divine seeds planted by God in the heart of man, must provide all guidance in issues of morality.

TMS and the Limits of Sentimental Virtue

In terms of the Adam Smith Problem, *TMS*, as I stated above, has been characterized as a book which "considers human nature as universally sympathetic, other-orientated, social and thus moral" and therefore as offering a disturbingly different vision of the world to *WN* which "treats human behavior as almost always self-interested and calculating"?[91] However, if we return to *TMS* in the light of the two poles of eighteenth-century sentimental discourse which I have identified above, the ideas in the text often seem to have more in common with pessimistic, "primitivist" visions of Rousseau and of Dodd's novel, than with the optimism of Hume's essays and Dodd's sermons. Indeed, this "primitivist" pessimism about uncultivated human nature in the world is increasingly emphasized in the later editions of the work. But even in the 1759 edition *TMS* seems to place surprisingly little faith in native benevolence either as an effective agent in the world or as a native instinct that is always capable of being refined into an effective agent in the world.

The famous opening statement of *TMS* in 1758, itself exemplifies a pretty lukewarm confidence in the virtuous propensities of human nature. This opening is often cited as an indictment of the Hobbesian proposition that human passions are not to be trusted and that strong government is therefore necessary.[92] Yet it lays claim only to "some principles in...[our] nature" which "interest...[us] in the fortune of others."[93] By the time Smith's second edition was published in 1761, his confidence in the innate moral sense seems to have waned further. He describes these innate principles of benevolence as a "feeble spark" "which Nature has lighted up in the human heart," one that is incapable of "counteracting the strongest impulses of self-love."[94] A more powerful source of virtue, Smith suggests, requires:

> reason, principle, conscience, the inhabitant of the breast, the man within, the great judge and arbiter of our conduct. It is he, who, whenever we are about to act so as to affect the happiness of others, calls to us with a voice capable of astonishing the most presumptuous of our passions...[95]

Certainly, as I argued above, this "man within" is envisaged by Smith to be the product of social commerce with the world. Indeed, this aspect of *TMS* is very much strengthened and elaborated in the subsequent editions. Society is figured as a mirror in which no man can see the "deformity of his own character, of the propriety or demerit of his own sentiments and conduct, of the beauty or deformity of his own mind."[96] Yet there is also a profound ambivalence in *TMS* as to whether this "feeble spark" is universally available to be cultivated into the highest form of virtue. In *TMS* virtue figures both as "humanity," and "generosity." "Humanity," or "benevolence" as Smith sometimes terms it, is native and spontaneous and requires "no self-denial, no self-command, no great exertion of the sense of propriety."[97] Acts of humanity, he tells us, consist "only in doing what this exquisite sense would of its own accord prompt us to do."[98] It is a virtue, but a very weak virtue. "Generosity," on the other hand, comprises "the great, the awful and respectable, the virtues of self-denial, of self-government." It is founded upon the effort "of the person principally concerned, to bring down his emotions to what the spectator can go along with."[99]

> Generosity is different from humanity. Those two qualities, which at first sight seem so nearly allied, do not always belong to the same person. Humanity is the virtue of a woman, generosity of a man.[100]

This gendering of virtues is reminiscent of Hume's essay "Of the Delicacy of Taste and Passion," where he argues that "woman naturally have a more "delicate Taste" both of the Ornaments of life… and the ordinary decencies of behaviour."[101] In Hume's argument "a delicacy of taste" is a goal that men should aim for and can only achieve through their cultivation of the liberal arts and their engagement in commerce. In Smith, however, this natural "delicacy of taste" which has its equivalent in the "soft virtue" of "humanity" is an inferior virtue, not something that men should aspire to. Indeed, in Smith's representation, this "humanity," which he has described as "the virtue of a woman," is almost indistinguishable from that classical-republican bugbear, effeminacy, particularly in *TMS*'s 1790 edition.[102] Here he tells us, "the soft virtue of humanity flourishes the most, and is capable of the highest improvement…[in] the mild sunshine of undisturbed tranquillity, in the calm retirement of undissipated and philosophical leisure."[103] All this sounds extremely positive, yet the remainder of this paragraph is devoted to classical-republican anxieties about the limits of humanity and the moral implications of luxury. Smith tells us "[t]he situations in which the gentle virtue of humanity can be most happily cultivated, are by no means the same with those which are best fitted for forming the austere virtue of self-command."[104] In such "undisturbed tranquillity," Smith concludes, "the greatest and noblest exertions of self-command have little exercise."[105] "Humanity" or "benevolence" in *TMS* is mostly figured as a separate and inferior virtue and where men are concerned is only a "perfect virtue" if it joins to "to all the soft, the amiable, and the gentle virtues...all the great, the awful, and the respectable."[106]

Indeed, by 1790, Smith is even more emphatic about the dangers of native sensibility. Here he tells us that when men are naturally in possession of this heightened sensibility it is:

> sometimes so strong as to render all self-command impossible. No sense of honour can control the fears of the man who is weak enough to faint, or to fall into convulsions, upon the approach of danger. Whether such weakness of nerves, as it has been called, may not, by gradual exercise and proper discipline, admit of some cure, may, perhaps, be doubtful.[107]

It is difficult not to hear in this paragraph distinct echoes of various descriptions of the dangers of native sensibility in William Dodd's novel, *The Sisters*. Smith's man of sensibility, is very like Mr. Jaison when he receives bad news: his "heart was too full for utterance: he cou'd not speak, it throbb'd too quick, and the faculties of his soul were too much tied up with eager expectation."[108] He is not an effective agent in the world.

"Benevolence" and "humanity" are undoubtedly recognized as virtues of some sort in Smith's *TMS*. However, as Smith complains of "those Systems which make Virtue consist in Benevolence," the defect is that they do not take into account the "virtues of prudence, vigilance, circumspection, temperance, constancy, firmness."[109] In Dodd's *The Sisters*, "humanity" and "benevolence" must be propped up both by a sense of propriety and by submission to the word of God; in Smith, the props are propriety and justice—which emerge from internal dialogue with the "impartial spectator," "the man within, the great judge and arbiter of our conduct."[110] The "man within" is the product of politeness, of commerce with the world in the broadest sense, there is no absolute confidence in *TMS* that "humanity" will turn into "generosity." Equally, as we saw above, Smith's subscription in *TMS* to the idea that the moral sense is refined through social commerce is not accompanied by any explicit commitment to the idea that this moral sense is refined through economic commerce. There is no explicit sense either that, even in its refined state, this moral sense might provide a bulwark against the excesses of luxury.

TMS, I suggest, does not really live up to its billing as a text which "considers human nature as universally sympathetic, other-orientated, social and thus moral."[111] *TMS*, it seems to me, is already inflected with a primitivist pessimism about the possibility of our native virtues of "benevolence" and "humanity" having any real agency in the world. I have argued elsewhere that this pessimism casts a shadow on even the most sanguine of the polite moral economists and can, I think, be traced to the origin of this discipline as a dialogue with classical-republican ideas.[112] The "Adam Smith question" has focused predominantly on the absence in *WN* of any significant role for the moral sense which had been so central to the *TMS*. It seems to me, however, that given the extent to which polite moral-sense philosophy of the mid-century was formulated both within and against the frame of classical-republican ideas, it is in many ways the absence of economic preoccupations from *TMS* which is the more significant question.

Is it perhaps the case that even as early as 1759, when Adam Smith wrote his first version of *TMS,* it was no longer possible to argue that benevolence and humanity might be refined by the rising tide of luxury into virtues strong enough to provide a bulwark against its morally corrosive properties. Two things are certainly clear. With the ascendancy of the primitivist sentimental discourse, we find that the virtues of refinement are increasingly figured in Rousseauvian terms, as having "the appearance of [a] virtue" without possessing any.[113] We find also that native sensibility increasingly features as a weak and wayward virtue, offering no true compass for navigating the world. Virtue is represented only as true virtue when it is supplemented by religion and propriety, or in the case of Smith, by propriety and justice in the form of the impartial spectator. But even then, as, we have seen, the true virtue of "generosity" which emerges from dialogue with the impartial spectator, does not seem to be available to all men and certainly not to all women. There is certainly no sense in *TMS* that we might expect our "dinner" from the "benevolence" of the "butcher, the brewer, or the baker," and absolutely no guarantee that "generosity" is a sufficiently widespread virtue in society for this to be a reliable source of sustenance.[114]

It seems possible to me that even as early as 1759 the rise of primitivist sentimental ideas had given a new currency to the classical-republican ideas which framed mid-century polite economic discourse: that the equation of refined manners with true virtue was becoming increasingly problematic. Smith's avoidance of economics in *TMS* might indeed be understood as a tacit admission that moral-sense theory had really reached its limits in this area. Certainly only eight years later, in 1767, that we find James Steuart writing, in An *Inquiry into the Principles of Political Economy*:

> As my subject is different from that of morals, I have no occasion to consider the term luxury in any other than a political sense, to wit, as a principle which produces employment, and gives bread to those who supply the demands of the rich. For this reason I have chosen the above definition of it, which conveys no idea, either of abuse, sensuality, or excess.[115]

There was, it seems, a perceived need to move discussions about economics beyond the impasse of the classical-republican parameters which had determined polite moral-sense economics. The "Adam Smith" problem, is much less conspicuous, I suggest, if we read his two key texts in relation to the gravitational shift in the discourse of sentiment: if we see *TMS* as a text already inflected with pessimism about the possibility that "benevolence" might have any agency in the world.

Notes

1 See "Introduction" to the present volume, p. 10.
2 Ibid.
3 See John Mullan, *Sentiment and Sensibility: The Language of Feeling in the Eighteenth Century* (Oxford: Oxford University Press, 1988) and Michael L. Frazer, *The Enlightenment of Sympathy: Justice and the Moral Sentiments in the Eighteenth Century and Today* (Oxford: Oxford University Press, 2010).
4 Adam Smith, *The Theory of Moral Sentiments* (hereafter *TMS* [1759]), (London: A. Millar, A. Kincaid and J. Bell, 1759), 168.
5 Ibid., 457.
6 Adam Smith, *TMS*, 2 vols. (hereafter *TMS* [1790]) (London: A. Strahan, A. Cadell, W. Creech and J. Bell, 1790), 2:213.
7 Adam Smith, *An Inquiry into the Nature and Causes of the Wealth of Nations* (hereafter *WN*), 2 vols. (London: W. Strahan: and T. Cadell, 1776), 1:17.
8 Ibid., 2:35.
9 D. D. Raphael and A. L. Macfie, "Introduction," in Adam Smith, *The Theory of Moral Sentiments* (Indianapolis: Liberty Fund, 1984), 20–21.
10 Dugald Stewart, "Account of the Life and Writings of Adam Smith, LLD," cited in Raphael and Macfie, "Introduction," 2.
11 Raphael and Macfie, "Introduction," 2.
12 Ibid., 21–22.
13 Ibid., 20.
14 David Hume, *An Enquiry Concerning the Principle of Morals* (London: A. Millar, 1751), 30.
15 Ibid., 30–31.
16 David Hume, "Of Luxury," in *Political Discourses* (Edinburgh: A. Kincaid and A. Donaldson, 1752), 30.
17 Ibid., 28.
18 Nigel Wood, "Adam Smith's *The Theory of Moral Sentiments* in 1759: Spectatorship, Duty, and Social Improvement," in *Reading 1759: Literary Culture in Mid-Eighteenth Century Britain and France*, eds. Shaun Regan (Lewisburg: Bucknell University Press), 57.
19 Adam Smith, *TMS* [1759], 256.
20 David Hume, *Essays and Treatises on Several Subjects*, 4 vols. (Edinburgh: Kincaid, and A. Donaldson, 1753), 4:27.
21 Hume, *Enquiry*, 30–31.
22 Eleanor Courtemanche, *The 'Invisible Hand' and British Fiction, 1818–1860: Adam Smith, Political Economy and the Genre of Realism* (Basingstoke: Palgrave Macmillan, 2011), 4.
23 Ibid., 1.

24 John Guillory, *Cultural Capital: The Problem of Literary and Canon Formation*, cited in ibid., 26.
25 Mullan, *Sentiment and Sensibility*, 13.
26 K-n-k, "A Letter from Mr. Rousseau, of Geneva, to Mr. d'Alembert, of Paris, Concerning the Effects of Theatrical Entertainments on the Manners of Mankind," *Monthly Review, or, Literary Journal* 20 (1759), 132.
27 Jean-Jacques Rousseau, *Discourse Which Carried the Praemium at the Academy of Dijon, In MDCCL. On this Question, Propos'd by the Said Academy, Whether the Re-Establishment of Arts and Sciences Has Contributed to the Refining of Manners* (London: W. Owen, 1761), 13.
28 William Boyer, "Translator's Preface," in Rousseau, *Discourse Which Carried the Præmium*, iii–iv.
29 Rousseau, *Discourse Which Carried the Præmium*, 36.
30 Ibid.
31 Jean-Jacques Rousseau, *The Miscellaneous Works of Mr. J. J. Rousseau*, 5 vols. (London: T. Becket and P. A. de Hondt, 1767), 2:18.
32 Jonas Hanway, *A Plan for Establishing a Charity-House or Charity-Houses, for the Reception of Repenting Prostitutes. To Be Called the Magdalen Charity* (London, 1758), 10.
33 Cited in Gerald Howson, *The Macaroni Parson: A Life of the Unfortunate Dr Dodd* (London: Hutchinson, 1973), 60.
34 S. B. P. Pearce, *An Ideal in the Working: The Story of the Magdalen Hospital, 1758–1795* (London: published privately, 1958), 44. Pearce notes: "The first anniversary of the formation of the Committee in April, 1758, was observed by a dinner followed by an anniversary service. The preacher was Dr Dodd, who afterwards offered to preach on Sunday evenings and to act as "Chaplain Extraordinary." These offers were accepted but the title never occurs again and he was never Chaplain."
35 Howson, *Macaroni Parson*, 45–46.
36 [Anon.], "Particulars of the Rev. Dr. Dodd's Trial for Forgery," *Sentimental Magazine, or, General Assemblage of Science, Taste, and Entertainment* (1777), 73.
37 Samuel Foote, *The Cozeners; A Comedy, in Three Acts. As It Is Performed at the Theatre-Royal in the Haymarket* (London: T. Sherlock, 1778), 24.
38 Howson, *Macaroni Parson*, 60–61.
39 William Dodd, "Memoirs of the Late Dr. William Dodd," *The Town and Country Magazine, or, Universal Repository of Knowledge, Instruction, and Entertainment* 9 (London, 1777), 372–7 (372).
40 Howson, *Macaroni Parson*, 58.
41 Edward Draper, "Doctor Dodd," *The Train: A First-Class Magazine* 1:6 (1856): 355.
42 William Dodd, *A Sermon on Job, Chap. xxix. Ver. 11–13. Preached at the Anniversary Meeting of the Governors of the Magdalen Charity on Thursday, March 18, 1762* (London: W. Faden, 1762), 5.
43 Ibid., 7.
44 Ibid., 31.
45 William Dodd, *The Sisters, or The History of Lucy and Caroline Sanson, Entrusted to a False Friend*, 2 vols. (London: T. Waller, 1754), 2:35.
46 Ibid., 2:90.
47 Ibid., 1:iv and iii.
48 Ibid., 1:x.
49 Ibid., 1:3.
50 Ibid., 1:24

51 Ibid., 1:76.
52 Ibid., 1:17.
53 Ibid., 1:iv.
54 Ibid., 2:64.
55 Ibid., 2:286.
56 Ibid., 2:240.
57 Ibid., 2:143.
58 Ibid., 1:17.
59 See Mary Peace, *Changing Sentiments and the Magdalen Hospital: Luxury, Virtue and the Senses in Eighteenth-Century Culture* (New York: Routledge, 2017), 88–98.
60 John Hill Burton, *The Life and Correspondence of David Hume* (Edinburgh: W. Tait, 1846), 108.
61 Thomas Edward Richie, *An Account of the Life and Writings of David Hume, Esq.* (London: T. Cadell, 1807), 160.
62 Hill Burton, *Life and Correspondence*, 304.
63 Ibid., 303.
64 Ibid., 313–14.
65 Mr. Rouet, "Mr. Rouet to Baron Mure, London, Jan. 25, 1766," in *Selections from the Family Papers Preserved at Caldwell MDCCLXV-MDCCCXXI*, 3 vols., ed. William Mure (Glasgow: np, 1854), 2:61.
66 See Robert Zaretsky and John T. Scott, *The Philosopher's Quarrel: Rousseau, Hume and the Limits of Human Understanding* (New Haven, CT: Yale University Press, 2010), 115.
67 Markman Ellis, *The Politics of Sensibility: Race, Gender and Commerce in the Sentimental Novel* (Cambridge: Cambridge University Press, 1996), 140 and C. E. Vaughan, "Henry Brooke, *The Fool of Quality*," in *The Cambridge History of English and American Literature*, 18 vols. (Cambridge: Cambridge University Press, 1907–1921), 10:3, §10.
68 See Mary Peace, "Sentimentality in the Service of Methodism: John Wesley's Abridgement of Henry Brooke's *Fool of Quality*," *Religion in the Age of Enlightenment* 4 (2013): 277–308.
69 Rousseau's *Discourse upon the Origin and Foundation of the Inequality among Mankind* had appeared in France in 1755, but was only published in England 1762 in the wake of Rousseau' s success with his novel.
70 [Anon.], Art. 26, "A New Estimate of Manners and Principles: Or, a Comparison between Ancient and Modern Times, in the Three Great Articles of Knowledge, Happiness, and Virtue. Part III. of Happiness; in which some Principles of Mr. Rousseau are Examined," *Critical Review, Or, Annals of Literature* 13 (1762): 270.
71 Oliver Goldsmith, *The Citizen of the World; Or Letters from a Chinese Philosopher, Residing in London, to His Friends in the East* (London: J. Newbery and W. Bristow, 1762), 75–76.
72 Ibid., 76.
73 Newton Ogle, *A Sermon Preached at the Anniversary Meeting of the Governors of the Magdalen Charity, on Thursday May 1, 1766* (London: W. Sandby and W. Faden, 1766), 6.
74 Ibid., 6–7.
75 Ibid., 7.
76 Ibid., 1.
77 Ibid., 10.
78 Ibid., 11.
79 Howson, *Macaroni Parson*, 42–43.

80 H. F. B. Compston, *The Magdalen Hospital: The Story of a Great Charity* (London: Society for Promoting Christian Knowledge, 1917), 120.
81 See ibid., 122.
82 Anon., "An Account of the Life and Writings of William Dodd, LL. D.," *The London Review of English and Foreign Literature* 5 (1777): 473–5 (474).
83 Anon., "Account of the Examination of the Rev. Dr Dodd, at Guildhall, for Forgery," *Universal Magazine of Knowledge and Pleasure* 60 (1777): 89–91 (91).
84 Ibid., 91.
85 Ibid.
86 Ibid.
87 Ibid.
88 Anon., "Particulars of the Rev. Dr Dodd's Trial for Forgery," *Sentimental Magazine, or, General Assemblage of Science, Taste, and Entertainment* (1777): 73–78 (73).
89 Anon., "Speech and Condemnation of Dr Dodd at the Session of the Old Bailey, which Ended on Friday the 16th instant," *The Gentleman's Magazine: And Historical Chronicle* 47 (1777): 226–7 (226–7).
90 Anon., "Dr William Dodd," *The Wesleyan-Methodist Magazine* 20 (1841): 12–13 (12).
91 Adelman and Packham, "Introduction," p. 10.
92 Wood, "Smith's *Theory of Moral Sentiments*," 61.
93 Smith, *TMS* [1759], 1:1
94 Adam Smith, *The Theory of Moral Sentiments*, 2 vols (hereafter *TMS* [1761]) (London: A. Millar, 1761), 2:213.
95 Ibid.
96 Adam Smith, *TMS* [1790], 1:277–8.
97 Smith, *TMS* [1759], 365.
98 Ibid., 365.
99 Ibid., 41.
100 Ibid., 364.
101 David Hume, *Essays Moral, Political and Literary* (Edinburgh: R. Fleming and A. Alison, 1741), 4.
102 Ibid., 364.
103 Smith, *TMS* [1790], 1:377.
104 Ibid.
105 Ibid., 1:378.
106 Smith, *TMS* [1759], 41.
107 Smith, *TMS* [1790], 1:387–8.
108 Dodd, *The Sisters*, 2:64.
109 Smith, *TMS* [1759],464.
110 Smith, *TMS* [1761], 2:213.
111 Adelman and Packham, "Introduction," p. 10.
112 Peace, *Changing Sentiments*, 96–98.
113 Rousseau, *Discourse Which Carried the Praemium*, 13.
114 Smith, *WN*, 1:17.
115 James Steuart, *An Inquiry into the Principles of Political Oeconomy: Being an Essay on the Science of Domestic Policy in Free Nations*, 2 vols. (London: A. Millar and T. Cadell, 1767), 1:32n.

8 The Anxiety of Inheritance

Work and the Impasses of Accumulation in Dickens's *The Old Curiosity Shop*

Joshua Gooch

In their introduction, our editors detail the ways in which Adam Smith introduces "the problematic of representation...at the heart of economic discourse" as well as how later political economists revise this visual problematic in order to bifurcate "sentiment and science." Rather than suggesting that this division can be readily overcome, they suggest a rediscovery of the liaison of empirical economics and moral philosophy that resides at the heart of Smith's work, an approach that authorizes the revision of theory in light of human and moral experience. This division of the visible and the invisible to distinguish the measured and the felt resonates with another description of nineteenth-century science, that of Henri Bergson. In *Time and Free Will*, Bergson argues that empiricism relies on a notion of quantity as homogenous, spacialized, and countable, and thus overlooks the analytic possibilities offered by quality, which he describes as heterogeneous, temporal, and uncountable. To rethink the division of the visible and the sensible in political economy, then, may demand a consideration of what escapes count, in particular the ever-ramifying processes of sensation, action, and memory that Bergson calls "duration."[1] In the following essay, I consider how the visible dimension of the political economic problematic may operate in a literary text as an articulation of the counted and the felt. This is to explore how quantity and quality may operate upon one another, and how the passage of objects and of intensities functions across different levels of being, modes of experience, and discourses of knowledge-making. It is to consider what, in a word, affects.

As we will see, questions of affect in nineteenth-century literature often produce sentimental solutions, perhaps most especially when confronting issues of political economy. The focus of my argument, Charles Dickens's *The Old Curiosity Shop* (1840–1841), has been extensively explored by critics for its sentimentality and its allegorization of an emergent capitalism.[2] As an extension of this work, I argue that inheritance as a political and economic discourse informs the novel's thematics, its representation of emotions, and its uses of sentimentality. I argue that the passage of money and objects between characters and across generations and the transfers of affect between characters and the novel's readers reveal a complex interweaving of the political and economic with the affective and the sentimental. The novel's initial pages articulate this connection of the economic and the affective through Nell's grandfather. He explains to the visiting Master Humphrey his plans for an extravagant bequest: "I would leave [Nell]—not with resources which could be easily spent or squandered away, but with what would place her beyond the reach of want for ever. You mark me, sir? She shall have no pittance, but a fortune."[3] To understand the radical fantasy that underlies this imagined inheritance, one must first gauge the size of this hoped-for fortune. By examining the fortunes and incomes of characters in Austen, Balzac, and James, economist Thomas Piketty estimates that extreme wealth during this era and beyond measures between 50 and 100 times the national average income.[4] Piketty estimates early nineteenth-century Britain's average income was about 35 l., a salary the novel's schoolmaster finds delightful.[5] This puts Nell's imagined yearly income between 1,750 l. and 3,500 l., sums that would demand a capital investment of 58,000–117,000 l. at an expected return of 3%. This is the size of Nell's grandfather's dream of leaving Nell a substantial inheritance. It is also the affective basis for his gambling and mental decline, and it will indeed eventually place Nell well "beyond the reach of want for ever"—in her grave, driven there by the desires attached to this imagined inheritance by characters such as the libidinous rage troll Quilp and Nell's own egoistic brother, Fred. In this novel, to count is to feel, and to feel is to count.

Although little is inherited in *The Old Curiosity Shop*, the novel's evocations and failures of inheritance can help unveil how questions of inheritance and bequest intertwined political economic discourses and the affective in Britain during the 1840s. These impasses and failures in some ways mirror ways in which the increasingly limited sphere of "proper" political economy framed inheritance as a political rather than economic concern, and offered only modest critiques insofar as inheritance law thwarted market exchanges. By contrast, popularizing and populist forms of political economy, most especially those offered by the Chartists, framed inheritance as fundamental to the economics of inequality by allowing wealth to further accumulate within an already well-off aristocracy. By the 1860s, this argument had lost its currency, in part due to the diminishing sway of Chartism and the success of the Anti-Corn Law League, whose arguments against the Corn Laws were premised on a critique of aristocratic privilege, and also due to a changing analysis of the politics and economics of inheritance. Even Karl Marx's thought bears evidence of this shift. In 1843, Marx subjected primogeniture to withering analysis in his *Critique of Hegel's Doctrine of the State*.[6] By 1869, however, he declared to the Fourth Annual Congress of the International Working Men's Association that "the right of inheritance is only of social import insofar as it leaves to the heir the power which the deceased wielded *during his lifetime*."[7] Marx further informed his audience—which included former Chartists—that "the abolition of the right of inheritance can never be the starting point of such a social transformation."[8] As we will see, Dickens's view of inheritance here reflects its political cast in the 1840s. While Dickens lacks a clear political alignment during this period, his views mix ideas from William Cobbet and Richard Cobden with broad sympathy for the plight of the working poor.[9] *The Old Curiosity Shop* thus may not intervene directly in political economic theorization, but its engagement with inheritance allows readers to trace economic fault lines in the moral sentiments, and to imagine the possibility of redress through the uneasy passage of affects and objects. And out of this implication of the one in the other, of affects as objects and of objects as affects, come the novel's key feelings, love, and anxiety.

Inheritance and Land Reform as Discourses of Inequality

Questions of inheritance are at once political and economic and no more so than in the 50 years following the French revolution. The issues at the heart of the post-Revolution debates about inheritance—the relation of the state to property owners, and the limitations that the state could place on testamentary freedom—may seem far removed from the world of *The Old Curiosity Shop*. However, British political economic discussions of inheritance grounded themselves in ways of seeing and feeling that fell well within the purview of Dickens's text, most especially their focus on familial feeling, paternal authority, and demands for equity. Jeremy Bentham had already taken such feelings into account in his 1795 argument in favour of limiting testamentary rights, *Supply Without Burthen*. Bentham lays out what becomes the general Utilitarian argument against inheritance, specifically that the state should receive and divide large estates; however, Bentham insists that such a programme should apply only to the estates of the childless wealthy. Similarly, Adam Smith argues against primogeniture by an appeal to familial fairness, noting that "nothing [could] be more contrary to the real interest of a numerous family, than a right which, in order to enrich one, beggars all the rest of the children too."[10] Dickens has Quilp turn to this line of argument when he tells Nell's brother, Fred: "I always will say...that when a rich relation having two young people—sisters or brothers, or brother and sister—dependent on him, attaches himself exclusively to one, and casts off the other, he does wrong."[11]

However, issues of inheritance in Dickens's novel are purely monetary. By contrast, primogeniture is an issue of "real property"—that is, titles, estates, land—and such issues of real property were central to arguments about inheritance in France following the revolution. In France, too, questions of familial feeling and paternal authority marked arguments about inheritance. Following Utilitarian thinking, the Marquis de Mirabeau proposed limiting testamentary freedom in order to expand the number of landowners and foster economic activity. Moreover, as sociologist Jens Beckert notes in his comparative history of inheritance law, Mirabeau saw this renovation of the social order as demanding the creation of familial equality, and he insisted in a letter that "the feelings and habits that are crucial to public happiness arise at the domestic hearth."[12] In a further bid for social equality, the Jacobins briefly eliminated testamentary freedom altogether in 1794.[13] Hence, while Edmund Burke's chief property focus in the *Reflections on the Revolution in France* belongs to the Church and precedes this Jacobin move, one should hear in his defence of inherited political rights a counter to attacks on intergenerational wealth transfers as well. Yet compared to the harsh regime of the Jacobins, post-revolutionary France's eventual restrictions of testamentary freedom were limited. The Code Civil enforced the equal division and sale of large estates among children and imposed new restrictions on the division of inheritances with an eye towards equality, and it also expanded the testamentary rights of smaller estate holders. As Beckert notes, "the expansion of testamentary freedom was supposed to restore paternal authority within the family."[14] Subsequent attacks on the Code Civil's limitations to inheritance would take paternal authority for their ground.[15] To the extent that interest provides an economic argument for private property, inheritance underlines an affective struggle between demands for equity and authority in both the family and society as a whole.

Renewed calls to limit testamentary freedom in France during the 1830s indicate an important shift in the ground of arguments about inheritance from aristocratic primogeniture to the demand to work. In 1830, the Saint-Simonians demanded, in their words,

> the abolition of all privileges of birth, without exception, and consequently the destruction of inheritance, the greatest of these privileges, the one which to-day embraces them all, and whose effect is to leave to chance the distribution of social privileges among the small number of those who wish to lay claim to them, and to condemn the most numerous class to depravity, ignorance and poverty.[16]

The demand for equity that marked prior discussions of inheritance now highlights the demand to work rather than the familial unfairness of primogeniture and entails. For the Saint-Simonians, inheritance must be eliminated because "it sanctions for some the impious privilege of idleness, that is to say, of living on the labor of others; only in so far as it leaves the social classification of individuals to the chance of birth."[17] In sum, inherited wealth not only authorizes the existence of a parasitic aristocratic class but also inhibits the distribution of work skills according to "the chance of birth."

John Stuart Mill interlaces the thread of this new critique of inheritance into mainstream British political economy. In his *Autobiography,* Mill admits that his initial encounter with the Saint-Simonian school came as "they were just beginning to question the principle of hereditary property" and that he "was by no means prepared to go with them even this length."[18] However, he contends that by the time of writing his *Principles of Political Economy*, he had become "far more heretical" than he "had been in the days of [his] most extreme Benthamism,"[19] and this heresy included a shift in his views about inheritance. Like Bentham, Mill had believed primogeniture and entails should be eliminated as a way of "mitigating the inequalities consequent on these institutions,"[20] but he came to focus instead on what he describes in a Biblical phrase as "the rule that they who do not work shall not eat."[21]

While the programme that Mill outlines in later editions of the *Principles* may seem tame, his positions are not far removed from that of the Saint-Simonians. Their shared emphasis on work reveals a crucial shift in political economic thought that allowed inheritance to become an increasingly non-economic category. For Physiocrats like François Quesnay, the productivity of land was the lynchpin of economic productivity.[22] One of the crucial innovations in Adam Smith's work was his insistence against Quesnay that productive labour was not reducible to agricultural labour but consisted of any labour that "adds to the value of the subject upon which it is bestowed."[23] Against Smith, T. R. Malthus took up the Physiocratic position in his famous argument that population increases faster than the means of subsistence, and he even castigates primogeniture because it limits access to land and its produce.[24] David Ricardo, however, stitches this problem of land and its produce back into the labour theory of value. Arguing against the idea that raises in land rents lead to higher food prices, Ricardo explains that "the reason why…raw produce rises in comparative value is because more labor is employed in the production of the last portion obtained, and not because a rent is paid to a landlord."[25] This economic focus on the labour that makes land productive allowed the inheritance of land to become an increasingly marginal question for later political economists, most especially J. S. Mill. Thus, while Mill offers his thoughts about inheritance in the context of his detailed exposition of political economy, he locates inheritance outside the realm of economics proper. Inheritance is an issue of distribution and public morals, not production, and he writes that the state should limit not the right of testamentary freedom but rather the maximum that one might inherit.[26] More broadly, Mill argues "it may be affirmed that in a majority of instances the good not only of society but of the individuals would be better consulted by bequeathing to them a moderate, than a large provision."[27] Mill elaborates this idea using familial feeling and asserts that all children should be provided for in terms no less generous than those society feels due illegitimate children:

"To such a child it is generally felt that there is due from the parent, the amount of provision for his welfare which will enable him to make his life on the whole a desirable one."[28] However, Mill admits that class expectations will likely intercede beyond this feeling:

> When the children of rich parents have lived, as it is natural they should do, in habits corresponding to the scale of expenditure in which the parents indulge, it is generally the duty of the parents to make a greater provision for them than would suffice for children otherwise brought up.[29]

A longstanding critic of unreflecting habit, he means to highlight a potentially corrosive class privilege and to encourage limits to inheritance that would foster industriousness[30]; however, he nonetheless understands that wealthier parents will likely provide portions that allow their children to remain comfortable members of the class in which they were raised. In sum, Mill tries to bolster the demand to work as a limit to inheritance without launching a full assault on class privilege.

Mill's discussion indicates the broader discursive shift in emphasis about inheritance from land to work in the 1840s. During this period, the two forms of discussion bleed into one another. Parliament's four reports on real property appear from 1829 to 1833, but political economic arguments cluster around 1848 with Mill's first edition of his *Principles* and John Ramsay McCulloch's full-throated defence of inheritance as inextricable from private property as such.[31] Against these middle-class perspectives, the working-class Chartists emphasized land reform in the 1840s. Indeed, the most immediately adjacent and suggestive version of land reform to Dickens's book is the Chartist land plan, which also attacked inheritance in favour of productive work. Although the Chartist Land Company was launched in 1845 after the novel's publication, Malcolm Chase notes that "commitment to agrarian reform...had been central to Chartism almost from its inception."[32] In 1839, the Chartist National Convention issued a declaration in favour of "taking into public ownership any land that had once been 'appropriated to public and general use',"[33] and Feargus O'Connor promoted reclaiming wastes for small landholders to work by hand in his 1841 pamphlet *Remedy for National Poverty and National Ruin*. Importantly, although the Chartist solution was, as Chase explains, "access to, rather than ownership of, the land,"[34] their focus on the mechanisms of inequality and capital accumulation drove their interest in land reform. An 1840 editorial in the *Northern Star* described this as a problem of "the acquisition and accumulation, in individual hands, of large heaps of wealth and property by the oppression and starvation of the people."[35] The Chartists understood inheritance as the problematic mechanism that transmitted "heaps of wealth and property" across generations, and initially the Chartists followed a Utilitarian line of argument that legal protections for inheritances should be eliminated in order to release land for small holders to work. However, by 1850 they had abandoned these positions as they came to believe that modifications of inheritance laws would neither break up the concentration of land capital nor make it accessible to working people.[36]

When brought to bear on *The Old Curiosity Shop,* such contemporary arguments about inheritance can significantly reframe its two central thematic concerns, death and objectification. Critics have long understood the two to be intertwined as in Claire Wood's analysis of the commercial culture of death and burial in the Victorian period, where she notes that the novel reveals "Dickens's ambivalent feelings about separating death and money by restaging the symbolic or sacred in a commercial context."[37] Without a doubt, the novel is ambivalent. However, I would argue that such ambivalence implicates the text's location in the midst of arguments about inheritance and economic inequality. As we have seen in the discussion of Chartism, the problem of inheritance as one of land and work is particularly located in popular political economic discourses of the 1840s—though pressure for land reform continues through the century—and is well established during the period of the initial run of *The Old Curiosity Shop* in *Master Humphrey's Clock* from April 1840 to February 1841. By the early 1840s, the demand to work had become a counterweight to problems of property ownership and intergenerational wealth transfer. The history of this discursive shift reveals that the novel's seemingly divergent narrative trajectories of its two central characters, Nell and Dick Swiveller, map the limits of respectable escapes from work, either through death or an acceptably modified inheritance, with the good-natured servant Kit providing the proper relation to work and wealth in its most limited form.

Nell's tale follows her decline from a seemingly well off middle-class position—"looked upon as affluent,"[38] in her relative's words—to a life of poverty marked by work and leading inexorably towards death. Her deterioration begins with her grandfather's failed inheritance plot, which first loads him with cares and then mortgages his belongings to Quilp. The failure of his plan to create an inheritance inaugurates Nell's turn to work. She pleads to her grandfather to flee the shop and his cares, telling him "we may beg, or work in the open roads or fields, to earn a scanty living, rather than live as we do now."[39] Nell may not be industrious enough to satisfy economically minded characters like Miss Monflathers, who asks her rhetorically, "Don't you know that the harder you are at work, the happier you are?"[40] but Nell tries her hand at a variety of work-like tasks throughout the text, from mending puppet clothes, making nosegays, and leading tours through Jarley's waxworks, to opening and closing a church. Much as Nell respects work, though, she sees little happiness in it, and instead seems to recognize it as intimately linked to the dead object world of the commodity. In his analysis of the novel, Theodor Adorno calls this "the object world of the bourgeois sphere"[41] and argues that because Nell can neither grasp nor escape this world she is finally sacrificed to it. However, when brought alongside the failure of Nell's great-uncle to find her in time to provide her with money—effectively a failure of intergenerational wealth transfer—this dead object world reveals the inability of inheritance to save the working poor. Adorno is right to see in the novel intimations that the object world of commodity production turns the worker into an object, but it is also important to distinguish, as he does, the novel's objects from Marx's critique of work and production. What Dickens has in his sights is not the worker's commodified labour time but the dead labour in the commodity as such. It is a near truism to term Nell's world a commodity world and liken it to Marx's talking table, most especially given its puppets and waxworks. What many overlook in this truism is that the world of Marx's talking table is the world of distribution, not production. The novel's commodity-centric world is part of a search for escape from the ways in which capitalism distributes wealth. In this way, the novel's interrogation of inheritance does not indicate an incipient critique of economic production so much as unease with the status of wealth distribution.

Thus, it is possible to see Dick Swiveller confronting a similar antagonism with work as a mechanism for wealth distribution against what he conceives to be his proper gentlemanly expectations. Gentlemen, he imagines, should not be sacrificed to the object world of work but rather freed from its demands by inherited wealth, in Dick's case either from his aunt or by marriage to Nell. When both his plots falter, Quilp inveigles him to accept a clerkship with Sampson Brass, a position that neither qualifies as work nor provides Dick the professional training that a law clerk would expect. With work too a dead letter, Swiveller reaches his financial nadir near the novel's end when he finds himself trapped in his room after an extended illness because all his clothes have been pawned for food. An unexpected but limited bequest from his aunt rescues him from pecuniary ruin, but, as Mr. Witherdeen informs him,

> If you had been another sort of nephew, you would have come into possession (so says the will, and I see no reason to doubt it) of five-and-twenty thousand pounds. As it is, you have fallen into an annuity of one hundred and fifty pounds a year.[42]

Swiveller's reduced expectations are of a piece with Mill's argument: his annuity allows him to maintain a semblance of his former class status without encouraging Dick to return to the bad habits that marked his character at the novel's start. Although this annuity does not push Dick into productive work, it does provide him with another Millian solution to the inheritance problem—the means to educate the Marchioness, whom the narrator hints to be the illegitimate offspring of Quilp and Sally Brass. Swiveller's subsequent marriage to the Marchioness even proves the basis for a recurrent joke from Swiveller who had "frequent occasion to remark at divers subsequent periods that there had been a young lady saving up for him after all."[43] Limited inheritances constrain the power of the gentlemanly while sentimental connections expand social relations.

Sentimentality as Distributionist Critique: Shared Feelings, Shared Wealth

Swiveller's turn from inheritance to familial feeling is part of the text's use of inheritance to reveal the power of sentimentality and to probe its limits. As critics have long noted, sentimentality imbues *The Old Curiosity Shop*. In *Sacred Tears*, Fred Kaplan argues that Victorian sentimentality reflects a late stage and problematic defence of positive social instincts that loosely follows a sense of the moral sentiments drawn from the eighteenth-century moral philosophy of Lord Shaftesbury, David Hume, Francis Hutcheson, and Adam Smith. In his discussion of the novel, Kaplan notes that Dickens's reliance on "the moral sentiments" does not keep him from creating villains seemingly devoid of the sentiments entirely, so that while Dickens often blames the social corruption of the sentiments for villainous behaviour, characters like Quilp can "challenge the assumption that moral sentiment is an innate human quality."[44] Others have challenged the use of eighteenth-century philosophy to explain a properly Victorian phenomenon bound to changes in social hierarchy.[45] Other critics have traced the novel's sentimental fault lines in political and generic terms. For instance, Sue Zemka claims that the novel's "hysteria of sentimentality" offers a successful "mass response" to block the potentially threatening "Jacobin carnivalesque" of the novel's more grotesque figures.[46] By contrast, Brad Fruhauff sees the novel's Gothicism and sentimentality as generic mechanisms to explore the threats to and promises of ethical actions in the world. And, of course, biographers correlate the novel's sentimentality with Mary Hogarth's death, drawing on Dickens's reflections in personal letters during the novel's composition.[47] In contrast to these approaches, attention to inheritance reveals a formal quality in the novel's sentimentality that binds the novel to a particular historical conjuncture in which arguments about social equality were conducted through economic arguments about inheritance. This appears in a tension in the passage of objects, bodies, and emotions in the text. On the one hand, the text wishes for the passage of objects, bodies, and emotions to act as a positive contagion or infection of the positive moral sentiments for its characters and its readers. Yet on the other hand, it solicits the possibility that these passages may disrupt the sentiments as much as reinforce them.

Nell and Kit are the characters that best capture the novel's sentimental urges, often through the use of the word "love," precisely because sentimentality is premised on the notion of shared, readily incited, and evoked affect. For these characters, the sentiments work, either on other characters or on readers, and do so as something infectious, perhaps most explicitly when the narrator insists that "there was something contagious in Kit's laugh."[48] In this way, one may see how the education or reintroduction of moral sentiments is, as Kaplan notes, what the novel means to achieve. However, the recurrent question within Dickens's sentimentality, of the efficacy of shared affect, reveals how particular emotions may become lexical markers of successful and failed affective incitements. For *The Old Curiosity Shop*, "love" marks the ways in which successful affective incitements cohere social relationships, while "anxiety" marks the troubling possibilities that they may fail. Little surprise, then, that the novel's villain, Quilp, entraps "the sole object of [Nell's grandfather's] love and anxiety into a connexion of which he knew he had a dread and hatred."[49] The phrase reflects two layers of care as fondness and concern, at once underlining the experience of love and imbuing it with instability. Indeed, anxiety often acts in the text in tandem with another affect to inflect the initial emotion with an additional level of concern, such as "sorrows and anxieties," "anxiety and distress," "depression and anxiety," "anxiety and surprise," and "anxiety and sorrow."[50] Anxiety seems omnipresent in this text, and yet, as phrases like "care and anxiety"[51] and "anxious and uneasy"[52] indicate, it is an emotion that seems to lack its own textures. Instead, it marks a heightening of and potential threshold with other emotions. In this way, it is an intensity that accompanies experiences of precarity. The text goes so far as to yoke anxiety to precarity late in the novel as an explicit descriptor of economic insecurity. When Nell's great-uncle describes how her grandfather opened the curiosity shop, he explains that "the tastes he had cultivated were not to yield him an anxious and precarious subsistence."[53] The objects within the curiosity shop themselves convey an economic anxiety that distribution may go wrong. Inheritance may fail.

I would suggest that the novel's distributionist concern with objects and wealth leads it to also map a precarity in a socially binding notion of the moral sentiments. Other critics have noted the importance of precariousness to the novel's sentimentality. Valerie Purton argues of the novel that "it is the knowledge of the precariousness of human identity against which the insistent rhetoric of sentimentalism militates."[54] Hilary Schor approaches a similar line of argument with her claim that Nell, in her age, flight, and death, represents both the commodification of the female body and resistance to this commodification. Schor rightly links this problematic to the issue of inheritance and writes, "the role of the good, quiet, daughter…may well be to represent a patrimony she cannot, yet, possess for herself."[55] However, Schor's focus falls on Nell's "pornographic" objectification[56] rather than the passages of objects and affects. My focus on affects and objects here draws on Sara Ahmed's argument in *The Cultural Politics of Emotion* that the passage of objects may reveal dissension in affective experiences and not simple emotional infections.[57] In a sense, the novel's persistent turn to commodification indicates a world in which the passing of objects between or away from characters should intensify sentimental connections but threatens instead to mark divisions within them. Hence, Master Humphrey emphasizes in the novel's early pages that objects reveal otherwise obscured deeper feelings:

> We are so much in the habit of allowing impression to be made upon us by external objects, which should be produced by reflection alone, but which, without such visible aids, often escapes us; that I am not sure I should have been so thoroughly possessed by this one subject, but for the heaps of fantastic things I had seen huddled together in the curiosity shop warehouse.[58]

That is, objects may impress upon us thoughts and feelings that we would otherwise miss. In this case, objects that are both "fantastic" and associated with Nell impress Master Humphrey with Nell's vulnerability. Yet, as Master Humphrey says, we should recognize these feelings without objects, "by reflection alone." The text thus strips objects from Nell in a clarifying sentimental process, encouraging readers to discover without the "visible aids" of objects sentimental connection. To find, in a way, feeling beyond the countable.

This objectless or dematerialized aspect of proper moral reflection in the novel resonates with its central discussion of inheritance and feeling. Here, anxiety that the sentiments may fail—that emotions may not transfer—becomes part of a discourse on inheritance and feeling that strips away possessions and their attendant vulnerability to misrecognition or capture. If the alienation of the object world reveals a wider problem of economic distribution, of inequalities and failed transfers, then one should expect to find an increased emphasis in the text on dematerialized forms of social connection. This extended passage near the novel's mid-point describing differences in emotional attachments based on class, then, is highly suggestive. Here, the narrator uses inheritance to contrast the landed elite's pride of ownership with a lower class homeless yet nationalist affective network:

> And let us linger in this place for an instant to remark that if ever household affections and loves are graceful things, they are graceful in the poor. The ties that bind the wealthy and the proud to home may be forged on earth, but those which link the poor man to his humble hearth are of the truer metal and bear the stamp of Heaven.

> The man of high descent may love the halls and lands of his inheritance as part of himself, as trophies of his birth and power; his associations with them are associations of pride and wealth and triumph; the poor man's attachment to the tenements he holds, which strangers have held before, and may to-morrow occupy again, has a worthier root, struck deep into a purer soil. His household gods are of flesh and blood, with no alloy of silver, gold, or precious stone; he has no property but in the affections of his own heart; and when they endear bare floors and walls, despite of rags and toil and scanty fare, that man has his love of home from God, and his rude hut becomes a solemn place.[59]

Andrew McCann rightly argues that in this passage "poverty is detached from any meaningful material context; it becomes the ennobling absence that frames more permanent, immaterial identifications."[60] This immateriality, however, is at once articulated as a critique of economic inequality via inheritance, and connected to a through line of affective immateriality in the novel itself. The problem of inheritance here adumbrates the material and affective as "associations of pride and wealth and triumph." Although the novel lacks aristocratic characters, its depiction of Quilp as a grasping, tyrannical man emphasizes his motivations as precisely those of pride (hence his plot against Fred and Dick due to sexual jealousy), wealth (his plot to defraud Nell's grandfather and then her great-uncle), and triumph (his plot against Kit due to Kit's honesty). Moreover, the narrator underlines Quilp's villainy as tyrannical both through Mrs. Quilp's mother's account of him as "the greatest tyrant that ever lived"[61] and by interpolating into the narration of Quilp language from Shakespeare's best-known tyrant, Richard III (including lines from Richard's announcement of his villainy in *3 Henry VI*).[62] The result presents Quilp as an aristocrat in literary terms while turning his physical appearance into a caustic comment on "the man of high descent." In this passage, the abstract contrast between landed wealth and "the poor man" thus carries implicit narrative and affective yield. The passage continues to exhort British political leaders "to improve the wretched dwellings in bye-ways where only Poverty may walk" to counteract such feelings and instead foster "that love of home from which all domestic virtues spring."[63] The narrator explains that this should be done because

> in love of home, the love of country has its rise, and who are truer patriots or the best in time of need—those who venerate the land, owning its woods, and stream, and earth, and all that they produce? Or those who love their country, boasting not a foot of ground in all its wide domain?[64]

In some respects, the narrator's pleas recall Adam Smith's response to the problem of stultification of the working-class mind: one must educate and support the working class to keep them embedded in the social order. However, where Smith advocates education to overcome such lost feeling, the narrator argues for a diffusive domestic sentimentality divorced from a stable notion of home and connected instead to feelings of good humour and hospitality. The novel's description of Chartists reiterates the sentimental portrait of home affections in the prior passage and marks this as a larger social uneasiness in the failure of the domestic virtues. In a chapter published in October 1840, the narrator describes how "maddened men, armed with sword and firebrand, [spurned] the tears and prayers of women who would restrain them, [and] rushed forth on errands of terror and destruction, to work no ruin half so surely as their own."[65] This use of women as the pleading avatars of the thwarted domestic virtues against masculine Chartist savagery has little basis in fact. As Dorothy Thompson notes, "women in the Chartist movement... were important, particularly between 1838 and 1843."[66] However, this gendering makes clear that the true source of terror for the novel is the destruction of the sentiments and their social connections they maintain, whether between employers or spouses.

For the narrator, the key to diffusing the horror of thwarted social sentiments is not to return to a sense of place and its associations via accumulated wealth but rather for the working man to embrace that he has "no property but in the affections of his own heart." Such an appeal is suited both to an emerging proletariat and a rising liberalism that dates back to Locke's *Second Treatise* and its individualistic defence of private property by insisting that a worker's only property is his labour. However, worker's dematerialization in Dickens's novel does not operate through an inchoate abstraction or demand for individualism so much as a demand that such affections—along with an attendant weak nationalism—operate with no objects passing between its subjects. As a result, one should consider Kit's quarter-holiday as an episode meant to capture an experience of affections dematerializing the objects that pass between characters. Claire Wood notes this tendency towards dematerialization in the novel as a problem of profiting off death, whether in fact or fiction. I agree that death marks dematerialization in the novel but would also emphasize that dematerialization means to find proper sentimental relations by evaporating the objects—like wealth—that may block them. Kit, of course, exemplifies the poor man and his portable domestic affections, whether working for Nell and her grandfather, at home with his mother, or with the Garlands. At first glance, his holiday, a family outing that includes a trip to the theatre and to an oyster house, seems merely to express these affections. Closer inspection, however, reveals it to consist of experiences of seemingly pure consumption of largely immaterial services that provides Kit and his family with pleasure and cheer while linking them to the wider world. From theatre going to restaurant eating, the only material accumulation of these experiences or the work they entail is the "grotto" of oyster shells that his brother Jacob builds on the table.[67] This emphasis on the dematerialization of objects through happy consumption runs through the novel, from Nell's dinner with the Punch men and the beer that Swiveller sends to Kit in prison to the restorative gifts of food from the single gentleman to an ailing Swiveller after he helps clear Kit's name, and the celebratory feast that the Garlands throw Kit upon his release. Objects that pass away clear the space for positive affective connection to bloom.

Home without Home: Nell and the Domestic Non-Place

This immaterial or dematerializing demand on objects passing between characters also marks Nell. Much like Kit, Nell too is a marker for the domestic virtues; however, Nell is imbued with the power to create through domestic virtues homes that are not homes. It is worth pausing here to reflect on the problem of place posed both by the working-man's home and Nell's constant flight. In a sense, they gesture towards what Marc Augé terms non-places, spaces dedicated to impersonal movement, and that he locates in twentieth- and twenty-first-century spaces of transit such as airports, train stations, and highways. Nell, too, is in transit, and her allegorical experience underlines what Augé calls the "melancholy pleasure"[68] of the isolated traveller that he argues first appears in nineteenth-century travelogues. Even more crucial to Nell's construction of domestic affections in passing is the way in which these moments occur as punctual events in increasingly derealized spaces. As Brian Massumi elaborates, the non-place reveals how late twentieth- and twenty-first-century societies of control create seemingly undisciplined spaces that in fact rely on checkpoints to identify and control movements of people, money, information, and such (Augé initially describes this relationship as "contractual"[69]).[70] Hence, the moments in which Nell expresses the domestic affections are punctual events of care and hospitality, checkpoints by which the domestic affections may be expressed without being bound to place—that is, to the land. Dickens thus gestures, long before the rise of the technologies necessary for societies of control, towards the ways that affective checkpoints compensate for the loss of striated space and stitch individuals into a new smooth political economic space. That is, how qualitative feeling may be stitched to quantitative space. Schor is thus right that Nell is effectively an object within the text but her objectification is part of the text's delocalized notion of home. Nell becomes the object that creates domestic virtue at crucial intervals, making her the contrasting affective centre to the selfish affects of inheritance—in other words, the poor man's "love of home." The novel's inheritance plots and their attendant misrecognitions are thus tightly bound to its affective form. Nell's non-existent inheritance creates a contrasting set of affects to the self-interest and double-dealing that otherwise surrounds her as the imagined heiress. Her subsequent spiritualization of domestic virtues through death thus operates as part of a broader construction of national virtues divorced from multigenerational landownership.

The novel's relentless focus on death turns in part on this sense that people are embedded in the land yet incapable of owning it. No episode makes this clearer than Nell's arrival at her final residence next to a decaying Gothic church. On the one hand, the narrator describes the turn to domestic virtue on their arrival as "to make these dwellings as habitable and full of comfort as they could was now their pleasant care."[71] Yet the Gothic carvings serve ends that a Graveyard poet like Robert Blair would recognize even if they lack the often solicited terror of mortality: "the aged walls" reveal "the solemn presence, within, of that decay which falls on senseless things the most enduring in their nature...of Death" and "filled [Nell] with deep and thoughtful feelings but with none of terror or alarm."[72] These reflections reach their apotheosis in Nell's discussion of the untended gardens left on the graves in the churchyard. The sexton tells her that some people tell him "it's melancholy to see these things all withering or dead" but that he insists "'tis a good sign for the happiness of the living."[73] Nell replies that "perhaps the mourners learn to look to the blue sky by day, and to the stars by night; and to think the dead are there, and not in graves,"[74] but nonetheless decides to tend the disused plots. In sum, death provides an opportunity to reflect on the punctual events of domestic virtues *and* their necessary dematerialization. The grave offers the central paradigm of one's relation to land as something held in trust, to be tended without ownership with the promise that one will pass into it, unavoidably, without pride or triumph, and outside questions of descent or inheritance.

As the crucial object mediating and cohering group feeling, Nell's death reveals how these shared affects are possible only by eliminating the objectification that figures their containment. Critics such as Wood and Mary Elizabeth Hotz have noted that Nell's dematerialized death coheres community without examining the centrality of the novel's shift between land and affect.[75] The narrator offers this lesson on Nell's passing: "When Death strikes down the innocent and young, for every fragile form from which he lets the panting spirit free, a hundred virtues rise, in shapes of mercy, charity, and love, to walk the world and bless it."[76] Nell's gender, youth, and death, then, mark the refusal of a quite specific patrimony, one that embeds national and domestic virtues in the land. Such objectified attachments must be buried, as it were, and virtues freed instead "to walk the world" like the emerging industrial working classes. This refusal of inheritance brings the novel to a close. The brother of Nell's grandfather, who has sought out Nell and her grandfather to restore their wealth through an intergenerational transfer, realizes the failure of this plan with Nell's death. He appeals to his brother to return with him, describing how together they would be "going home with no hope realized, that had its growth in manhood—carrying back nothing that we brought away, but our old yearnings to each other—saving no fragment from the wreck of life, but that which first endeared it."[77] Nothing can be saved, nothing can be inherited. When this too fails, the brother becomes an avatar of the now unleashed virtues; he "went forth into the world, a lover of his kind,"[78] the narrator implying that, unlike the inheritance that becomes a gift in Dickens's much later *Our Mutual Friend,* here what had been meant to pass as inheritance becomes instead a series of charitable gifts. The narrator tells readers that "those who had been kind to them [Nell and her grandfather], did not escape his search."[79] This subversion of inheritance seems to infect the land itself. An aged Kit returns to the neighbourhood of the curiosity shop after it has been torn down, but he is uncertain where it had once stood, and this change of environment solicits the novel's closing exclamation: "Such are the changes which a few years bring about, and so do things pass away, like a tale that is told!"[80] What passes, passes away, an inescapable change. In this respect, the novel's focus on death—so clearly laden with other affective strains than those of wealth and inequality—nonetheless offers a counter to the specific historical implications of landed inheritance, as the Biblical language conjures a final and total passage of objects out of sight, dematerialized as words lost in the telling.

Conclusion: The Anxiety of Inheritance

The novel's closing appeal to sentimentality and death may obscure the novel's economic and political resonances with inheritance even as it leaves readers with a sense that nothing can be inherited beyond the affective freight of compensatory "virtues" and "gentler nature." Such an answer may be resistant in its historical moment—it refuses to endorse land and inheritance as the basis of political power—but it also is to one side of the political and economic problems posed by inherited wealth. Whether this response is a sleight of hand, a substitution or exchange of feeling for economic value, or part of a construction of a specifically literary humanist value in contrast to the economic is difficult to say. The novel's sentimentality evokes each possibility without fully endorsing any one. Certainly, the novel's affective critique of inherited wealth is of a piece with other affective distinctions that evoke problems in inequality, perhaps most clear in its two concluding narrative strands of Kit's persecution and Nell's death. There too, affect turns questions of inequality away from conflict by making poverty an existential problem, and locating potential class antagonisms in personal grievance instead. Dickens intervenes in the 1840s political economy of emotions, then, with a critique of inheritance and landed wealth more attuned to middle-class arguments against aristocratic privileges like those of the Anti-Corn Law League. The multiple lines of argument mounted by Anti-Corn Law League leaders such as Cobden and Bright, however, take on landed wealth not via an attempted reform of inheritance but rather by advocating the benefits of free trade for workers and their employers as well as claiming that stronger trading ties would end international conflict.[81] The novel's use of dematerialization, then, may carry one further valence: a freedom of movement that brings material and moral benefits to all. It may seem cynical to suggest that Nell's death is the emotional equivalent of an end of protectionist tariffs, yet those "hundred virtues" thereby released are nonetheless the beneficial result of freer trade in sentiment. Its use of anxiety, however, unsettles such economic homologies. Anxiety is, as Gilbert Simondon would argue nearly 100 years later, *pace* Heidegger, a result of mistaking the formative potentials that precede subjectivity for an interiority of subjectivity itself.[82] The result, as Massumi explains, is "an unliveable tension,"[83] a drive towards death as the subject confronts a fundamentally impossible demand. In a sense, *The Old Curiosity Shop* intimates this notion of anxiety as a response to an impossible internalization and coagulation of capitalism's preeminent bearer of potential, wealth, and treats its release as an unveiling of the affective network that Dickens understood best, the moral sentiments. Perhaps more broadly, then, inheritance may solicit anxiety as a mechanism able to capture and internalize accumulations of wealth, mistaking social potentials for the pride of personal possession. This, I would hazard, is one of the affective pathways through the political economic problematic, a culturally embedded and historically specific involution of the division of counting from feeling.

Notes

1 Henri Bergson, *Key Writings*, eds. Keith Ansell Pearson and John Mullarkey (London: Bloomsbury, 2014), 77.

2 For readings of sentimentality in the novel, see Brad Fruhauff, "The Devil You Know: Sentimentalism and Gothic Threat in *The Pickwick Papers* and *The Old Curiosity Shop*," *Victorians: A Journal of Culture and Literature* 122 (2012): 77–89; Mary Elizabeth Hotz, *Literary Remains: Representations of Death and Burial in Victorian England* (Albany, NY: SUNY Press, 2009), 67–79; Nicola Brown, "Introduction: Crying Over Little Nell," *19: Interdisciplinary Studies in the Long Nineteenth Century* 4 (2007), accessed 22 June 2017, www.19.bbk.ac.uk/articles/abstract/10.16995/ntn.453/; Miriam Bailin, "'Dismal Pleasure': Victorian Sentimentality and the Pathos of the Parvenu," *ELH* 66:4 (1999), 1015–32; Fred Kaplan, *Sacred Tears: Sentimentality in Victorian Fiction* (Princeton, NJ: Princeton University Press, 1987), 39–70; Valerie Purton, *Dickens and the*

Sentimental Tradition: Fielding, Richardson, Sterne, Goldsmith, Sheridan, Lamb (London: Anthem Press, 2012), 102–109; Hilary Schor, *Dickens and the Daughter of the House* (Cambridge: Cambridge University Press, 1999), 19–46; Claire Wood, *Dickens and the Business of Death* (Cambridge: Cambridge University Press, 2015), 58–105; and Sue Zemka, "From the Punchmen to Pugin's Gothics: The Broad Road to a Sentimental Death in The Old Curiosity Shop," *Nineteenth-Century Literature* 48:3 (1993): 291–309. For readings of the novel as an allegory of capitalism, see Theodor W. Adorno, *Notes to Literature*, ed. Rolf Tiedemann, trans. Sherry Weber Nicholsen, vol 2., (New York: Columbia University Press, 1992), 171–77; and John Bowen, *Other Dickens: Pickwick to Chuzzlewit* (Oxford: Oxford University Press, 2000), 132–56. Gareth Cordery offers one of the few historicizations of the novel's economics, but he focuses on Quilp as a demonic embodiment of Cain and Hopkins's gentlemanly capitalism; see "Quilp, Commerce, and Domesticity: Crossing Boundaries in *The Old Curiosity Shop*," *Dickens Quarterly* 26:4 (2009): 209–33.

3 Charles Dickens, *The Old Curiosity Shop*, ed. Norman Page (New York: Penguin Classics, 2000), 34.

4 See Thomas Piketty, *Capital in the Twenty-First Century* (Cambridge: Harvard University Press, 2014), 410–14.

5 Dickens, *The Old Curiosity Shop*, 46.

6 See *Early Writings*, trans. Rodney Livingstone and Gregor Benton (New York: Penguin, 1992), 57–198, esp. 164–87.

7 Marx, "Report of the Fourth Annual Congress of the International Working Men's Association, held at Basle, in Switzerland, 1869," accessed 19 June 2017, www.marxists.org/history/international/iwma/documents/1869/inheritance-report.htm.

8 Ibid.

9 On Dickens's relation to the radical press, see Sally Ledger, *Dickens and the Popular Radical Imagination* (Cambridge: Cambridge University Press, 2010), 106–41; for the influence of Cobdenite radicalism, see Michael Shelden, "Dickens, 'The Chimes,' and the Anti-Corn Law League," *Victorian Studies* 25:3 (1982): 329–53.

10 Adam Smith, *The Wealth of Nations*, ed. Edwin Cannan, 2 vols. (Chicago, IL: University of Chicago Press, 1976), 1:409.

11 Dickens, *The Old Curiosity Shop*, 182.

12 Quoted in Jens Beckert, *Inherited Wealth*, trans. Thomas Dunlap (Princeton, NJ: Princeton University Press, 2008), 31.

13 Ibid., 35–36.

14 Ibid., 37.

15 See Beckert, *Inherited Wealth*, 39–46 on Frederic Le Play's 1864 attack on testamentary freedom and subsequent political arguments.

16 Quoted in Adolphe-Jérôme Blanqui, *History of Political Economy in Europe*, trans. Emily J. Leonard (New York: GP Putnam's Sons, 1880), 501.

17 Ibid.

18 John Stuart Mill, *Autobiography*, ed. Jack Stillinger (Boston, MA: Houghton Mifflin, 1969), 98.

19 Ibid., 137.

20 Ibid.

21 Ibid., 138.

22 See Ronald Meek, *The Economics of Physiocracy: Essays and Translations* (Cambridge: Harvard University Press, 1963), 128–37.

23 Smith, *Wealth of Nations* 1:351; see also 1:351–71.

24 See Thomas. R. Malthus, *An Essay on the Principle of Population*, ed. Geoffrey Gilbert (Oxford: Oxford University Press, 1993), 139.
25 David Ricardo, *The Works of David Ricardo*, ed. John Ramsay McCulloch (London: John Murray, 1888), 38.
26 John Stuart Mill, *Principles of Political Economy* (Amherst, NY: Prometheus, 2004), 232.
27 Ibid., 229.
28 Ibid., 230.
29 Ibid.
30 See Stefan Collini, *Public Moralists: Political Thought and Intellectual Life in Britain 1850–1930* (Oxford: Clarendon Press, 1991), 121–69, esp. 154–55.
31 Mill returns to this issue with the Land Tenure Reform Association toward the end of his life. Arguments of the late 1860s and early 1870s, as part of the great moderation of the mid-century, are politically and economically distinct from those of the tumultuous forties. See Mill, *Programme of the Land Tenure Reform Association with an Explanatory Statement by John Stuart Mill* (London: Longmans, Green, Reader, and Dyer, 1871).
32 Malcolm Chase, "Chartism and the Land: 'The Mighty People's Question,'" in *The Land Question in Britain, 1750–1950*, eds. Matthew Cragoe and Paul Readman (New York: Palgrave Macmillan, 2010), 57–73 (65).
33 Ibid., 64.
34 Ibid., 70.
35 Quoted in Chase, "Chartism and the Land," 66.
36 See ibid.
37 Wood, *Dickens*, 59.
38 Dickens, *The Old Curiosity Shop*, 363.
39 Ibid., 79–80.
40 Ibid., 240.
41 Adorno, *Notes*, 177.
42 Dickens, *The Old Curiosity Shop*, 504.
43 Ibid., 552.
44 Kaplan, *Sacred Tears*, 62–63.
45 See Michael Bell, *Sentimentalism, Ethics, and the Culture of Feeling* (Houndsmills, UK: Palgrave, 2000), 120–22; Bailin, "Dismal Pleasure," 1027.
46 Zemka, "From the Punchmen to Pugin's Gothics," 296.
47 See Peter Ackroyd, *Dickens* (New York: Harper Collins, 1990), 226–27 and 318–19; and Kaplan, *Dickens: A Biography* (Baltimore, MD: Johns Hopkins University Press, 1988), 120–21.
48 Dickens, *The Old Curiosity Shop*, 173.
49 Ibid., 181.
50 Ibid., 58, 76, 85 and 98.
51 Ibid., 133.
52 Ibid., 154.
53 Ibid., 526.
54 Purton, *Dickens and the Sentimental Tradition*, 108.
55 Schor, *Dickens and the Daughter of the House*, 45.
56 Ibid., 34.
57 See Sara Ahmed, *The Cultural Politics of Emotion* (New York: Routledge, 2015), 1–16.
58 Dickens, *The Old Curiosity Shop*, 20.
59 Ibid., 289.
60 Andrew McCann, "Ruins, Refuse, and the Politics of Allegory in *The Old Curiosity Shop*," *Nineteenth-Century Literature* 66:2 (2011): 170–94 (191).

61 Dickens, *The Old Curiosity Shop*, 39.
62 See ibid., 388 and 504.
63 Ibid., 289.
64 Ibid.
65 Ibid., 341.
66 Dorothy Thompson, *The Chartists: Popular Politics in the Industrial Revolution* (New York: Pantheon Books, 1984), 150.
67 Dickens, *The Old Curiosity Shop*, 301.
68 Marc Augé, *Non-places: An Introduction to Supermodernity*, (London: Verso, 2008), 70.
69 Ibid., 82.
70 See Brian Massumi, *The Politics of Affect* (Malden, MA: Polity, 2015), 24–28.
71 Dickens, *The Old Curiosity Shop*, 392.
72 Ibid., 393.
73 Ibid., 407.
74 Ibid.
75 See Wood, *Dickens and the Business of Death*, 57–58; and Hotz, *Literary Remains*, 91.
76 Dickens, *The Old Curiosity Shop*, 544.
77 Ibid., 538.
78 Ibid., 545.
79 Ibid.
80 Ibid., 556.
81 See Donald Read, *Cobden and Bright: A Victorian Political Partnership* (London: Edward Arnold, 1967), 41–68, esp. 66–67.
82 Simondon's major works have yet to be translated in English. I draw here on discussions of Simondon's ideas in Massumi, *The Politics of Affect*, 159–65; and David Scott, *Gilbert Simondon's Psychic and Collective Individuation* (Edinburgh, UK: Edinburgh University Press, 2014), 85–87.
83 Massumi, *The Politics of Affect*, 160.

Part III

Modelling Political Economy Today

Section 5

Models and Their Consequence

9 From the South Sea Bubble to Modern Finance

The Legacy of Two Eighteenth-Century Economic Ideas

Mary Poovey

When the global economic system began to slide towards recession in 2007, most professional economists were caught flat-footed. With a few notable exceptions, economists had failed to notice early warning signs, and, as banks around the world scrambled for liquidity, bond markets froze, and Lehman Brothers finally collapsed, most were unable to explain why these events were happening. In the long winter of 2008, there was a lot of professional soul-searching, widespread calls for economists to examine their assumptions and models, and a general sense that something had gone terribly wrong in the dismal scientists' ability to explain the economic world we inhabit.

While some of the disenchantment with economists has faded, the fact remains that the assumptions that made economics a science came up short in some fundamental ways.[1] In this paper, I examine two sets of ideas, each of which lies at the heart of modern economics, and both of which are implicated in the discipline's failure to anticipate the Great Recession. I identify the eighteenth-century roots of these two ideas and explore their lasting legacy, which persists even as economic conditions have changed since the eighteenth century. My argument is that, while neither set of ideas is exclusively responsible for modern economists' inability to anticipate financial crises, the combination of the two is—and will continue to be—detrimental to the discipline's efforts to predict and analyse such events.

The two clusters of ideas should be familiar to anyone who has studied eighteenth-century Britain. The first holds that economic processes, like their natural counterparts, belong to a self-organizing and self-regulating system. The second assumes that human beings are, by nature, rational, self-maximizing agents who can model risk in probabilistic terms. Each is critical to today's mainstream economics. The idea of a self-organizing economic system allows economists to assume that, if left to guide themselves, both national and global economies will tend towards a state of equilibrium, in which supply and demand balance each other and labourers distribute themselves to fill available jobs. The idea of rational, self-maximizing economic agents who can model risk allows economists to subject human behaviour to mathematical analysis so that the notoriously unpredictable vicissitudes of human emotion and some kinds of economic events fit neatly into a regime of calculation, where principles of logic obtain. As a predictive enterprise, guided by the unambiguous methods of mathematics, mainstream economics is now recognized as a science, which is, arguably, as powerful as physics, its natural-scientific counterpart.

Idea One: The Economy Is a Self-organizing System

Adam Smith did not invent the idea that economic processes naturally tend towards equilibrium, as components of a self-organizing system.[2] Indeed, as Jonathan Sheehan and Dror Wahrman have argued, the image of a self-organizing system began to rival the dominant model of mechanistic causality as early as the 1720s.[3] In its earliest version, the image of self-organization retained some of the theological overtones associated with providentialism: the early eighteenth-century truism that God made man and nature in His own image could easily be extended to the emergent image of market society. We see one version of providentialism in the early nineteenth-century Bridgewater treatises, in which British clerics celebrated the fit between the forms of natural creatures and the functions those forms served.[4] The most recent version of this idea appears in the campaign rhetoric of American conservative politicians, who resist increasing taxes or government oversight with appeals to the self-regulating nature of the market—a position that generates an aura of providentialism without always explicitly stating that God made markets in His image too.

Sheehan and Wahrman offer a helpful way of conceptualizing the relationship between ideas and images that retain their hold on a culture's collective imaginary even after new ideas emerge and the ideas that are just beginning to displace their predecessors—what Raymond Williams called "residual" and "emergent" ideas, each of which jostles for a place alongside ideas that are at least temporarily "dominant" or hegemonic.[5] Writing of the early eighteenth-century turn from providentialism to the first intimations of self-organizing systems, Sheehan and Wahrman explain that providence gave "a shape and a language for thinking about and describing nature's dynamic processes. Providence was also, in turn, a shelter under which the ideas of self-organization could grow."[6] One articulation of the residual power providentialism continued to have even as images of self-organization sprouted under its protective wing are these lines from Alexander Pope's *Epistle to Bathurst*:

> Hear then the truth: "'Tis Heav'n each Passion sends,
> And diff'rent Men directs to diff'rent Ends.
> Extremes in Nature equal Good produce,
> Extremes in Man concur to general Use.["][7]

Epistle to Bathurst was published in 1733, but it was written in response to an event that had occurred 13 years earlier, memories of which were resurrected in the 1733 political debate over a company called the Charitable Corporation. The 1720 event that was still reverberating through British culture over a decade later occurred not in the domain of nature but in the newly prominent realm of finance. This event, the dramatic inflation and collapse of the South Sea Bubble (addressed in detail in Claire Wilkinson's contribution to this volume), provoked two, diametrically opposed reactions from contemporaries. On the one side, many responded to the financial bubble as a prime example of the chaos inherent in a world God seemed to have abandoned. Some called the bubble a "Monster"; others compared it to the flood that had drowned most of humanity in Noah's day. One anonymous writer saw in the sell-off that deflated the bubble a sign of the ungovernable contagion of human emotion:

> one Man selling alarms another, and makes him sell, and thus the Stock has run down insensibly, till all the People are put into a Fright; and such has been the panick Fear, that it has brought great Confusion along with it.[8]

Inspired by Isaac Newton's ability to master gravity through mathematical language, many victims of the crash tried to subject the wild swings of stock market prices to numerical discipline, but the "Madness of the People" and the collapse of "Public Credit" seemed immune to the soothing power of numbers. The rise and fall of the South Sea shares remained "a Mystery, that Figures were incapable of demonstrating."[9]

On the other side—and this is the side Sheehan and Wahrman emphasize—some Britons resurrected from the chaos a new version of providentialism, this one robust enough to accommodate not only the idea that God made form fit function but also the operations of chance. If events like the South Sea bubble were viewed as the outcomes of *aggregate* actions, not isolated events, then it would be possible to imagine that what looked like unpredictable randomness could also be seen, at a greater scale, as an orderly process. Chance and Providence, in other words, could be seen to coexist—if one stood at sufficient distance from unfolding events. This is the image of the economy advanced by the English director of another early eighteenth-century corporation in the aftermath of the crash. In a plea for Parliament to reject the Bubble Act, which outlawed almost all British corporations for over a century, Isaac Gervaise described the economy in terms most historians attribute to Adam Smith.

> If Trade was not curbed by Laws, or disturbed by those Accidents that happen in long Wars, etc., which break the natural Proportion,

> either of People, or of private Denominators; Time would bring all trading Nations of the World into that Equilibrium, which is proportioned, and belongs to the number of their inhabitants.[10]

Here is the more familiar version of this idea, from book ten of Smith's *Wealth of Nations.*

> The whole of the advantages and disadvantages of the different employments of labour and stock must, in the same neighborhood, be either perfectly equal or continually tending to equality. If in the same neighborhood, there was any employment evidently either more or less advantageous than the rest, so many people would crowd into it in the one case, and so many people would desert it in the other, that its advantages would soon return to the level of other employments. This at least would be the case in a society where things were left to follow their natural course, where there was perfect liberty, and where every man was perfectly free both to chuse what occupation he thought proper, and to change it as often as he thought proper.[11]

This image of free markets still persists today, as the basis for both mainstream economic theory and political conservatism. I want to call attention to something that may be obvious: the foundation for this image of a self-organizing, self-regulating market is an *analogy* between natural processes and their economic counterpart: economic markets are like nature. If this analogy holds true, then economics can become a science that resembles natural sciences like astronomy and physics—even though economists cannot conduct experiments, as physicists can. This is how the argument-by-analogy goes: just as physics discovers the laws of the physical world (e.g. gravity), so economics can discover the laws that govern economic transactions (e.g. supply and demand).

Almost all modern economists assume this analogy holds. In the early part of the twentieth century, Irving Fisher, one of America's preeminent economists and the first American to embrace mathematics as a suitable method for economic analysis, built a physical model designed to demonstrate this analogy. Fisher's device used a system of cisterns floating in water and connected to each other by rods to show that, as the amount of money in the economic system rose (with money represented by water), the cisterns rose too, in a fixed relation to each other (a relation fixed by the inflexible rods). Fisher was also fond of using the illustration of a physical scale or balance, weighted at one end with commodities and at the other with money, to show how equilibrium worked (again, the analogy links the gravity that operates in the physical world with price ratios). As twentieth-century economists began to represent economic processes in mathematical language—the supply and demand curve, for example, or the graphs and tables that represented index numbers—they reinforced the analogy between physical and economic processes by using the language considered most suitable for the former. The analogy everyone assumed to obtain was bolstered by the universal language of mathematics—and, in the process, the irregularities visible in everyday economic processes were smoothed into the regularities that could be observed in scaled-up "trends" and "tendencies."

A few heterodox economists—like George Soros—have questioned whether economic processes actually resemble their natural counterparts or whether the economy is simply made to *look* like it is governed by natural laws through a combination of reification (turning economic transactions into "the economy") and the application of logic-based methods like mathematical modelling. This is a complicated question, but rather than worrying it at this level of abstraction, let's take just one part of the modern economy and test the foundational analogy. The part I want to consider is *finance*, a complex of transactions and relationships that plays an increasingly prominent role in the economies of developed nations and the global economy as well. The South Sea Bubble, of course, occurred in the domain of finance—it was a financial bubble whose rise and fall depended less on the changing value of the product the company traded (slaves) than on the market price of the shares that represented the company. In passing, I want to suggest that the weakness of Sheehan and Wahrman's provocative book (*Invisible Hands*) is that they treat the theories of self-organization provoked by this *financial* event as interchangeable with theories designed to capture the dynamics of physical and biological processes. They do not stop to ask, as George Soros does, whether finance might be a phenomenon different in kind not only from natural processes but also from other kinds of economic processes. Because they are interested in the "language of self-organization," Sheehan and Wahrman do not worry about whether their examples belong to "the realm of ontology: things actually *do* organize themselves" or the "realm of epistemology: however things actually are, we humans understand them *as if* they organized themselves."[12] In the domain of finance and in financial markets in particular, the relationship between ontology and epistemology is exceedingly important precisely because it is almost impossible to distinguish between ontology—the nature of being—and epistemology—which is a function of knowledge. This distinction is so difficult because the way financial actors think about financial factors and behave in relation to them influences the nature—which is to say, the value—of many components of finance. To understand why this matters, and how finance relates to the second idea I want to explore, we need to pause for a moment over the peculiar nature of *finance*.

What Is Finance?

In general, finance refers to *claims* or contracts that provide ownership of *future* returns, and financial markets allow households, governments, and institutions to save and invest in order to meet their current and future spending or consumption requirements. In one sense, financial markets are very old—in the form of trading agricultural futures, like the value of a future harvest of olives, they date to Aristotle's time. Modern financial markets, especially since the advent of digital communications and data processing, resemble these old financial markets in their future-orientation and their stated intention, which is to manage investment over time under conditions of uncertainty. But they also differ from earlier financial markets in significant ways. Because digital communication has linked markets across the globe, trading in financial markets is now almost continuous, and information about the constantly changing prices of securities is transmitted almost instantaneously. This means that investors, who are making decisions about investment or consumption over a lifetime, are involved in a continuous decision-making process, based on the information at hand. Financial theorists tend to treat this information as if it were perfect and equally accessible to all investors, but, in fact, the information is not perfect or equally available to everyone. The information is not perfect partly because some kinds of financial products (like derivatives) trade outside of public exchanges. Information is not equally available to everyone because of the fragmented nature of trading systems and the different information structures that govern the way various exchanges generate information. This means, for example, that some investors, using high-speed trading programs, are able to take advantage of discrepancies among exchanges to profit from what is essentially an asymmetrical distribution of information.

Because finance is inherently oriented to the future—costs and benefits are spread over time and no one can know in advance the outcome of financial investments—finance inevitably contains an element of uncertainty. One might say that this uncertainty is analogous to the uncertainty that obtains in the physical world: there are simply too many instances of natural phenomena to test; there is too much data, and the best way to deal with the overabundance of data is to use probability estimates. Or, one might say, as a few brave economists have, that in this sense, finance is *not* analogous to the natural world. One might say, in other words, that because we cannot know the future, and because finance is all about the future, finance contains a form of uncertainty that simply lies beyond the capability of human beings.

The distinction between these two kinds of unknowability—one that results from an overabundance of evidence and one that marks the limits of human knowledge—was introduced in 1921 by Frank Knight, an economist at the University of Chicago. Knight called the first kind of unknown "uncertainty" and the second "risk." Risk, he argued, can be managed or hedged through strategies based on mathematical principles, the law of large numbers, and logic. These strategies were manifest as early as the eighteenth century in actuarial tables, and they are also found in all kinds of insurance policies that price risk. The second kind of unknown, uncertainty, cannot be managed or calculated because these events occur too infrequently to conform to probability distributions. This kind of unknown was elaborated in the 1930s by John Maynard Keynes, one of the century's greatest economic theorists. But the vast majority of theorists simply collapse the two kinds of unknowns and treat the uncertainty of the anomalous event as if it were identical to the uncertainty of risky events. This has led them to develop financial theories that radically simplify both the nature of actors and the observable characteristics of financial markets. That discrepancies have opened between the professional economists' theories, and the models spun from them, and the actual behaviours of actors and prices, is a shorthand way of explaining why economists have been unable to predict or explain the financial crises that now occur more frequently than in the past.

Idea Two: Every Individual Is a Rational Self-maximizer in a World of Calculable Risk

In financial theory, the conflation between risk and uncertainty began in the 1940s, as economists tried to figure out how to factor into their economic theories the vicissitudes of human decision-making. To include human choice in the economic equation required some kind of theory about human beings themselves. Eighteenth-century political economists realized this, and they built their accounts of markets on a set of assumptions about human nature. Famously, Adam Smith invoked a "propensity," "common to all men": "the propensity to truck, barter, and exchange one thing for another."[13] Nearly every modern economist agrees with Smith's claim that everyone is fundamentally alike in this way, but few remember just how cautious Smith was in accounting for this propensity.

> Whether this propensity be one of those original principles in human nature, of which no further account can be given; or whether, as seems more probable, it is the necessary consequence of the faculties of reason and speech, it belongs not to our present subject to enquire.[14]

Whatever the origin of the propensity to exchange, Smith continues, its nature is clear.

> [M]an has almost constant occasion for the help of his brethren, and it is vain for him to expect it from their benevolence only. He will be more likely to prevail if he can interest their self-love in his favor, and shew them that it is for their own advantage to do for him what he requires of them. Whoever offers to another a bargain of any kind, proposes to do this. Give me that which I want, and you

> shall have this which you want, is the meaning of every such offer; and it is in this manner that we obtain from one another the far greater part of those good offices which we stand in need of. It is not from the benevolence of the butcher, the brewer, or the baker, that we expect our dinner, but from their regard to their own interest. We address ourselves, not to their humanity but to their self-love.[15]

The idea that all human beings are in essence the same, like the idea that nature is a self-organizing system, sheltered under, but also adjusted, the theological notion to which I have already alluded: the Biblical claim that God made the human species in His own image. Of course, in Smith's version, human beings must aspire to realize God's ideal because they are both dependent on each other and must address this by appealing to the self-interest of others. With or without its theological overtones, this idea continued to inform economic theory for at least the next century. It was essential to the procedural move of aggregation, upon which the discipline of economics rests, because it was key to economists' ability to theorize demand as an aggregate of the desires of like-minded individuals rather than the outcome of warring anarchists, each motivated by a different kind of desire.[16] In 1871, W. Stanley Jevons noted that aggregation played a critical role in economics and that aggregation rests on the assumption that all human beings are the same.

> Though the theory [of consumer demand] presumes to investigate the condition of a mind, and bases upon this investigation the whole of Economics, practically it is an aggregate of individuals which will be treated. The general forms of the laws of Economics are the same in the case of individuals and nations; and, in reality, it is a law operating in the case of multitudes of individuals which gives rise to the aggregate represented in the transactions of a nation.[17]

By the third decade of the twentieth century, economic theorists had begun to reconsider whether simply positing a universal human nature was sufficient to explain the decision-making processes of aggregate populations and individuals. This was not a response to developments in psychological research or theory but an attempt to keep economics aligned with the natural sciences. To preserve the foundational analogy between the economic and natural or physical sciences, economic theorists tried to incorporate advances in the theory and mathematics of probability, which had been roiling the natural sciences for several years. In the natural sciences and physics, these advances addressed changes in the way scientists understood the natural world and the usefulness of probability theory. Instead of thinking of nature and the physical world as essentially law-governed and viewing probability techniques as necessary because of an excess of data, physicists began to believe that randomness or stochasticity is an integral part of nature. In this view, which Werner Heisenberg formalized in 1925, the stochastic properties that had previously made probability estimates seem necessary because the set was too large, came to be viewed not as an epistemic matter—a function of the observer's ignorance—but an ontological matter—a function of nature itself. While scientists might still say that natural laws exist, they were increasingly likely to say that these laws are statistical, not causal, and they were increasingly apt to say that degrees of probability, not certainty, constitute the limits of human knowledge. If laws are statistical, then statistical methods like correlation and inference constitute the only way we can infer any regularities that might resemble laws.

Many economists writing in the 1930s and early 1940s followed this lead by adding probability theory to the received economic axioms about a universal human nature. This combination gave economists an "objective" way to factor probability into economic predictions because it allowed them not only to make generalizations about probable economic events but also to generate an account of how individuals make decisions that did not require speculations about psychological motivation. Instead of having to assume that the economic agent based his decisions on perfect information, foreknowledge about what would serve him best, or a psychological preference for maximal "utility," the economist could simply assume that individuals make probabilistic decisions—somehow factoring into their choices the likelihood that one outcome is more probable—and more desirable—than others. In the 1930s and 1940s, Jacob Marschak, one of the preeminent economic theorists of the day, asserted that economists had to recast the universal economic agent Adam Smith's *homo economicus*—as a statistical agent, an individual who assesses the objective probability of various outcomes as he seeks to further his own interests. "Instead of assuming an individual who thinks he knows the future events, we assume an individual who thinks he knows the probabilities of future events."[18] Marschak defined this behaviour as "rational," and this is what most economists now understand the economic agent to be a rational self-maximizer, who factors the probability of various outcomes into his decisions, which are designed to maximize the likelihood of increasing his own well-being.

We might want to note at this point how the assumption of the rational self-maximizer, who can factor into decisions the probability of various outcomes, simply sidesteps the dilemma we have already encountered in the conflation of ontology and epistemology. Paradoxically, it does so by retaining the foundational analogy between economic and physical processes while ignoring the radical implications of the Heisenbergian revolution in the way physicists understand the natural world. In other words, economists continue to assume that, because the physical and economic worlds are analogous to each other, economists can emulate physicists in using mathematical strategies to understand their object of study, but most fail to consider that some economic processes might be more like quarks than sharks—they might be inherently stochastic, not regular, uniform, or homogeneous. This is the point John Maynard Keynes tried to make about uncertainty in the 1930s when he questioned whether the statistical methods other economists were applying to national economies were appropriate. Other theorists resisted Keynes, however, they neglected Frank Knight, and they simply translated "uncertainty," which is a statement about the non-stationary nature of the universe and the limits of human knowledge, into "risk," which accommodates a statistical approximation.

Finance, Again

In an article published in the *New York Times* in July 2015, Harvard economist Sendhil Mullainathan pondered the opacity of financial markets and tried to explain why economic principles might not apply so well to financial markets. In markets for consumer goods, he explains, competition helps bring prices down as consumers gain more information and make choices among various products. If many consumers buy and like iPhones, for example, other producers of mobile phones will either try to imitate and improve on Apple's device or they will introduce new or cheaper products to rival the iPhone. Consumers will benefit as choices proliferate and prices fall on these devices, and reviews and social media outlets will help consumers make informed decisions.

In financial markets, by contrast, several factors disrupt this economic paradigm. First, information is not readily available in the markets where investors spend their money. As we've already seen, information is always deferred, rarely perfect, and often asymmetrical as well. Here is the way Mullainathan describes this.

> Once I've used a phone for a few weeks, I can tell whether it was worth the money. By contrast, I may not know for decades (if ever) whether an investment was wise or foolish. Does a low return signal a prudent choice or a missed opportunity? And by the time the answer becomes clear, it's already too late. You've got to live with your bad choice. What's more, the invisible hand of competition does not do well by consumers with limited understanding. Rather than eliminating biases, markets often cater to them. For example, many consumers choose a mutual fund by looking at last year's returns, despite warnings that they should not do so. This creates a winner-take-all situation with the highest-performing funds getting most of the investors… What this [in turn] produces is a perverse incentive for fund companies to take risks. That's because investors often choose what to do with their money once, and leave it there for a long time. Faced with that reality, the most profitable strategy

> for a mutual fund company can be to simply take risks in the hope of gaining high short-term returns. Win this high-return lottery and you can draw many investors from whom you will earn fees for decades. Big families of funds can start new funds regularly, each with a different risk strategy. For the companies, it's like buying many lottery tickets. It doesn't matter for the company if many of the funds are clunkers as long as they end up with a few near the top of the performance rankings. For the consumers of these funds, though, it's a losing proposition.[19]

Here again we see the conflation of ontology and epistemology in the domain of finance, now complicated by the behaviour of another set of rational self-maximizers, the fund managers whose incentive to exploit investors' lack of perfect understanding is increased by the way their own remuneration is typically determined: most are compensated on the basis of some combination of the investment dollars they attract (hence the incentive to spin off new funds) and the quarterly increase (or loss) in the value of the company's stock price (which typically follows successful high-risk, short-term strategies). In the short term, which is what matters to the fund manager, attracting investors by using a range of high-risk, possibly high-return strategies is an unalloyed benefit. But in the long run, which is what matters to investors, these high-risk strategies may not yield high returns and—here's the killer—the investor can't know in the present what the future return will be because deferral lies at the heart of financial markets. In the case of financial markets, epistemology—what the investor can (or cannot) know—*is*, for all intents and purposes, ontology—the nature of value—because there is no way to separate the two.

Theorists of modern finance, who have proliferated since 1970, must treat investors the way economists treat other economic agents—as rational self-maximizers—if they want to use the mathematical tools that underwrite the discipline's claim to be a science. The assumptions that investors have perfect or at least probabilistic knowledge and free choice are also essential to the available mathematical methods. Even if individual investors are motivated by their own financial interest, however, perfect knowledge is not possible in financial markets, nor does probability analysis always work: participants are not equal; information is not symmetrical; and the future is, by definition, unknowable. Applying theories and strategies developed in relation to nature, or even to economic processes as a whole, can lead to critical misunderstandings of what happens in financial markets—as we see in a whole slew of recent financial events like the collapse of Long Term Capital Management in 1987, the flash crash of 2010, or the near-meltdown of the global financial system in 2008.

In order to protect some of their foundational assumptions, financial theorists have had to ignore not only the nature of financial markets but also some inconvenient lessons of history. Among these are the fact that the frequency of financial bubbles has increased in recent decades—from the approximately one-a-decade that characterized the entire nineteenth century to the one-every-five-or-so years we have seen since the Dot. Com Bubble of the 1990s. Bubbles in financial markets may well not be departures from the norm or improbable events but constitutive features of these markets. This is what George Soros argued in 2008 when he wrote that securities markets are subject to a dynamic that virtually guarantees that bubbles will occur, regardless of the economists' assertion that markets are efficient.[20] In certain cases, Soros explains, the market can affect the fundamentals it is supposed to reflect. This occurs, for example, when the value of an underlying asset, like a house, is affected by a financial decision—the bank's willingness to lend money for its purchase. It happens when global financial institutions like the IMF are willing to lend money to a nation whose sovereign debt ratio is high, as happened when Greece wanted to enter the Euro zone. It can happen when an individual's ability to borrow money is increased by taking on debt, which theoretically establishes the debtor's credit-worthiness. In such situations, prices on the financial market do not passively reflect values established by underlying assets or the efficient management of information; they actively affect either the flows of information or present value and future prices. Securities markets are not immune to politics, social relationships, or the statements made about them (especially by influential individuals like the head of the Federal Reserve in the U.S., or Warren Buffet). Financial theorists do not typically acknowledge the reality of these dynamics because, thus far at least, they do not have mathematical models that can render them predictable.

The desire to preserve the idea that economics—and financial theory—is a mathematical science is intimately bound up with the discipline's desire to protect what one team of social scientists has called "the superiority of economists."[21] This social scientific observation refers to the distinctive behaviour displayed by economists as a group: in publications, they refer only to each other's papers more than do counterparts in political science or sociology; they consistently rank the same small group of graduate programs as the most prestigious and tend to hire from these programs whenever possible; as a group, they enjoy higher salaries than other social scientists; and they exercise more visible and consequential influence over public policy than political scientists or sociologists. The authority governments and corporations now accord to economists as a group gives these individuals a vested interest in defending the foundational assumptions and methods of their discipline. This vested interest carries over to financial theorists—but with a decisive twist: economists may sometimes "donate" their expertise to government commissions (albeit with copious indirect benefits), but financial professionals are explicitly engaged in making money for themselves (and their clients).

The fact that few financial professionals acknowledge that history and financial markets tell a story that runs counter, in important ways, to the stories economists have told helps protect them from too much scrutiny from regulators. Few are eager to acknowledge that the statistical tools that have made irregularities in the physical world mathematically manageable may fail in analyses of financial markets, where time series are non-stationary and skewed, insufficient data exists to evaluate the success of portfolio managers, and rare events—like the crashes of 1987 or 2008—keep defying explanatory models. I grant that we continue to need experts in matters financial, but those who proclaim to guide investors must learn from what history has told us, not simply from the models upon which the authority of their discipline rests.

Representation and Ontology: Is Finance Exemplary or the Limit Case?

In their introduction, the editors of this volume have provocatively extended Timothy Mitchell's notion of "the idea of the economy" into a general claim: "Economics is a science which has created its object." In this paper, I have explored two ideas that inform mainstream economics and, in so doing, form part of what Peter De Bolla calls the "architecture" of the discipline. These ideas have been silently written into the models and visualization techniques by which economists have both represented and given form to the amorphous, dispersed, and literally incalculable transactions and interrelations that, collectively, constitute what we know as "the economy." In this sense—in using mathematical models, graphs, indices (such as the Dow Jones Industrial Average), and statistical aggregates (such as the gross national product)—economists have undeniably created the object of their discipline. They have created what we can know *of* and *as* "the economy"; they have created our collective *experience* of "the economy," even though these representational techniques cannot alter the disparate ways individuals suffer or enjoy specific economic ups and downs, such as rises and falls in wages or the value of the particular stocks an individual owns.

I have also raised an additional question in this paper, which does not undermine the editors' general claim so much as add to it an additional level of complexity. My question has to do with the nature of finance, which is a subfield of the discipline of economics but also a set of practices routinely deployed by traders to make money. Traders and broker-dealers make money not by exchanging things or services but by making wagers about the future. My question is whether the engagement with an uncertain future, which is central to finance, renders financial practices the very type of economic representation or some kind of outlier, whose flirtation with uncertainty takes the performative potential of economics to a logical (but not necessarily definitive) extreme. In other words, it makes sense to say that "economics is a science which has created its object" and still to assume that this object *must* be created because it is nowhere visible in and of itself. But if this object—and that which it pretends to represent—is not simply too dispersed to be apprehended all at once but actually unknowable (because of its properties or the limits to human knowledge), then our inquiry must proceed with even more momentous scepticism.

John Maynard Keynes raised this question in the 1930s when he suggested that financial markets may exhibit non-stationary patterns: as economists have known since the early twentieth century, future movements of financial markets have no determinate relation to their past movements and may, in fact, defy existing laws of probability, which are based on the properties of the physical world. George Soros raised the question again in 2008 when he challenged mainstream economists' assertion that financial markets resemble the physical world in their regularity. According to Soros, the financial crisis that began in 2007 occurred because of features peculiar to financial markets, not to economic markets in general. These features include the recursive or performative nature of financial markets: the actions of individual traders and trading programs can affect market prices and movements. If the complex relationship between ontology and epistemology that characterizes financial markets in particular takes the principle our editors identify in economics to an extreme, then we need to direct at least part of our analysis of economics to modern finance in particular. Certainly, it is the case that the macroeconomic models used by most economists leading up the 2007 crisis, the dynamic stochastic equilibrium models, did not even try to represent financial markets. What lies outside the representational technologies of mainstream economic models may include not simply psychological factors that challenge the idea of a rational economic agent or externalities that trouble the notion that the economy is a self-contained, self-regulating system, but properties intrinsic to financial markets. Mathematical models, which assume and deploy the regularities of logic, may simply not work when it comes to finance.

Notes

1 A small sample of economists' self-interrogation can be found in Paul Krugman, "How Did Economists Get It So Wrong?" *New York Times* 6 September 2009; Edmund L. Andrews, "Greenspan Concedes Error on Regulation," *New York Times* 23 October 2008; Geoffrey M. Hodgson, "The Great Crash of 2008 and the Reform of Economics," *Cambridge Journal of Economics* 33:6 (2009): 1205–21; and Jean-Phillippe Bouchard, "Economics Needs a Scientific Revolution," *Nature* 455 (October 2008): 1181.

2 See Catherine Packham, "The Physiology of Political Economy: Vitalism and Adam Smith's *Wealth of Nations*," *Journal of the History of Ideas* 63:3 (2002): 465–81.

3 Jonathan Sheehan and Dror Wahrman, *Invisible Hands: Self-Organization and the Eighteenth Century* (Chicago, IL: University of Chicago Press, 2015).

4 Inspired by William Paley's *Natural Theology; or, Evidences of the Existence and Attributes of the Deity* (1802), the eight treatises were commissioned by Francie Henry Egerton, Earl of Bridgewater, and published between 1833 and 1840.

5 Raymond Williams, "Dominant, Residual, and Emergent," *Marxism and Literature* 1 (1977): 121–27.

6 Sheehan and Wahrman, *Invisible Hands*, 45.

7 Quoted in ibid., 161–64.

8 Quoted in ibid., 106.

9 Quoted in ibid., 116.

10 Quoted in ibid., 129.

11 Adam Smith, *An Inquiry into the Nature and Causes of the Wealth of Nations*, eds. R. H. Campbell, A. S. Skinner, and William B. Todd, 2 vols. (Oxford: Oxford University Press, 1976), 1:116.

12 Sheehan and Wahrman, *Invisible Hands*, xiii.

13 Smith, *Wealth of Nations*, 1:25.

14 Ibid.

15 Ibid., 26–27.

16 Elisabeth Wallmann's essay in this volume historicizes "aggregation" in French physiocratic thought.

17 W. Stanley Jevons, *Theory of Political Economy* (London: Macmillan, 1871), 14–15.

18 Jacob Marschak, "Neumann's and Morgenstern's New Approach to Static Economics," *Journal of Political Economy* 54:2 (April 1946): 97–115 (109).

19 Sendhil Mullainathan, "The Confusing Chore of Retirement Investing," *New York Times* 12 July 2015.

20 George Soros, *The Crash of 2008 and What It Means: The New Paradigm for Financial Markets* (New York: PublicAffairs, 2009).

21 Marion Fourcade, Etienne Ollion, and Yann Algan, "The Superiority of Economists," *Maxpo Discussion Paper* 14/3 (2014). Issued by the Max Planck Sciences Po Center on Coping with Instability in Market Societies.

10 Afterword

Modelling the Political Economy in the Twenty-First Century

Nicky Marsh

Political Economy, Literature and the Formation of Knowledge, 1720–1850 provides an important historical corrective to our understanding of the necessity of the idea of political economy, the return of politics to economics. It complicates the dominant assumptions of contemporary economics, its turn to finance and to technocracy, and offers new ways of historicizing the discipline in its fullest social, political, cultural, and philosophical contexts. It is a collection that understands very well the irony that attends on the fact that contemporary economics' biggest problem is that it has *no* "Adam Smith Problem," that it retained Smith's interest in *homo economicus* at the cost of the moral and political philosophies that could made sense of him. These brief concluding comments offer, by way of a contemporary parallel, an account of how recent visual culture has also responded to the now-familiar history of economics' technocratic turn and has implied the possibility for imagining alternatives.

In his lectures on *The Birth of Biopolitics* in the early 1970s, Michel Foucault takes us to the failure of the political economy, suggesting that its two terms became "heterogeneous and incompatible" when the economy, comprised of the dispersed actions of Smith's rational and self-serving individuals, emerged as distinct from the totalizing sovereignty that the political had hitherto demanded. According to Foucault, the new figure of *homo economicus* "strips the sovereign of power" by revealing their "essential, fundamental and major incapacity," which is that they "cannot fail to be blind *vis-a-vis* the economic domain" because the "whole set of economic processes cannot fail to elude a would-be central, totalising bird-eye view."[1] Yet the essays in this collection demonstrate one of the central ironies of the economic: that the apparent dispersal of the sovereign's totalizing authority was almost immediately countermanded by financial technologies of visual representation that were able to successfully reconstitute the whole from the singular. As Mary Poovey argues, events as chaotic as the South Sea bubble could be perceived "as the outcomes of *aggregate* actions" in ways that made it "possible to imagine that what looked like unpredictable randomness could also be seen, at a greater scale, as an orderly process."[2] I want to trace the ways in which these visualized abstractions denuded economics of its political concerns, by naturalizing its authority and narrowing its concerns, before exploring the ways in which more recent visual culture has offered us ways of interrupting this trajectory.

The history of the economic model frequently begins, as it does here, with Francois Quesnay's *Tableau Economique* of 1758, the economic model that Mary S. Morgan has described as "the great grandfather" of economic models because its visualization sought not merely to represent the economy but to provide the "internal resources" through which its workings can be reasoned.[3] The Physiocratic tradition that Quesnay led, as Elisabeth Wallmann's essay in this collection observes, was one that used the close observation of nature to draw the collective from the singular in ways that could generate a general theory of government and perceived nature as the very foundation of their thought. Yet this act of close observation, as John O'Brien's reading of Malthus argues, also came to provide political economy with a visual methodology that organized its naturalized model through what he tellingly describes as "a sovereign vantage point" familiar from contemporary economics. Were "Malthus writing today," O'Brien suggests,

> it is a certainty that his description of these relationships would come accompanied by a set of graphs and charts that would provide numerical support, but would at the same time constitute something closer to a literal picture of the situation that the narrative is describing:

a picture that created a single point of knowledge through which Malthus was able to make authoritative claims even as he came to face a "new kind of sovereign, the modern corporation," which challenges the transparency of the prospect that his prose aims to construct.[4] This ability to realize the total from the single through the metaphor of visualization can also be discerned in the work of Harriet Martineau, as Sarah Dredge's citation from "Weal and Woe" suggests, in which Martineau states that "when observation is exercised in a narrow range, the truth becomes immediately apparent."[5]

The growth of an interest in the ideas of finance over those of the political economy that were consolidated in the nineteenth century, the shift from the land-based economy of the Physiocrats to a monetary-based symbolic and urban economy meant that the ability to realize the whole from the singular becomes the preserve of a narrowed class that was far less concerned with understanding the broad social problems, of food, population, and growth, that had exercised Quesnay, Malthus, and Martineau.[6] The technologies of financial abstraction that developed in the second half of the nineteenth century, notably the stock ticker and the market index, continued to naturalize the existence of the economy, often representing it as a single body, but did so in ways that attributed an ironically mysterious omniscience, not incomparable to those of the sovereign that Foucault claims economics had dispersed into the body politic, to the financial professional who could bring it to health. Alex Preda's account of the stock ticker, for example, makes clear that this was a form of representation that resulted in a profoundly restricted "form of scientific knowledge" but that it was one whose authority was paradoxically understood to be founded not simply upon rationality but upon "a vital force" because it was "charisma, not knowledge" that kept "markets in their place."[7] Marieke de Goede's account of the development of financial indices, meanwhile, notes that they produced a similarly ironically "modern conceptualization of time and numbers where human agency is seen to be able to have a bearing on a still divinely ordered cosmos."[8]

This discovery of an omniscient form of knowledge derived from a visual abstraction continued to be evident in the twentieth century where, as Phillip Mirowski has demonstrated, the organicist language of the economy gave way in the 1930s to the neo-classical language of physics[9] (which was to be similarly usurped by evolutionary psychology, network sociology, and cybernetics by the neo-liberal economists of the 1970s).[10] Yet the use of the language of vision in the financial models suggested by economists such as Irving Fisher, who Mirowski singles out for his dependence on a faulted model of physics, continued to contrast the apparently rational desire of the economist who only wants to "*see*, to picture the interplay of economic elements" with a more elusively dramatic sense of the economist's power to *realize* the world they see. Fisher, notably, sees the "economic world [as] a misty vision. The first explorers used unaided vision. Mathematics is the lantern by which that was before dimly visible now looms up in firm, bold outlines" and his aggrandizing account of how the "old phantasmagoria disappear. We see better. We also see further" implicitly acknowledges that this is a production of knowledge that creates as much as it reveals.[11] This performativity of the financial model resulted by the end of the twentieth century in a state of almost constant financial crisis. It is now synonymous with the Black-Scholes formula that made derivative trading possible (and which carries the name of two of its three Nobel prize winning inventors, Fischer Black, Myron Scholes, and Robert Merton), which was celebrated in the 1990s for having successfully calculated risk out of financial markets. Yet, as financial sociologist Donald McKenzie's analysis has made clear, the changes in financial markets that rendered realistic its assumptions were "at first grossly at variance with market conditions." These models assumed not only faster trading and financial deregulation but also, "by making options trading seem legitimate," they also "contributed to the emergence of the high-volume, efficient, low-transaction cost liquid market the theory posited." They did this because, in short, "'reality' was not a stable backdrop against which testing could take place: finance theory's effects on its object of study were growing."[12]

The hubristic effects of this performative conflation of epistemology and ontology—to use Mary Poovey's neat phrase for finance capital's misrecognition of the distinction between knowing and being—have a powerful counterpart in the visual world as artists have critically engaged with the power of its technologies of representation. The stock market index and the financial formula, for example, have been made central to an emerging but important tradition of work and are evident in pieces such as Lise Autogen and Josh Portway's *Black Shoals Stock Market Planetarium* (1998), Matthew Cross and David Cornford's *Lost Horizon* (2003) and *Black Narcissus* (2014), and Beate Geissler and Oliver Sann's *Volatile Smile* (2010).[13] Each piece is supported by a detailed knowledge of a quite specific operation of financial abstraction—Autogen and Portway and Cornford and Cross work with real-time stock market data; Geissler and Sann with the Black-Scholes formula—in order to critically reflect upon the assumptions that follow from these totalizing surveys of the market. Each piece, albeit in different ways, renders an ironic version of the financial sublime that highlights the unacknowledged but absolute political authority that this financial vision produces.

Black Shoals (Figure 10.1) represents real-time stock market data as a planetarium that the observer stands below. It was first developed in the late 1990s as the technology boom came to a sudden end, specifically

Figure 10.1 First Sketch for *Black Shoals Stock market planetarium*/ Black Shoals Dark Matter by Lise Autogena and Joshua Portway (2000/2015). Photo credit: Lise Autogena and Joshua Portway.

in response to the Black-Scholes formula's failure to "take into account its own effect on the market and the feedback loops it would create when others started copying the model. It led to a sudden spiral of collapse, like a galaxy imploding into dark matter."[14] The work translates real-time market data into a planetarium, its slowly moving stars correspond to real traded companies and their movement

> is based on calculated correlations between the histories of each stock and those of its near neighbours. The stronger the correlation between the histories of the stock prices of any two companies, the more powerful the gravitational attraction between them...[D]ifferent industries naturally start to emerge as galaxies.[15]

Black Shoals achieves a powerful contradiction. On the one hand, its algorithms deliver a sophisticated analysis of the movement of shares in relation to one another, a

> disturbance in a section of the market will have a visible effect on the sky—the collapse of Enron, for instance, would have caused a sort of black hole—all the companies affected would glow very brightly due to the level of trading and would be pulled in to a single point in a very powerful vortex.[16]

Yet, on the other, it refuses to yield this knowledge, we don't know what each star represents and instead of knowledge we are presented with a mute natural order, a cosmos, in which interpretation becomes divination. The larger irony of the contradiction, that speaks precisely to the ways in which the naturalization of this market knowledge was concurrent with a professional restriction that disavowed its political claims, is that it was Reuters who provided this information but then refused to allow the piece to reveal it, lest its analysis be made available to those who had not paid for access to the data.

Cross and Cornford's pieces *Lost Horizon* and *Black Narcissus* were also designed using live stock market data, but their translation of it positioned the observer of the sublime against a computer-generated fantasy mountain landscape rather than under a sparkling sky. *Lost Horizons* used stock data provided by American Express to provide a screen saver that represented the day's trading, and *Black Narcissus* fused the "abstract profile of financial graphs" from between 2003 and 2013, with "the illusory space of computer-generated imagery."[17] The hyperbolic promise of human conquest and achievement that the clearly fabricated nature of these mountain ranges both imply and belie, evoking Fisher's sense of the economist-explorer creating the economic models of the 1930s, can be compared to the tension between the trader's abstract and real effects on the world. As Alistair Robinson who commissioned the piece for the 2014

Show Me the Money exhibition suggested, the peaks and troughs of the graphic mountain mimic the experience of the trader who observes the markets from the "safety and isolation of a computer screen" but whose interconnection with "real-time software" also means that betraying "merely an inkling of fear, or of hope through their actions...has repercussions worldwide, despite the apparent abstraction of their actions."[18]

Beate Geissler and Oliver Sann's *Volatile Smile* was similarly concerned with the encompassingly self-realizing energies of these financial models but captures instead the perplexing tenacity of this model in the self-evident face of crisis, rather than the heady turbulence suggested in the work of Cornford and Cross or Autogene and Portway. The piece is comprised of photographs of a series of large computer monitors sitting on an untidy desk that is strewn with papers and keyboards. Paul Crosthwaite has explained the piece's relationship to financial modelling, noting that the volatility smile is an "anomaly in the pricing of US options contracts" that became apparent after the crash of October 1987 when the assumption that "options on the same underlying asset with the same time to expiration date formed a flat line on a graph, as the famous Black-Scholes-Merton model of options pricing dictated" was replaced by a skew—or "smile"—as investors learnt that stock markets could fall in what had previously been considered to be mathematically impossible amounts.[19] Crosthwaite uses McKenzie's analysis to suggest that this smile represents the acceptance of a "collective trauma," the mathematical incorporation of the "*fear* that the 1987 crash would be repeated"[20] into the financial model itself, and he suggests that

> perhaps somewhere around the blank and impassive screens pictured in Geissler and Sann's photographs, then, hovers a Cheshire Cat grin, a wry smile at the faith (and capital) that humans have invested in their equations, and the machines that perform them.[21]

Each of these pieces—the planetarium, the mountainscape, and the blank smile of the screen—demonstrates how the metaphorical presentation that financial technology has adopted for itself has naturalized the effects of its abstraction, and the unwieldy political powers that flow from it. They achieve this by literalizing the cultural work that the metaphorical, as well as financial, abstractions achieve. In each case, their parodic representations of the financial sublime both counter and replicate the mysterious omniscience of a human agency that "is seen to be able to have a bearing on a still divinely ordered cosmos."[22] As Rita Raley has suggested of the *Black Shoals Planetarium*, such works "attempt to make the mysterious workings of financial capitalism comprehensible to the viewer" by participating

> in a Deleuzian project of using the virtual to enact the actual. That is to say, the old axioms about the material significance of models

> and narrative frames apply: with critically reflective visualization tactics, we might produce counter-simulations and, as a result, new modes of understanding the past and imagining the futures of finance capitalism.[23]

Yet this ability to use these "critically reflective visualization tactics" to suggest an alternative future for "finance capitalism" seems to be much less available in these art pieces than perhaps Raley suggests. The power of the works at least partly derives from the fact that they are placed *within* the financial and technological modes of knowledge that they critique. It is not only that they use an insider's knowledge of the data and the formula: it is that they literally and deliberately identify themselves with the sharply delineated spaces of financial knowledge. *Black Shoals* was "originally designed to be installed in a restaurant next door to the London Stock Exchange" with the idea "that traders would be able to eat underneath the dome—that it would be a kind of ironic 'Mount Olympus' from which they would be able to look down and oversee their creation during their lunch time"; *Lost Horizons* was "installed as a screensaver throughout the LSE for a whole year, being updated daily in response to new FTSE figures";[24] and a still from *Black Narcissus*' damming representation of financial crisis and ecological destruction adorns the front cover of 2015's *The Oxford Handbook of Financial Regulation*.[25] Even *Volatile Smile* suggests this relationship, as its inclusion of the untidy desks of the traders evokes a stage from which they have only momentarily departed and the photographs hang with the palpable presence of those who, like the Reuters or American Express analysts, have a privileged knowledge denied to the observer of the artwork. Hence, although the pieces call attention to the boundaries that they are operating within, it is far from clear that they are able, or even really seek, to escape their knowingly self-referential assumptions.

I want to conclude, finally, with a reading of Ellie Harrison's piece *Vending Machine* (2009) (Figure 10.2) that also uses real-time market data but seeks a form of representation, and a relationship with the observer, that actively works to confront the depoliticizing effects that finance's simultaneous naturalization and restriction of its knowledge achieves. The piece, which was initially shown in exhibitions that took place in student unions, cinemas, and bars around the UK before being included in Somerset House's *Big Bang Data* exhibition in 2015–2016, is comprised of a "rundown but functional old vending machine"[26] that is linked not to the propriety data of the financial industry but to the publically available data distributed by the BBC's RSS feed, which it displays on a screen next to the vending machine. Although the observer who stands and reads the machine's information, waiting to act upon its

Figure 10.2 The Vending Machine by Ellie Harrison, 2010. Photo credit: Ellie Harrison.

implications, seems to mimic that of the stock ticker reader described so well by Peter Knight, the fact that they are reading headlines rather than stock prices complicates the market's assumption that all political news is contained by price—an assumption that reached its pinnacle in Eugene Fama's Efficient Market Hypothesis that regarded prices as the sum of all possible information.[27]

Instead, Harrison's vending machine contains a processor that is searching the newsfeed for keywords associated with finance or crisis, and upon registering them it releases a packet of crisps. The action mimics but reverses that normally associated with market data as it replaces the response that market news imagines it engenders—to buy, to sell, to imagine buying, or selling—with a consumable object that opens the economy to the logic of the gift. Yet the piece is well aware that this is no utopian logic: the giving of crisps in response to information about finance or crisis acerbically mocks the austerity agenda that has been seen as the only political response to economic crisis. The radical insufficiency, the sheer random silliness of distributing bags of Walkers crisps in pubs in the face of crisis, bathetically evokes the dramatic rise of food poverty in the UK since 2008. The machine, in other words, is both the stock ticker and the food bank.

Yet although this combination appears harshly absurd in the contemporary moment, it also revives the possibility of an economic modelling that, like that of the political economists of the eighteenth century, assumed holistic connections and political responsibilities for the crucial connections between, for example, food and finance. The squat material

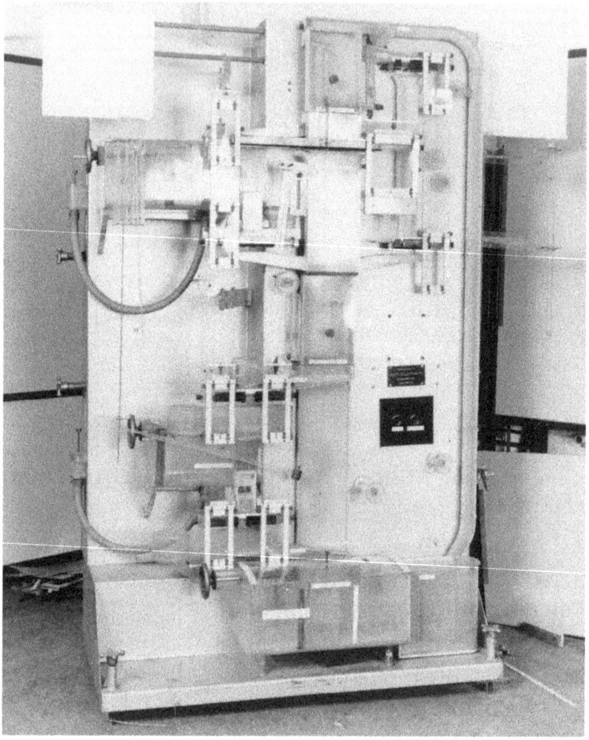

Figure 10.3 Restored *Phillips Machine*, 1993. Photo credit: LSE Library.

functionality of Harrison's vending machine—its visible machinery, vertical levers, rectangular boxes, clear points of entry and exit—evokes not the slickly transcendent financial models of American Express or Reuters captured by Autogene and Portwey and Cornford and Cross but rather the MONIAC machine of the post-war era (Figure 10.3). This machine—also known as the Phillips Machine, the Phillips-Newlyn Machine, the Phillips Hydraulic Computer, and the Financephalograph—was developed by Bill Phillips and Walter Newlyn in the post-war moment in an attempt to represent the connections between politics and economics that a Keynesian managed economy required, a set of liberal assumptions that have become almost radical to describe in the contemporary moment. The machine was a macroeconomic hydraulic marvel: a system of tanks, pumps, sluices, channels, and levers that simulated the action of money as it moved around the economy and could allow the economist to see the interconnected effects of taxation, spending, stock prices, and inflation.

Harrison's *Vending Machine* evokes the quaintly anachronistic sense of the MONIAC machine, quaint because of their shared and visible DIY aesthetic—Phillips was apparently given free room and board, with one cinema visit and a packet of cigarettes a week, during the summer in which the machine was built—suggests a sense of both endurance and optimism. Both are also quaint, more significantly, because they suggest that politics and economics are imbricated but also independent from one another. Harrison's use of the news feed rather than of market prices implies a critical distance from the now ubiquitous assumption that prices *are* news and news *are* prices. This distance is suggested in a different way by the MONIAC's machine assumption that the State has a central role in price setting, in controlling the movement of money in the economy, with a clear political view in mind. As David Vines has more specifically argued, the machine was progressive because the connections between employment, inflation, and money supply that it made apparent led Phillips to develop the Phillips Curve in the late 1950s, the formula that tracked the relationship between unemployment and inflation and profoundly influenced the post-war mixed economy.[28] Ellie Harrison's *Vending Machine*, then, can be read as offering a quite different way of intervening in the history of the visual cultures of the economic model: it offers an appropriately provisional but deeply elegiac response to the very idea of political economy in the twenty-first century, of a model that thought that the "national economy—with great care and attention—could be made not just to run like a machine but be set up to run better."[29]

It is in providing the historical and theoretical resources necessary to imagine this possibility in the contemporary, an economy that would not simply "run better" but could reflect on what, and for whom, the act of running involves, that the real significance of this collection lies. Hence, although the essays included in the collection can be usefully marshalled, as I have suggested here, to tell one kind of story about the development of the modern economy, they also indicate the presence of the stories, and the forms of knowledge and knowing, that were until very recently never considered by economists. Lesa Scholl's account of the ways in which Harriet Martineau's fiction gave voice to those dispossessed by imperialism, Joshua Gooch's attention to Charles Dicken's ability to find ways of representing the affect of financial knowledge, that "to count is to feel, and to feel is to count,"[30] Alex Dean's analysis of the ways in which Malthus's strictures produced a moral surveillance of everyday life, for example, all indicate not only the historical but also the methodological importance of the humanities in thinking about an economy that can "run better." The collection is so important, in other words, because it contributes in careful and scholarly ways to the ongoing project of acknowledging, and beginning to more fully realize, the importance and relevance of the disciplines of the humanities to the discipline of economics.[31]

Notes

1 Michel Foucault, *The Birth of Biopolitics*, ed. Arnold I. Davidson, trans. Graham Burchell (Basingstoke: Palgrave, 2008), 292.
2 See Mary Poovey's essay in the present volume, p. 207.
3 Mary S. Morgan, *The World in the Model: How Economists Work and Think* (Cambridge: Cambridge University Press, 2012), 3.
4 See John O'Brien's essay in the present volume, pp. 124 & 128.
5 See Sarah Dredge's essay in the present volume, p. 110.
6 Ole Bjerg, *The Parallax of Growth: The Philosophy of Ecology and Economy* (London: Polity, 2016).
7 Alex Preda, *Framing Finance: The Boundaries of Markets and Modern Capitalism* (Chicago, IL: Chicago University Press, 2009), 20.
8 Marieke de Goede, *Virtue, Fortune and Faith: A Genealogy of Finance* (Minneapolis: University of Minnesota Press, 2005), 108.
9 Philip Mirowski, "Shall I compare thee to a Monkowski-Ricardo-Leontief-Metzler matrix of the Mosak-Hicks type," in *The Consequences of Economic Rhetoric*, eds. Arjo Klamer, Donald N. McCloskey and Robert M. Solow (Cambridge: Cambridge University Press, 1988), 121.
10 Philip Mirowski, "Postface: Defining Neoliberalism," in *The Road from Mont Pèlerin: The Making of the Neoliberal Thought Collective*, eds. Dieter Plehwe and Philip Mirowski (Cambridge, MA: Harvard University Press, 2009), 435.
11 Irving Fisher, *Mathematical Investigation in the Theory of Value and Price* (New Haven, CT: Yale University Press, 1925), 119; cited in Mary S. Morgan, The World in the Model, 94.
12 Donald MacKenzie, *An Engine, Not a Camera: How Financial Models Shape Markets* (Cambridge, MA: MIT Press, 2006), 256 and 88.
13 Twentieth-century literature has also long been interested in the implications of these technologies: the quotron, the first electronic version of the stock ticker that appeared in 1960, is represented as an uncontrollable force in William Gaddis' 1973 novel JR; the involvement of the Black-Scholes formula in the failure of Long Term Capital Management in 1998 is dramatized as a form of dementia in Kate Jenning's 2003 novel *Moral Hazard*, and a version of the CBOE Volatility Index (Vix), the so-called "fear index," becomes an AI monster that destroys the economy in Robert Harris 2011 thriller *The Fear Index*.
14 Oliver Wainwright, "The Stock Market Planetarium that could have a big bang any minute," *The Guardian*, Tuesday 1st December 2015.
15 Anon., "The Project", in *Black Shoals: Stock Market Planetarium*, accessed 10 August 2017, www.blackshoals.net/the-project-1/.
16 Ibid.
17 Matthew Cornford and David Cross, *Black Narcissus*, accessed 10 August 2017, www.cornfordandcross.com/projects/2014/blacknarcissus/index.html.
18 Alistair Robinson, "Booms and Busts: End of Season Thought" in *Show Me the Money: The Image of Finance, 1700 to the Present*, eds. Paul Crosthwaite, Peter Knight and Nicky Marsh (Manchester: Manchester University Press, 2014), 145.
19 Paul Crosthwaite, "Framing Finance," in *Show me the Money: The Image of Finance*, 60–61.
20 Donald MacKenzie, *An Engine, Not a Camera*, 205; quoted in Paul Crosthwaite, "Framing Finance," 60–61.
21 Paul Crosthwaite, "Framing Finance," 61.

22 Marieke de Goede, *Virtue, Fortune and Faith: A Genealogy of Finance* (Minneapolis: University of Minnesota Press, 2005), 108.
23 Rita Raley, *Tactical Media* (Minneapolis: University of Minnesota Press, 2009), 115.
24 Anon., "The Project."
25 See *The Oxford Handbook of Financial Regulation*, eds. Niamh Moloney, Eilis Ferran and Jennifer Payne, (Oxford: Oxford University Press, 2015).
26 Anon., "Vending Machine," in *Ellie Harrison*, accessed 16 August 2017, www.ellieharrison.com/vendingmachine/.
27 Peter Knight, *Reading the Market: Genres of Financial Capitalism in Gilded Age America* (Baltimore, MD: John Hopkins University Press, 2016).
28 David Vines, "The Phillips Machine: A Progressive Model," in *A. W. H. Phillips: Collected Works in Contemporary Perspective* (Cambridge: Cambridge University Press, 2000). It was, of course, this Phillips curve that was challenged by Milton Friedman during the stagflation of the early 1970s, and although it is now regarded as too simplistic a modified version remains influential upon the new-Keynesianism of figures such as Joseph Stiglitz.
29 Mary S. Morgan, *The World in the Model: How Economists Work and Think* (Cambridge: Cambridge University Press, 2012), 183.
30 See Joshua Gooch's essay in the present volume, p. 184.
31 It was an acknowledgement most notably led by Thomas Piketty's use of the works of Jane Austen in Capital in the Twenty-First Century but has been more recently followed in the writing of economists, such as Gary Saul Morson and Morton Schapiro in *Cents and Sensibility: What Economics Can Learn from the Humanities* (Princeton, NJ: Princeton University Press, 2017), Jans Beckert in *Imagined Futures: Fictional Expectations and Capitalist Dynamics* (Harvard, MA: Harvard University Press, 2016) and Mihir Desai in *The Wisdom of Finance: Discovering Humanity in the World of Risk and Return* (Boston, MA: Houghton Mifflin Harcourt, 2017).

Bibliography

Ablow, Rachel. *The Marriage of Minds: Reading Sympathy in the Victorian Marriage Plot*. Stanford, CA: Stanford University Press, 2007.

Ackroyd, Peter. *Dickens*. New York: Harper Collins, 1990.

Adorno, Theodor W. *Notes to Literature*. Vol. 2. Edited by Rolf Tiedemann. Translated by Sherry Weber Nicholsen. New York: Columbia University Press, 1992.

Agamben, Giorgio. *The Kingdom and the Glory: For a Theological Genealogy of Economy and Government*. Translated by Lorenzo Chiesa. Stanford, CA: Stanford University Press, 2011.

Ahmed, Sara. *The Cultural Politics of Emotion*. New York: Routledge, 2015.

Anderson, Adam. *An Historical and Chronological Deduction of the Origin of Commerce, from the Earliest Accounts*. 4 vols. London: Printed for J. Walter, 1787.

Andrews, Edmund L. "Greenspan Concedes Error on Regulation." *New York Times* 23 October 2008.

Andriopoulos, Stefan. "The Invisible Hand: Supernatural Agency in Political Economy and the Gothic Novel." *ELH* 66 (1999): 739–58.

Anonymous. "Art. 26. A New Estimate of Manners and Principles: Or, a Comparison between Ancient and Modern Times, in the Three Great Articles of Knowledge, Happiness, and Virtue. Part III. of Happiness; in Which Some Principles of Mr. Rousseau are Examined." *Critical Review, Or, Annals of Literature* 13 (1762): 270.

———. *Journal Oeconomique, ou Memoires, notes et avis sur l'Agriculture, les Arts, le Commerce, & tout ce qui peut avoir rapport à la santé, ainsi qu'à la conservation & à l'augmentation des biens des Familles, &c*. Paris: chez Antoine Boudet, 1766.

———. "Account of the Examination of the Rev. Dr. Dodd, at Guildhall, for Forgery." *Universal Magazine of Knowledge and Pleasure* 60 (1777): 89–91.

———. "An Account of the Life and Writings of William Dodd, LL. D." *The London Review of English and Foreign Literature* 5 (1777): 473–75.

———. "Particulars of the Rev. Dr. Dodd's Trial for Forgery." *Sentimental Magazine, or, General Assemblage of Science, Taste, and Entertainment* (February, 1777): 73–78.

———. "Speech and Condemnation of Dr. Dodd at the Session of the Old Bailey, Which Ended on Friday the 16th instant." *The Gentleman's Magazine: And Historical Chronicle* 47 (May, 1777): 226–27.

———. "Dr. William Dodd." *The Wesleyan-Methodist Magazine* 20 (November, 1841): 12–13.

———. "Review" of Bessie Rayner Parkes, *Remarks on the Education of Girls* (1854). Girton College Archive, University of Cambridge.

———. "The 'Saturday Review' and the 'English Woman's Journal': The Reviewer Reviewed." *English Woman's Journal* 1 (1858): 201–4.

———. "Queen Bees or Working Bees?" *Saturday Review* 8 (November, 1859): 575–76.

Augé, Marc. *Non-Places: An Introduction to Supermodernity*. London: Verso, 2008.

Bailin, Miriam. "'Dismal Pleasure': Victorian Sentimentality and the Pathos of the Parvenu." *ELH* 66:4 (1999): 1015–32.

Baker, Keith Michael. "A Script for a French Revolution: The Political Consciousness of the Abbé Mably." *Eighteenth-Century Studies* 14:3 (1981): 235–63.

———. *Inventing the French Revolution: Essays on French Political Culture in the Eighteenth Century*. Cambridge: Cambridge University Press, 1990.

Barrell, John. *English Literature in History: An Equal, Wide Survey*. New York: St. Martin's Press, 1983.

Beckert, Jans. *Inherited Wealth*. Translated by Thomas Dunlap. Princeton, NJ: Princeton University Press, 2008.

———. *Imagined Futures: Fictional Expectations and Capitalist Dynamics* Harvard, MA: Harvard University Press, 2016.

Bell, Michael. *Sentimentalism, Ethics and the Culture of Feeling*. Basingstoke: Palgrave, 2000.

Bennett, David, ed. *Loaded Subjects: Psychoanalysis, Money and the Global Financial Crisis*. London: Lawrence & Wishart, 2012.

Bentham, Jeremy. *Supply without Burthen or Escheat vice Taxation*. London: J. Debrett, 1795.

Berg, Maxine. *The Machinery Question and the Making of Political Economy, 1815–1848*. Cambridge: Cambridge University Press, 1980.

Bergson, Henri. *Key Writings*. Edited by Keith Ansell Pearson and John Mullarkey. London: Bloomsbury Press, 2014.

Bjerg, Ole. *The Parallax of Growth: The Philosophy of Ecology and Economy*. London: Polity, 2016.

Blanqui, Adolphe-Jérôme. *History of Political Economy in Europe*. Translated by Emily J. Leonard. New York: GP Putnam's Sons, 1880.

Blum, Carol. *Strength in Numbers: Population, Reproduction, and Power in Eighteenth-Century France*. London: The Johns Hopkins University Press, 2012.

Bodichon Papers, Girton College Archive, University of Cambridge.

Bouchard, Jean-Phillippe. "Economics Needs a Scientific Revolution." *Nature* 455 (October, 2008): 1181.

Bowen, John. *Other Dickens: Pickwick to Chuzzlewit*. Oxford: Oxford University Press, 2000.

Brown, Nicola. "Introduction: Crying Over Little Nell." *19: Interdisciplinary Studies in the Long Nineteenth Century* 4 (2007). Accessed 22 June 2017. www.19.bbk.ac.uk/articles/abstract/10.16995/ntn.453/.

Brown, Stewart J. *Thomas Chalmers and the Godly Commonwealth in Scotland*. Oxford: Oxford University Press, 1982.

Brown, Vivienne. *Adam Smith's Discourse: Canonicity, Commerce and Conscience*. London: Routledge, 1994.

Buck-Morss, Susan. "Envisioning Capital: Political Economy on Display." *Critical Inquiry* 12:2 (1995): 434–67.

Burdick, Anne, Johanna Drucker, Peter Lunenfeld, Todd Presner, and Jeffrey Schnapp. *Digital_Humanities*. Boston, MA: MIT Press, 2012.

Burnett, Joyce. "Women Workers in the British Industrial Revolution." *Economic History Net*. Accessed 31 January 2017. http://eh.net/encyclopedia/women-workers-in-the-british-industrial-revolution-2/.

Burrow, John W. "Intellectual History in English Academic Life: Reflections on a Revolution." In *Palgrave Advances in Intellectual History*. Edited by Richard Whatmore and Brian Young. Basingstoke: Palgrave, 2006, pp. 8–24.

Burton, John Hill. *The Life and Correspondence of David Hume*. Edinburgh: W. Tait, 1846.

Cantillon, Richard. *Essai sur la Nature du Commerce en général. Traduit de l'Anglois*. London: Fletcher Gyles, 1755.

Carswell, John. *The South Sea Bubble*. London: Cresset, 1960.

Chalmers, Thomas. "Minutes of the Evidence Taken before the Committee Appointed by the House of Commons, to Inquire into the State of Mendicity and Vagrancy in the Metropolis and Its Neighbourhood." *Edinburgh Review* 28:55 (March, 1817): 1–31.

———. *The Christian and Civic Economy of Large Towns*. 3 vols. Glasgow: Printed by J. Starke for Chalmers & Collins, 1821–1826.

Chang, Ha-Joon. *Economics: The User's Guide*. London: Penguin, 2004.

Charbit, Yves. *The Classical Foundations of Population Thought: From Plato to Quesnay*. Dordrecht: Springer, 2010.

Chase, Malcolm. "Chartism and the Land: 'The Mighty People's Question.'" In *The Land Question in Britain, 1750–1950*. Edited by Matthew Cragoe and Paul Readman. New York: Palgrave Macmillan, 2010, pp. 57–73.

Clark, Geoffrey. *A Farewell to Alms: A Brief Economic History of the World*. Princeton, NJ: Princeton University Press, 2007.

Cockburn, Henry. *Memorials of His Time*. Edinburgh: Adam and Charles Black, 1856.

Codr, Dwight. *Raving at Usurers: Anti-Finance and the Ethics of Uncertainty in England, 1690–1750*. Charlottesville: University of Virginia Press, 2016.

Cohen, Michèle. "The Pedagogy of Conversation in the Home: 'Familiar Conversation' as a Pedagogic Tool in Eighteenth- and Nineteenth-Century England." *Oxford Review of Education* 41 (2015): 447–63.

Cole, Joshua. *The Power of Large Numbers: Population, Politics, and Gender in Nineteenth-Century France*. Ithaca, NY: Cornell University Press, 2000.

Cole, Lucinda. *Imperfect Creatures: Vermin, Literature, and the Sciences of Life, 1600–1740*. Ann Arbor: University of Michigan Press, 2016.

Collini, Stefan. *Public Moralists: Political Thought and Intellectual Life in Britain 1850–1930*. Oxford: Clarendon Press, 1991.

Collini, Stefan, Richard Whatmore and Brian Young, eds. *Economy, Polity and Society: British Intellectual History, 1750–1950*. Cambridge: Cambridge University Press, 2000.

Compston, H. F. B. *The Magdalen Hospital: The Story of a Great Charity*. London: Society for Promoting Christian Knowledge, 1917.

Connell, Phillip. *Romanticism, Economics and the Question of 'Culture'*. Oxford: Oxford University Press, 2001.

Copley, Stephen, and Kathryn Sutherland, eds. *Adam Smith's Wealth of Nations: New Interdisciplinary Essays*. Manchester: Manchester University Press, 1995.

Coppel, Harry C., and James W. Mertins. *Biological Insect Pest Suppression*. Berlin and Heidelberg: Springer, 1977.

Cordery, Gareth. "Quilp, Commerce, and Domesticity: Crossing Boundaries in *The Old Curiosity Shop*." *Dickens Quarterly* 26:4 (2009): 209–33.

Courtemanche, Eleanor. *The "Invisible Hand" and British Fiction, 1818–1860: Adam Smith, Political Economy, and the Genre of Realism*. Basingstoke: Palgrave, 2011.

Crashaw, Richard. *The Complete Poetry of Richard Crashaw*. Edited by George Walton Williams. Translated by Phyllis S. Bowman. New York: New York University Press, 1972.

Crosthwaite, Paul. "Framing Finance." In *Show Me the Money: The Image of Finance, 1700 to the Present*. Edited by Paul Crosthwaite, Peter Knight and Nicky Marsh. Manchester: Manchester University Press, 2014, pp. 35–61.

Crosthwaite, Paul, Peter Knight, and Nicky Marsh, eds. *Show Me the Money*. Manchester: Manchester University Press, 2014.

Dalley, Lana L. "Domesticating Political Economy: Language, Gender and Economics in the *Illustrations of Political Economy*." In *Harriet Martineau: Authorship, Society and Empire*. Edited by Ella Dzelzainis and Cora Kaplan. Manchester: Manchester University Press, 2010, pp. 103–117.

Damilaville, Étienne-Noël. "Population, (Physique, Morale, Politique)." In *L'Encyclopédie*. Edited by Jean le Rond d'Alembert and Denis Diderot. ARTFL Encyclopédie Project. Edited by Robert Morrissey and Glenn Roe. Chicago, IL: University of Chicago, 2016. Accessed 11 August 2017. http://encyclopedie.uchicago.edu.

Daston, Lorraine. "On Scientific Observation." *Isis* 99 (2008): 97–110.

Daston, Lorraine, and Peter Galison. *Objectivity*. Boston, MA: MIT Press, 2007.

David, Deirdre. *Intellectual Women and Victorian Patriarchy: Harriet Martineau, Elizabeth Barrett Browning, George Eliot*. London: Macmillan, 1987.

De Bolla, Peter. "Mediation and the Division of Labor." In *This Is Enlightenment*. Edited by Clifford Siskin and William Warner. Chicago, IL: University of Chicago Press, 2010, pp. 87–101.

De Goede, Marieke. *Virtue, Fortune and Faith: A Genealogy of Finance*. Minneapolis: Minnesota Press, 2005.

Deleuze, Gilles. "Postscript on the Societies of Control." *October* 59 (1992): 3–7.

De Mably, Gabriel Bonnot. *Doutes proposés aux philosophes économistes, sur l'ordre naturel et essentiel des sociétés politiques*. Paris: Nyon et Veuve Durand, 1768.

De Réaumur, René Antoine Ferchault. *Mémoire pour servir à l'histoire des insectes: Sur les chenilles & sur les papillons*. Paris: Imprimerie royale, 1734.

———. *Mémoires pour servir à l'histoire des insectes. Suite de l'histoire des chenilles & des papillons; & l'histoire des insectes ennemis des chenilles*. Paris: Pierre Mortier, 1737.

Derham, William. *Physico-Theology; Or, A Demonstration of the Being and Attributes of God from His Works of Creation: Being the Substance of Sixteen Sermons Preached in St. Mary-Le-Bow Church, London, at the*

Honourable Mr. Boyle's Lectures, in the Years 1711, and 1712 : With Large Notes, and Many Curious Observations. London: W. and J. Innys, 1720.

Desai, Mihir. *The Wisdom of Finance: Discovering Humanity in the World of Risk and Return.* Boston, MA: Houghton Mifflin, 2017.

Dickens, Charles. *The Old Curiosity Shop.* Edited by Norman Page. New York: Penguin, 2000.

Dickson, P. G. M. *The Financial Revolution in England: A Study in the Development of Public Credit, 1688–1756.* London: Macmillan, 1967.

Dodd, William. *The Sisters, or the History of Lucy and Caroline Sanson, Entrusted to a False Friend.* 2 vols. London: T. Waller, 1754.

———. *A Sermon on Job, Chap. Xxix. Ver. 11–13. Preached at the Anniversary Meeting of the Governors of the Magdalen Charity on Thursday, March 18, 1762.* London: W. Faden, 1762.

———. "Memoirs of the Late Dr. William Dodd." *The Town and Country Magazine, or, Universal Repository of Knowledge, Instruction, and Entertainment* 9 (1777), 372–77.

Doward, Jamie, Larry Elliott, Rod Ardehali, and Terry Macalister. "The World Has Glimpsed Financial Crisis. But Is the Worst to Come?" *The Observer* 24 January 2016.

Draper, Edward. "Doctor Dodd." *The Train: A First-Class Magazine* 1:6 (1856): 353–60.

Du Monceau, Henri-Louis Duhamel, and Matthieu Tillet. *Histoire d'un Insecte, qui devore les grains de l'angoumois. Avec les moyens que l'on peut employer pour le détruire.* Paris: H. L. Guerin & L. F. Delatour, 1762.

Dumont, Louis. *From Mandeville to Marx: The Genesis and Triumph of Economic Ideology.* Chicago, IL: University of Chicago Press, 1977.

Dwyer, John. "Ethics and Economics: Bridging Adam Smith's *Theory of Moral Sentiments* and *Wealth of Nations.*" *Journal of British Studies* 44:4 (2005): 662–87.

Dzelzainis, Ella. "Feminism, Speculation and Agency in Harriet Martineau's *Illustrations of Political Economy.* In *Harriet Martineau: Authorship, Society and Empire.* Edited by Ella Dzelzainis and Cora Kaplan. Manchester: Manchester University Press, 2010, pp. 118–37.

Eliot, George. *Middlemarch.* Edited by W. J. Harvey. London: Penguin, 1965.

Elliott, Larry. "Beware the Great 2016 Financial Crisis." *The Guardian* 12 January 2016.

Ellis, Markman. *The Politics of Sensibility: Race, Gender and Commerce in the Sentimental Novel.* Cambridge: Cambridge University Press, 1996.

Ellis, Sarah. *The Women of England, Their Social Duties, and Domestic Habits.* London: Fisher, Son & Co., 1839.

Engell, James. "Wealth and Words: Pope's *Epistle to Bathurst.*" *Modern Philology* 85 (1988): 433–46.

Engels, Friedrich. *Condition of the Working Class in England.* London: G. Allen & Unwin: 1891.

Evensky, Jerry. "Adam Smith's *Theory of Moral Sentiments*: On Morals and Why They Matter to a Liberal Society of Free People and Free Markets." *The Journal of Economic Perspectives* 19:3 (2005): 109–30.

Féraud, Jean F. *Dictionnaire critique da la langue française: O-Z.* 3 vols. Marseille: Chez Jean Mossy, Père et fils, 1788.

Firth, Ann. "From Oeconomy to 'the Economy:' Population and Self-Interest in Discourses on Government." *History of the Human Sciences* 11:3 (1998): 19–35.

Fisher, Irving. *Mathematical Investigation in the Theory of Value and Price.* New Haven, CT: Yale University Press, 1925.

Fissell, Mary. "Imagining Vermin in Early Modern England." *History Workshop Journal* 47 (1999): 1–29.

Foote, Samuel. *The Cozeners; a Comedy, in Three Acts. As It Is Performed at the Theatre-Royal in the Haymarket.* London: T. Sherlock, 1778.

Forget, Evelyn L. "Jane Marcet as Knowledge Broker." *History of Economics Review* 65:1 (2016): 15–26.

Foucault, Michel. *Discipline and Punish: The Birth of the Prison.* Translated by Alan Sheridan. London: Penguin, 1991.

———. *The Foucault Effect: Studies in Governmentality.* Edited by Graham Burchell, Colin Gordon, and Peter Miller. London: Harvester Wheatsheaf, 1991.

———. *Security, Territory, Population: Lectures at the Collège de France, 1977–1978.* Basingstoke: Palgrave Macmillan, 2007.

———. *The Birth of Biopolitics: Lectures at the Collège de France, 1978–1979.* Edited by Michel Senellart. Translated by Graham Burchell. Basingstoke: Palgrave, 2008.

Fourcade, Marion, Etienne Ollion, and Yann Algan. "The Superiority of Economists." Maxpo Discussion Paper 14/3 (2014). Issued by the Max Planck Sciences Po Center on Coping with Instability in Market Societies.

Frazer, Michael L. *The Enlightenment of Sympathy: Justice and the Moral Sentiments in the Eighteenth Century and Today.* Oxford: Oxford University Press, 2010.

Fruhauff, Brad. "The Devil You Know: Sentimentalism and Gothic Threat in *The Pickwick Papers* and *The Old Curiosity Shop*." *Victorians: A Journal of Culture and Literature* 122 (2012): 77–89.

Gaddis, William. *JR.* New York: Alfred A. Knopf, 1975.

Gagnier, Regenia. "On the Insatiability of Human Wants: Economic and Aesthetic Man." *Victorian Studies* 36:2 (1993): 125–53.

———. *The Insatiability of Human Wants: Economics and Aesthetics in Market Society.* Chicago, IL: University of Chicago Press, 2000.

Gallagher, Catherine. *The Industrial Reformation of English Fiction: Social Discourse and Narrative Form, 1832–1867.* Chicago, IL: University of Chicago Press, 1985.

———. *The Body Economic: Life, Death, and Sensation in Political Economy and the Victorian Novel.* Princeton, NJ: Princeton University Press, 2006.

Gaskell, Elizabeth. *Mary Barton.* Edited by Stephen Gill. London: Penguin, 1970.

Gay, John. *The Letters of John Gay.* Edited by C.F. Burgess. Oxford: Clarendon, 1966.

———. *Poetry and Prose.* Edited by Vinton A. Dearing and Charles E. Beckwith. 2 vols. Oxford: Oxford University Press, 1974.

Gerrard, Christine. "Political Passions." In *The Cambridge Companion to Eighteenth-Century Poetry.* Edited by John Sitter. Cambridge: Cambridge University Press, 2001.

Glass, D. V. *Numbering the People: The Eighteenth-Century Population Controversy and the Development of Census and Vital Statistics in Britain.* London: Gordon and Cremosi, 1978.

Goldsmith, Oliver. *The Citizen of the World; or Letters from a Chinese Philosopher, Residing in London, to His friends in the East.* London: J. Newbery and W. Bristow, 1762.

Gordon, Robert. *The Rise and Fall of American Growth.* Princeton, NJ: Princeton University Press, 2016.

Graeber, David. *Debt: The First 5000 Years.* London: Melville House, 2011.

Grampp, William D. "Adam Smith and the Economic Man." *Journal of Political Economy* 56:4 (1948): 315–36.

Green, Michele. "Conflicting Principles or Completing Counterparts? J. S. Mill on Political Economy and the Equality of Women." *Utilitas* 6:2 (1994): 267–85.

Greenwell, Dora. "Our Single Women." *North British Review* 36 (1862): 62–87.

Gupta, Akhil. "Farming as a Speculative Activity: The Ecological Basis of Farmers' Suicides in India." In *The Routledge Companion to the Environmental Humanities.* Edited by Ursula K. Heise et al. New York: Routledge, 2017, pp. 185–93.

Guy, Josephine. *The Social Problem Novel: The Market, the Individual and Communal Life.* London: Macmillan, 1996.

Guy-Bray, Stephen. "'Pulchrum Spargitur Hic Chaos': Crashaw's Meta-Commentary." *Journal for Early Modern Cultural Studies* 9 (2009): 147–59.

Hammond, Brean S. "'A Poet, and a Patron, and Ten Pound': John Gay and Patronage." In *John Gay and the Scriblerians.* Edited by Peter Lewis and Nigel Wood. London: Vision Press, 1989, pp. 23–43.

Hanway, Jonas. *A Plan for Establishing a Charity-House or Charity-Houses, for the Reception of Repenting Prostitutes. To Be Called the Magdalen Charity.* London: [no publisher,] 1758.

Harris, Robert. *The Fear Index.* London: Hutchinson, 2011.

Hill, Mike, and Warren Montag. *The Other Adam Smith.* Stanford, CA: Stanford University Press, 2015.

Hilton, Boyd. *The Influence of Evangelicalism on Social and Economic Thought, 1785–1865.* Oxford: Clarendon, 1988.

Hirschman, Albert O. *The Passions and the Interests: Political Arguments for Capitalism before Its Triumph.* Princeton, NJ: Princeton University Press, 1977.

Hirschmann, Nancy. "Mill, Political Economy, and Women's Work." *The American Political Science Review* 102:2 (2008): 199–213.

Hobart, Ann. "Harriet Martineau's Political Economy of Everyday Life." *Victorian Studies* 37 (1994): 223–51.

Hochstrasser, T. J. "Physiocracy and the Politics of Laissez-Faire." In *The Cambridge History of Eighteenth-Century Political Thought.* Edited by Mark Goldie and Robert Wokler. Cambridge: Cambridge University Press, 2006, pp. 419–42.

Hodgson, Geoffrey M. "The Great Crash of 2008 and the Reform of Economics." *Cambridge Journal of Economics* 33:6 (2009): 1205–21.

Hollis, Hilda. "The Rhetoric of Jane Marcet's Popularizing Political Economy." *Nineteenth-Century Contexts* 24:4 (2002): 379–96.

Hont, Istvan, and Michael Ignatieff, eds. *Wealth and Virtue: The Shaping of Political Economy in the Scottish Enlightenment*. Cambridge: Cambridge University Press, 1983.

Hoppit, Julian. "Myths of the South Sea Bubble." *Transactions of the Royal Historical Society* 12 (2002): 141–65.

Horrell, Sara, and Jane Humphries. "Women's Labour Force Participation and the Transition to the Male-Breadwinner Family, 1790–1865." *Economic History Review* 48 (1995): 89–117.

Hotz, Mary Elizabeth. *Literary Remains: Representations of Death and Burial in Victorian England*. Albany, NY: SUNY Press, 2009.

Howlett, John. *An Examination of Dr. Price's Essay on the Population of England and Wales*. Maidstone: J. Blake, 1781.

Howson, Gerald. *The Macaroni Parson: A Life of the Unfortunate Dr. Dodd*. London: Hutchinson, 1973.

Hume, David. *A Treatise of Human Nature: Being an Attempt to Introduce the Experimental Method of Reasoning into Moral Subjects*. 3 vols. London: John Noon, 1739–1740.

———. *Essays Moral, Political and Literary*. Edinburgh: R. Fleming and A. Alison, 1741.

———. *An Enquiry Concerning the Principle of Morals*. London: Printed for A. Millar, 1751.

———. "Of Luxury." In *Political Discourses*. Edited by David Hume. Edinburgh: A. Kincaid and A. Donaldson, 1752.

———. *Essays and Treatises on Several Subjects*. Edinburgh: A. Kincaid, and A. Donaldson, 1753.

Jacobs, Michael, and Mariana Mazzucato, eds. *Rethinking Capitalism*. Oxford: Wiley-Blackwell, 2016.

Jacobs, Steve, and Dennis Calvin. "Angoumois Grain Moth." Department of Entomology (Penn State University), 1990. Accessed 14 September 2016. http://ento.psu.edu/extension/factsheets/angoumois-grain-moth.

James, Patricia. *Population Malthus: His Life and Times*. London: Routledge and Keegan Paul, 1979.

Jameson, Fredric. "Culture and Finance Capital." *Critical Inquiry* 24 (1997): 246–65.

Jennings, Kate. *Moral Hazard*. New York: Harper Collins, 2002.

Jevons, W. Stanley. *Theory of Political Economy*. London: Macmillan, 1871.

Johnson, Samuel. *A Dictionary of the English Language*. 2 vols. London: Printed for J. Knapton, 1755.

———. *Lives of the English Poets*. 2 vols. London: Oxford University Press, 1906.

Jones, Tom. "Pope's *Epistle to Bathurst* and the Meaning of Finance." *Studies in English Literature* 44 (2004): 487–504.

Jonsson, Fredrik Albritton. "Rival Ecologies of Global Commerce: Adam Smith and the Natural Historians." *The American Historical Review* 115:5 (2010): 1342–63.

Kaplan, Fred. *Sacred Tears: Sentimentality in Victorian Fiction*. Princeton, NJ: Princeton University Press, 1987.

———. *Dickens: A Biography*. Baltimore, MD: Johns Hopkins University Press, 1988.

Keats, John. "Ode on a Grecian Urn." In *Keats's Poetry and Prose*. Edited by Jeffrey N. Cox. London: Norton, 2009.

Kent, Eddy. *Corporate Character: Representing Imperial Power in British India, 1786–1901*. Toronto, ON: University of Toronto Press, 2014.

Klaus, Ian. *Forging Capitalism: Rogues, Swindlers, Frauds, and the Rise of Modern Finance*. New Haven, CT: Yale University Press, 2014.

Klaver, Claudia. *A/Moral Economics: Classical Political Economy and Cultural Authority in Nineteenth-Century England*. Columbus: Ohio State Press, 2003.

Kleer, Richard. "Riding a Wave: The Company's Role in the South Sea Bubble." *Economic History Review* 68 (2015): 264–85.

Knight, Peter. *Reading the Market: Genres of Financial Capitalism in Gilded Age America*. Baltimore, MD: John Hopkins University Press, 2016.

Krieger, Murray. *Ekphrasis: The Illusion of the Natural Sign*. Baltimore, MD: Johns Hopkins University Press, 1992.

Krieger, Nancy. "Who and What Is a 'Population?' Historical Debates, Current Controversies, and Implications for Understanding 'Population Health' and Rectifying Health Inequities." *Milbank Quarterly* 90:4 (2012): 634–81.

Krugman, Paul. "How Did Economists Get It So Wrong?" *New York Times* 6 September 2009.

Kwass, Michael. "Consumption and the World of Ideas: Consumer Revolution and the Moral Economy of the Marquis de Mirabeau." *Eighteenth-Century Studies* 37:2 (2004): 187–213.

Lanchester, John. *Whoops! Why Everyone Owes Everyone and No One Can Pay*. London: Penguin, 2010.

Landry, Adolphe. "Idées de Quesnay Sur La Population." *Revue d'Histoire Des Doctrines Économiques et Sociales* 2 (1909): 41–87.

Ledger, Sally. *Dickens and the Popular Radical Imagination*. Cambridge: Cambridge University Press, 2010.

Leitner, Helga, Emma Colven, and Eric Sheppard. "Ecological Security for Whom? The Politics of Flood Alleviation and Urban Environmental Justice in Jakarta, Indonesia." In *The Routledge Companion to the Environmental Humanities*. Edited by Ursula K. Heise et al. New York: Routledge, 2017, pp. 194–205.

Levine, Caroline. *Forms: Whole, Rhythm, Hierarchy, Network*. Princeton, NJ: Princeton University Press, 2015.

Logan, Deborah. *Harriet Martineau, Victorian Imperialism, and the Civilizing Mission*. Farnham: Ashgate, 2010.

MacKenzie, Donald. *An Engine, Not a Camera: How Financial Models Shape Markets*. Cambridge, MA: The MIT Press, 2006.

Maginn, William. "On National Economy: Review of Miss Martineau's 'Cousin Marshall.'" *Fraser's Magazine for Town and Country* 6 (1832): 403–13.

Malthus, Thomas Robert. *An Essay on the Principle of Population, as It Affects the Future Improvement of Society, with Remarks on the Speculations of Mr. Godwin, M. Condorcet, and Other Writers*. London: 1798.

———. *An Essay on the Principle of Population*. London: T. Bensley, 1803.

———. *An Essay on the Principle of Population; or a View of Its Past and Present Effects on Human Happiness*. London, 1803.

———. *A Letter to the Right Honorable Lord Grenville Occasioned by Some Observations of His Lordship on the East India Company's Establishment for the Education of Their Civil Servants*. London: J. Johnson, 1813.

———. *Statements Respecting the East-India College with an Appeal to Facts in Refutation of the Charges Lately Brought Against It in the Court of Proprietors*. London: John Murray, 1817.
———. *Principles of Political Economy*. London: John Murray, 1820.
———. *Principles of Political Economy*. Edited by John Pullen. Cambridge: Cambridge University Press, 1989.
———. *An Essay on the Principle of Population, or a View of Its Past and Present Effects on Human Happiness; with an Inquiry into Our Prospects Respecting the Future Removal or Mitigation of the Evils Which It occasions*. Edited by Donald Winch. Cambridge: Cambridge University Press, 1992.
———. *An Essay on the Principle of Population*. Edited by Geoffrey Gilbert. Oxford: Oxford University Press, 1993.
———. *An Essay on the Principle of Population*. Edited by Philip Appleman. New York: Norton, 2004.
Manning, Paul. "Owning and Belonging: A Semiotic Investigation of the Affective Categories of a Bourgeois Society." *Comparative Studies in Society and History* 46:2 (2004): 300–25.
Marcet, Jane. *Conversations on Political Economy*. London: Spottiswoode, 1816.
Marlow, Ben. "World Economy Stands on the Cusp of Another Crash." *The Telegraph* 27 February 2016.
Marschak, Jacob. "Neumann's and Morgenstern's New Approach to Static Economics." *Journal of Political Economy* 54:2 (1946): 97–115.
Martineau, Harriet. *Illustrations of Political Economy*. London: Charles Fox, 1832.
———. "On the Duty of Studying Political Economy." *Monthly Repository* 6 (1832): 24–34.
———. *Cinnamon and Pearls*. London: Charles Fox, 1833.
———. "England's Foreign Policy." *Westminster Review* 61 (1854): 190–232.
———. *Illustrations of Political Economy: Selected Tales*. Edited by Deborah Anna Logan. Peterborough, ON: Broadview, 2004.
Marx, Karl. "Report of the Fourth Annual Congress of the International Working Men's Association, held at Basle, in Switzerland, 1869." Accessed 21 June 2017. www.marxists.org/history/international/iwma/documents/1869/inheritance-report.htm.
———. *A Contribution to the Critique of Political Economy*. Translated by N.I. Stone. Chicago, IL: Charles H. Kerr, 1904.
———. *Capital: A Critique of Political Economy*. Translated by Ben Fowkes. London: Penguin, 1976.
———. *Capital*. Translated by David Fernbach. 3 vols. London: Penguin, 1981.
———. *Early Writings*. Translated by Rodney Livingstone and Gregor Benton. New York: Penguin, 1992.
Masami, Yuki. "Meals in the Age of Toxic Environments." In *The Routledge Companion to the Environmental Humanities*, Edited by Ursula K. Heise et al. New York: Routledge, 2017, pp. 56–63.
Massumi, Brian. *The Politics of Affect*. Malden, MA: Polity, 2015.
McCann, Andrew. "Ruins, Refuse, and the Politics of Allegory in *The Old Curiosity Shop*." *Nineteenth-Century Literature* 66:2 (2011): 170–94.

McCulloch, John Ramsay. *Treatise on Succession to Property Vacant by Death.* London: Longman, Brown, Green, and Longmans, 1848.

McNally, David. *Political Economy and the Rise of Capitalism: A Reinterpretation.* Berkeley: University of California Press, 1988.

Meek, Ronald. *The Economics of Physiocracy: Essays and Translations.* Cambridge, MA: Harvard University Press, 1963.

Mill, John Stuart. *Programme of the Land Tenure Reform Association with an Explanatory Statement by John Stuart Mill.* London: Longmans, Green, Reader, and Dyer, 1871.

———. *Principles of Political Economy.* In *Collected Words of John Stuart Mill.* Edited by J. M. Robson. 33 vols. London: Routledge, 1965.

———. *Autobiography.* Edited by Jack Stillinger. Boston, MA: Houghton Mifflin, 1969.

———. *Principles of Political Economy.* Amherst, MA: Prometheus, 2004.

Millgate, Murray, and Shannon C. Stimson. *After Adam Smith: A Century of Transformation in Politics and Political Economy.* Princeton, NJ: Princeton University Press, 2011.

Millman, Sara, and Robert W. Kates. "Toward Understanding Hunger." In *Hunger in History: Food Shortage, Poverty, and Deprivation.* Edited by Lucile F. Newman. Oxford: Blackwell, 1995, pp. 3–24.

Mirabeau, Victor Riqueti, marquis de. *L'ami des hommes ou traité de la population, nouvelle édition corrigée.* Avignon: [no publisher,] 1758.

Mirabeau, Victor Riqueti, marquis de, and François Quesnay. *Philosophie rurale, ou économie générale et politique de l'agriculture.* 3 vols. Amsterdam: Les Libraires associés, 1763.

Mirowski, Philip. "Shall I Compare Thee to a Monkowski-Ricardo-Leontief-Metzler Matrix of the Mosak-Hicks Type." In *The Consequences of Economic Rhetoric.* Edited by Arjo Klamer, Donald N. McCloskey and Robert M. Solow. Cambridge: Cambridge University Press, 1988, pp. 117–45.

———. "Postface: Defining Neoliberalism." In *The Road from Mont Pèlerin: The Making of the Neoliberal Thought Collective.* Edited by Dieter Plehwe and Philip Mirowski. Cambridge, MA: Harvard University Press, 2009, pp. 417–56.

Mitchell, Robert. *Sympathy and the State in the Romantic Era: Systems, State Finance, and the Shadows of Futurity.* New York: Routledge, 2007.

Mitchell, Timothy. *Rule of Experts: Egypt, Techno-Politics, Modernity.* Berkeley: University of California Press, 2002.

Mitchell, W. J. T. *Picture Theory.* Chicago, IL: University of Chicago Press, 1994.

Moloney, Niamh, Eilis Ferran, and Jennifer Payne, eds. *The Oxford Handbook of Financial Regulation.* Oxford: Oxford University Press, 2015.

Morgan, Mary S. *The World in the Model: How Economists Work and Think.* Cambridge: Cambridge University Press, 2012.

Morson, Gary Saul, and Morton Schapiro. *Cents and Sensibility: What Economics Can Learn from the Humanities.* Princeton, NJ: Princeton University Press, 2017.

Mullainathan, Sendhil. "The Confusing Chore of Retirement Investing." *New York Times* 12 July 2015.

Mullan, John. *Sentiment and Sensibility: The Language of Feeling in the Eighteenth Century*. Oxford: Oxford University Press, 1988.

Nicholson, Colin. *Writing and the Rise of Finance*. Cambridge: Cambridge University Press, 1994.

Nokes, David. *John Gay: A Profession of Friendship*. Oxford: Oxford University Press, 1995.

O'Connor, Feargus. *Remedy for National Poverty and National Ruin*. Leeds: J. Hobson, 1841.

Ogilvie, Brian W. "Order of Insects." In *The Life Sciences in Early Modern Philosophy*. Edited by Ohad Nachtomy and Justin E. H. Smith. Oxford: Oxford University Press, 2014, pp. 222–46.

Ogle, Newton. *A Sermon Preached at the Anniversary Meeting of the Governors of the Magdalen Charity, on Thursday May 1, 1766*. London: W. Sandby and W. Faden, 1766.

Oncken, August. "Das Adam Smith Problem." *Zeitschrift für Sozialwissenschaft* 1 (1898): 25–33, 101–8, 267–87.

Owen, Robert. *New View of Society: Or, Essays on the Principle of the Formation of the Human Character*. London, 1817.

Packham, Catherine. "The Physiology of Political Economy: Vitalism and Adam Smith's *Wealth of Nations*." *Journal of the History of Ideas* 63:3 (2002): 465–81.

———. "Feigning Fictions: Imagination, Hypothesis, and Philosophical Writing in the Scottish Enlightenment." *The Eighteenth Century* 48:2 (2007): 149–71.

Palmer, Clare. "Taming the Wild Profusion of Existing Things?" *Environmental Ethics* 23:4 (2001): 339–58.

Parkes, Bessie Rayner. "Apropos Political Economy." *English Woman's Journal* 12 (1863–1864): 73–80.

Paul, Helen J. *The South Sea Bubble: An Economic History of Its Origins and Consequences*. New York: Routledge, 2011.

Peace, Mary. "Sentimentality in the Service of Methodism: John Wesley's Abridgement of Henry Brooke's *Fool of Quality*." *Religion in the Age of Enlightenment* 4 (2013): 277–308.

———. *Changing Sentiments and the Magdalen Hospital: Luxury, Virtue and the Senses in Eighteenth-Century Culture*. New York: Routledge, 2017.

Pearce, S. B. P. *An Ideal in the Working: The Story of the Magdalen Hospital, 1758–1795*. London: published privately, 1958.

Pentland, Gordon. "'Betrayed by Infamous Spies'? The Commemoration of Scotland's 'Radical War' of 1820." *Past and Present* 201:1 (2008): 141–73.

Persky, Joseph. "Retrospectives: Adam Smith's Invisible Hands." *The Journal of Economic Perspectives* 3:4 (1989): 195–201.

Piketty, Thomas. *Capital in the Twenty-First Century*. Cambridge, MA: Harvard University Press, 2014.

Pocock, J. G. A. *The Machiavellian Moment: Florentine Political Thought and the Atlantic Republican Tradition*. Princeton, NJ: Princeton University Press, 1975.

Poovey, Mary. "Aesthetics and Political Economy in the Eighteenth Century: The Place of Gender in the Social Constitution of Knowledge." In *Aesthetics and Ideology*. Edited by George Levine. New Brunswick, NJ: Rutgers University Press, 1994, pp. 79–105.

———. *The Making of the Social Body: British Cultural Formation 1830–1864*. Chicago, IL: University of Chicago Press, 1995.

———. *A History of the Modern Fact, Problems of Knowledge in the Sciences of Wealth and Society*. Chicago, IL: University of Chicago Press, 1998.

———. "The Liberal Civil Subject and the Social in Eighteenth-Century British Moral Philosophy." *Public Culture* 14:1 (2002): 125–45.

———. *Genres of the Credit Economy: Mediating Value in Eighteenth- and Nineteenth-Century Britain*. Chicago, IL: University of Chicago Press, 2008.

Pope, Alexander. *The Poems of Alexander Pope*. Edited by John Butt. 11 vols. London: Methuen, 1939–1967.

Preda, Alex. *Framing Finance: The Boundaries of Markets and Modern Capitalism*. Chicago, IL: Chicago University Press, 2009.

Price, Richard. *Essay on the Population in England, from the Revolution to the Present Time*. London: T. Cadell, 1780.

Pujol, Michèle. *Feminism and Anti-Feminism in Early Economic Thought*. Aldershot: Edward Elgar, 1992.

Purton, Valerie. *Dickens and the Sentimental Tradition: Fielding, Richardson, Sterne, Goldsmith, Sheridan, Lamb*. London: Anthem Press, 2012.

Quesnay, François. *Discourse Which Carried the Praemium at the Academy of Dijon, In MDCCL. On This Question, Propos'd by the said Academy, Whether the Re-Establishment of Arts and Sciences Has Contributed to the Refining of Manners*. London: W. Owen, 1761.

———. "Hommes." In *Oeuvres économiques complètes et autres textes: Textes polémiques, Documents associés*. Edited by Christine Théré, Loïc Charles and Jean-Claude Perrot. Paris: INED, 2005.

———. "Fermiers." In *L'Encyclopédie*. Edited by Jean le Rond d'Alembert and Denis Diderot. ARTFL Encyclopédie Project. Edited by Robert Morrissey and Glenn Roe. Chicago, IL: University of Chicago, 2016. Accessed 11 August 2017. http://encyclopedic.uchicago.edu.

Raley, Rita. *Tactical Media*. Minneapolis: University of Minnesota Press, 2009.

Raphael, D. D., and Macfie, A. L., eds. "Introduction." In *The Theory of Moral Sentiments*. Edited by Adam Smith. Indianapolis, IN: Liberty Fund, 1984.

Ratcliff, Marc J. "Duchesne's Strawberries: Between Growers' Practices and Academic Knowledge." In *Heredity Produced: At the Crossroads of Biology, Politics, and Culture, 1500–1870*. Edited by Staffan Müller-Wille and Hans-Jörg Rheinberger. Boston, MA: MIT Press, 2007.

Read, Donald. *Cobden and Bright: A Victorian Political Partnership*. London: Edward Arnold, 1967.

Ricardo, David. *On the Principles of Political Economy, and Taxation*. London: John Murray, 1821.

———. *The Works of David Ricardo*. Edited by J. R. McCulloch. London: John Murray, 1888.

———. *On the Principles of Political Economy and Taxation. Library of Economics and Liberty*. Accessed 1 May 2017. www.econlib.org/library/Ricardo/ricP.html.

Richie, Thomas Edward. *An Account of the Life and Writings of David Hume, Esq*. London: T. Cadell, 1807.

Richmond, Alexander B. *Narrative of the Condition of the Manufacturing Population and the Proceedings of Government Which Led to the State Trials in Scotland*. New York: Augustus M. Kelley, 1971.

Roach, W. M. "Alexander Richmond and the Radical Reform Movements in Glasgow in 1816–1817." *The Scottish Historical Review* 51:151 (1972): 1–19.

Robinson, Alistair. "Booms and Busts: End of Season Thought." In *Show Me the Money: The Image of Finance, 1700 to the Present*. Edited by Paul Crosthwaite, Peter Knight and Nicky Marsh. Manchester: Manchester University Press, 2014, pp. 132–56.

Rodrik, Dani. *Economics Rules*. Oxford: Oxford University Press, 2015.

Rogers, Pat. "Plunging in the Southern Waves: Swift's Poem on the Bubble." *Yearbook of English Studies* 18 (1988): 41–50.

———. "South Sea Bubble Myths." *TLS* 9 April 2014. Accessed 19 June 2017. http://the-tls.co.uk/tls/public/article1397751.

Rostek, Joanna. "Female Authority and Political Economy: Jane Marcet's and Harriet Martineau's Contradictory Strategy in Disseminating Economic Knowledge." In *Proceedings of the Conference of the German Association of University Teachers of English*. Vol. 35. Edited by Silvia Mergenthal and Reingard M. Nischik. Trier: Wissenshaftlicher Verlag Trier, 2013, pp. 21–33.

———. "Managing the Unmanageable: Paradoxes of Poverty in Harriet Martineau's *Illustrations of Political Economy*." In *Narrating Poverty and Precarity in Britain*. Edited by Barbara Korte and Frederic Regard. Berlin: De Gruyter, 2014, pp. 33–55.

Rothschild, Emma. *Economic Sentiments: Adam Smith, Condorcet, and the Enlightenment*. Cambridge, MA: Harvard University Press, 2001.

Rouet, Mr. "Mr. Rouet to Baron Mure, London, January 25, 1766." In *Selections from the Family Papers Preserved at Caldwell MDCCLXV–MDCCCXXI*. Edited by William Mure. 3 vols. Glasgow: np, 1854.

Rousseau, Jean-Jacques. "A Letter from Mr. Rousseau, of Geneva, to Mr. d'Alembert, of Paris, Concerning the Effects of Theatrical Entertainments on the Manners of Mankind." *Monthly Review, or, Literary Journal* 20 (February, 1759): 131–32.

Rousseau, Jean-Jacques. "Translator's Preface." In *The Discourse Which Carried the Præmium at the Academy of Dijon*. Translated by William Boyer. London: W. Owen, 1761, pp. iii–x.

Rousseau, Jean-Jacques. *The Miscellaneous Works of Mr. J. J. Rousseau*. London: T. Becket & P. A. de Hondt, 1767.

Sahlins, Peter. "The Royal Menageries of Louis XIV and the Civilizing Process Revisited." *French Historical Studies* 35:2 (2012): 237–67.

Samuels, Warren J. *Erasing the Invisible Hand*. Cambridge: Cambridge University Press, 2014.

Schliesser, Eric. "Adam Smith's Benevolent and Self-Interested Conception of Philosophy." In *New Voices on Adam Smith*. Edited by Leonidas Montes and Eric Schliesser. London: Routledge, 2006, pp. 328–57.

Scholl, Lesa. *Translation, Authorship and the Victorian Professional Woman*. Farnham: Ashgate, 2011.

Schor, Hilary. *Dickens and the Daughter of the House*. Cambridge: Cambridge University Press, 1999.

Schwartz, Janelle A. *Worm Work: Recasting Romanticism*. Minneapolis: University of Minnesota Press, 2012.

Schwartze, Michelle A., and John T. Scott. "Spontaneous Disorder in Adam Smith's *Theory of Moral Sentiments*: Resentment, Injustice, and the Appeal to Providence." *The Journal of Politics* 77:2 (2015): 463–76.

Scott, David. *Gilbert Simondon's Psychic and Collective Individuation*. Edinburgh: Edinburgh University Press, 2014.

Scott, William R. *The Constitution and Finance of English, Scottish, and Irish Joint-Stock Companies to 1720*. Cambridge: Cambridge University Press, 1910.

Seigel, Jerrold. "Necessity, Freedom, and Character Formation from the Eighteenth Century to the Nineteenth." In *Character, Self, and Sociability in the Scottish Enlightenment*. Edited by Susan Manning and Thomas Ahnert. Basingstoke: Palgrave Macmillan, 2011, pp. 249–66.

Sen, Amartya. *Poverty and Famines: An Essay on Entitlement and Deprivation*. Oxford: Clarendon, 1981.

Shapin, Steven, and Simon Schaffer. *Leviathan and the Air-Pump: Hobbes, Boyle, and the Experimental Life*. Princeton, NJ: Princeton University Press, 1985.

Shaw, Katy. *Crunch Lit*. London: Bloomsbury, 2015.

Sheehan, Jonathan, and Dror Wahrman. *Invisible Hands: Self-Organization and the Eighteenth Century*. Chicago, IL: University of Chicago Press, 2015.

Shelden, Michael. "Dickens, 'The Chimes,' and the Anti-Corn Law League." *Victorian Studies* 25:3 (1982): 329–53.

Shonkwiler, Alison. *The Financial Imaginary: Economic Mystification and the Limits of Realist Fiction*. Minneapolis: University of Minnesota Press, 2017.

Shovlin, John. *The Political Economy of Virtue: Luxury, Patriotism, and the Origins of the French Revolution*. Ithaca, NY: Cornell University Press, 2007.

Singer, Peter. "Preface." In *Animal Philosophy: Ethics and Identity: Essential Readings in Continental Thought*. Edited by Matthew Calarco and Peter Atterton. New York: Continuum, 2004, pp. xi–xiii.

Siskin, Clifford. "Novels and Systems." *Novel* 34 (2001): 202–15.

———. *System: The Shaping of Modern Knowledge*. Cambridge, MA: MIT Press, 2016.

Siskin, Clifford, and William Warner, eds. *This Is Enlightenment*. Chicago, IL: University of Chicago Press, 2010.

Sleigh, Charlotte. "Inside Out: The Unsettling Nature of Insects." In *Insect Poetics*. Edited by Eric C. Brown. Minneapolis: University of Minnesota Press, 2006, pp. 281–97.

Smith, Adam. *The Theory of Moral Sentiments*. 2 vols. London: A. Millar, A. Kincaid & J. Bell, 1759–1761.

———. *An Inquiry into the Nature and Causes of the Wealth of Nations*. 2 vols. London: Strahan and Cadell, 1776.

——— *The Theory of Moral Sentiments*. London: A. Strahan and T. Cadell; Edinburgh: W. Creech and J. Bell, 1790.

———. *The Theory of Moral Sentiments*. Philadelphia, PA: Anthony Finley, 1817.

———. *An Inquiry into the Nature and Causes of the Wealth of Nations*. Edited by R. H. Campbell, A. S. Skinner, and W. B. Todd. Oxford: Oxford University Press, 1976.

———. *The Theory of Moral Sentiments*. Edited by D. D. Raphael and A. L. Macfie. Oxford: Clarendon, 1976.

———. *Wealth of Nations*. Edited by Edwin Cannan. Chicago, IL: University of Chicago Press, 1976.

———. "*A Letter to the* Edinburgh Review." In *Essays on Philosophical Subjects*. Edited by W. P. D. Wightman and J. C. Bryce. Oxford: Clarendon Press, 1980.

———. "Of the External Senses." In *Essays on Philosophical Subjects*. Edited by W. P. D. Wightman and J. C. Bryce. Oxford: Clarendon Press, 1980.
———. "The Principles Which Lead and Direct Philosophical Enquiries; Illustrated by the History of Astronomy." In *Essays on Philosophical Subjects*. Edited by W. P. D. Wightman and J. C. Bryce. Oxford: Clarendon Press, 1980.
———. *Wealth of Nations: A Selected Edition*. Edited by Kathryn Sutherland. Oxford: Oxford World Classics, 1998.
———. *The Theory of Moral Sentiments. Library of Economics and Liberty*. Accessed 1 May 2017. www.econlib.org/library/Smith/smMS1.html.
Sonenscher, Michael. "Physiocracy as Theodicy." *History of Political Thought* 23:2 (2002): 326–39.
———. *Before the Deluge: Public Debt, Inequality, and the Intellectual Origins of the French Revolution*. Princeton, NJ: Princeton University Press, 2007.
Soros, George. *The Crash of 2008 and What It Means: The New Paradigm for Financial Markets*. New York: PublicAffairs, 2009.
Sperling, John G. *The South Sea Company*. Boston, MA: Harvard Graduate School of Business Administration, 1962.
Steiner, Philippe. *La "science nouvelle" de l'économie politique*. Paris: Presses universitaires de France, 1998.
Steuart, James. *An Inquiry into the Principles of Political Oeconomy: Being an Essay on the Science of Domestic Policy in Free Nations*. London: A. Millar and T. Cadell, 1767.
Stockland, Etienne. "'La Guerre Aux Insectes': Pest Control and Agricultural Reform in the French Enlightenment." *Annals of Science* 70:4 (2013): 435–60.
Stroup, Alice. *A Company of Scientists: Botany, Patronage, and Community at the Seventeenth-Century Parisian Royal Academy of Sciences*. Berkeley: University of California Press, 1990.
Sutherland, Kathryn. "Adam Smith's Master Narrative: Women and the *Wealth of Nations*." In *Adam Smith's Wealth of Nations: New Interdisciplinary Essays*. Edited by Stephen Copley and Kathryn Sutherland. Manchester: Manchester University Press, 1995, pp. 97–121.
Swift, Jonathan. *The Poems of Jonathan Swift*. Edited by Harold Williams. 3 vols. Oxford: Clarendon, 1937.
———. *The Prose Writings of Jonathan Swift*. Edited by Herbert Davis et al. 16 vols. Oxford: Clarendon, 1939–1975.
———. *The Poems of Jonathan Swift*. Edited by Harold Williams. 3 vols. 2nd edn. Oxford: Clarendon, 1958.
———. *Jonathan Swift: The Complete Poems*. Edited by Pat Rogers. New Haven, CT: Yale University Press, 1983.
Teichgraeber, Richard III. "Rethinking Das Adam Smith Problem." *Journal of British Studies* 20:2 (1981): 106–23.
Terrall, Mary. *Catching Nature in the Act: Réaumur and the Practice of Natural History in the Eighteenth Century*. Chicago, IL: University of Chicago Press, 2014.
Théré, Christine, and Jean-Marc Rohrbasser. "L'emploi du terme 'population' dans *l'Encyclopédie*." *Recherches sur Diderot et sur l'Encyclopédie* 31–32 (2002): 103–22.
Thompson, Dorothy. *The Chartists: Popular Politics in the Industrial Revolution*. New York: Pantheon Books, 1984.

Thompson, E. P. "The Moral Economy of the English Crowd in the Eighteenth Century." *Past and Present* 50 (1971): 76–136.

Tribe, Keith. "Professors Malthus and Jones: Political Economy at the East India College, 1806–1858." *The European Journal of the History of Economic Thought* 2:2 (1995): 327–54.

———. *The Economy of the World: Language, History, and Economics.* Oxford: Oxford University Press, 2015.

Tufte, Edward. *The Visual Display of Quantitative Information* Berkeley: University of California Press, 1983.

Vardi, Liana. *The Physiocrats and the World of the Enlightenment.* Cambridge: Cambridge University Press, 2012.

Vaughan, C. E. "Henry Brooke, *The Fool of Quality.*" In *The Cambridge History of English and American Literature.* 18 vols. Cambridge: Cambridge University Press, 1907–1921.

Vernon, James. *Hunger: A Modern History.* Cambridge, MA: Harvard University Press, 2007.

Viner, Jacob. *The Role of Providence in Social Order.* Philadelphia, PA: Philadelphia University Press, 1972.

Vines, David. "The Phillips Machine: A Progressive Model." In *A. W. H. Phillips: Collected Works in Contemporary Perspective.* Cambridge: Cambridge University Press, 2000, pp. 39–67.

Wainwright, Oliver. "The Stock Market Planetarium That Could Have a Big Bang Any Minute." *The Guardian*, Tuesday 1st December 2015.

Wakefield, Priscilla. *Reflections on the Present Condition of the Female Sex: With Suggestions for Its Improvement.* Cambridge: Cambridge University Press, 2015.

Wales, William. *An Inquiry into the Present State of Population in England and Wales.* London: C. Nourse, 1781.

Wallace, Robert. *A Dissertation on the Numbers of Mankind.* Edinburgh: G. Hamilton and J. Balfour, 1753.

Wasserman, Earl R. *Pope's Epistle to Bathurst: A Critical Reading with an Edition of the Poem.* Baltimore, MD: Johns Hopkins University Press, 1960.

Whatmore, Richard. *What Is Intellectual History?* Cambridge: Polity, 2015.

Whatmore, Richard, and Brian Young, eds. *Palgrave Advances in Intellectual History.* Basingstoke: Palgrave, 2006.

———, eds. *A Companion to Intellectual History.* Oxford: Wiley Blackwell, 2015.

Wille, Sheila. "The Ichneumon Fly and the Equilibration of British Natural Economies in the Eighteenth Century." *The British Journal for the History of Science* 48:4 (2015): 639–60.

Williams, Abigail. "Literary and Intellectual History." In *Palgrave Advances in Intellectual History.* Edited by Richard Whatmore and Brian Young. Basingstoke: Palgrave, 2006, pp. 49–65.

Williams, Raymond. "Dominant, Residual, and Emergent." *Marxism and Literature* 1 (1977): 121–27.

Wilson, Charles H. *Anglo-Dutch Commerce and Finance in the Eighteenth Century.* Cambridge: Cambridge University Press, 1941.

White, Mark D. "Adam Smith and Immanuel Kant: On Markets, Duties, and Moral Sentiments." *Social Economics* 39 (2010): 53–60.

Winch, Donald. "Marginalism and the Boundaries of Economic Science." *History of Political Economy* 4:2 (1972): 325–43.

———. *Riches and Poverty: An Intellectual History of Political Economy in Britain, 1750–1834*. Cambridge: Cambridge University Press, 1996.

Wood, Claire. *Dickens and the Business of Death*. Cambridge: Cambridge University Press, 2015.

Wood, Nigel. "Adam Smith's *The Theory of Moral Sentiments* in 1759: Spectatorship, Duty, and Social Improvement." In *Reading 1759: Literary Culture in Mid-Eighteenth Century Britain and France*. Edited by Shaun Regan. Lewisburg, PA: Bucknell University Press, 2012, pp. 57–74.

Wright, Johnson Kent. *A Classical Republican in Eighteenth-Century France: The Political Thought of Mably*. Stanford, CA: Stanford University Press, 1997.

Zaretsky, Robert, and John T Scott. *The Philosopher's Quarrel: Rousseau, Hume and the Limits of Human Understanding*. New Haven, CT: Yale University Press, 2010.

Zemka, Sue. "From the Punchmen to Pugin's Gothics: The Broad Road to a Sentimental Death in *The Old Curiosity Shop*." *Nineteenth-Century Literature* 48:3 (1993): 291–309.

Index

For Product Safety Concerns and Information please contact our EU representative GPSR@taylorandfrancis.com
Taylor & Francis Verlag GmbH, Kaufingerstraße 24, 80331 München, Germany

www.ingramcontent.com/pod-product-compliance
Ingram Content Group UK Ltd.
Pitfield, Milton Keynes, MK11 3LW, UK
UKHW022001180926
475701UK00003B/141

* 9 7 8 1 0 3 2 0 9 5 6 8 4 *